CW00530395

Everyday Life

Everyday Life

How the Ordinary
Became Extraordinary

Joseph A. Amato

REAKTION BOOKS

To those loyal to gifts given and
generous in crafting their own lives.

Published by Reaktion Books Ltd
Unit 32, Waterside
44–48 Wharf Road
London N1 7UX, UK
www.reaktionbooks.co.uk

First published 2016

Printed and bound in Great Britain by TJ International, Padstow, Cornwall

A catalogue record for this book is available from the British Library

ISBN 978 1 78023 663 6

Permission to quote from the poems 'Hands', 'Prairie Storm' and
'The Routine is What We Remember' granted by Dana R. Yost

Contents

Writing Daily and Everyday Life

And how can we place ourselves above the past if we are in it
and it is in us?

Benedetto Croce

Countless peoples, places and periods have won and still call out for
an everyday history of their own. Such histories can be characterized by a scarcity or abundance of evidence. Reconstructing the
early days of deep history, to use a recent term, depends principally
on archaeological artefacts and anthropological cases and analogies
to modern and contemporary times, whereas, beginning in the
eighteenth and nineteenth centuries, written and visual evidence
literally overflows and drives historians with the full use of the social
sciences to select themes and narrative. Everyday histories, or daily
histories (a synonym throughout this work), have focused, especially in classical and medieval times, on all classes: royalty,
aristocracy, courts, warriors and also craftspeople, artists and religious leaders, including members of monasteries, religious orders
and heretics – to choose a single example like the dualistic Cathars
of thirteenth-century Languedoc.[1] Increasingly in the nineteenth
and twentieth centuries historians, differentiated into social, economic and cultural fields, have focused on the foundations, ways
and beliefs of urban and rural peoples: those at the top, the bottom
and along the fringe of society; the working class, the bourgeoisie
and the diverse underclasses who constitute the landless and homeless. Multiple theories and disciplines generated in conjunction with
the social sciences account for new subjects, methodologies and

insights in the writing and discussion of the content and value of everyday life.

This work, chronological in development, will seek the boundaries of thinking and writing about everyday history. It will seek to examine the making of everyday life across a trajectory from the material and social to the mental and cultural, reaching to modern times with the accelerating move from the industrial and democratic to the primacy of abundance, consumption, design and invention, and individual choice, consciousness and imagination. At some point, beyond history and the social sciences, as I suggest in the Conclusion, inner explorations of daily life increasingly belong to the penetration of literature and poetry.

Neither a survey nor a guide, *Everyday Life* is, above all, a reflective work on the elements that compose everyday life. It is mediated through two essential forms of historical writing. First, it derives from my writing of intellectual, cultural and social histories covering long trajectories on subjects including the small, walking and, most recently, surfaces. Second, and more pertinently, my interest in everyday life grows out of numerous works I have written on family history and local and regional history. As I attributed a distinct value to them as a means to explore places and times and as productive paths to knowledge, so too have I here sought to make everyday history a means to enter the past and gain what the best histories provide – self-knowledge.

AWAKENED BY NOSTALGIA

My writing on family, local and regional history carries with it a sense of urgency and moral imperative: to secure, if only in word and understanding, home and family in heart and hearth and to save the uniqueness of place as a reservoir of variety in a time when the local, rural and traditional lose out to the encroachment and encapsulation of national and global forces.

With great exaggeration, the local southwestern Minnesota writer, conservationist and newspaper editor Paul Gruchow (1947–2004) gets at the truth of the autobiographical foundation of history in saying, in the Introduction to *Grass Roots*, 'All history is ultimately local and personal. To tell what we remember, and keep on telling it, is to keep the past alive in the present.' And he adds, to know a place is to inhabit it, which 'means literally to have made a habit of it . . . to wear it like a familiar garment . . . What is strange to us – unfamiliar – can never be home.'[2]

John Berger elaborates on 'home', an old Norse word meaning village. 'Originally home meant the center of the world – not in a geographical, but in an ontological sense.' Home, Berger draws from the historian of religion Mircea Eliade, 'was the place from which the world could be founded'. Finally, 'without a home at the center of the real, one was not only shelterless, but also lost in non-being . . . everything was fragmentation.'[3] And without home as an anchor in place, I would add, the everyday loses its assured coherence.

Gruchow gets at a second truth about the centring and anchoring powers of home by affirming the validity of nostalgia. A Greek compound word, nostalgia, combines *nóstos*, meaning homecoming, a Homeric word, and *álgos*, meaning pain and ache. (It was coined in the seventeenth century to describe the illness suffered by Swiss soldiers longing for home.) Gruchow has it that home, the ever-sought centre, 'is a place in time – and that we cannot know where we are now unless we can remember where we have come from'.[4]

Out of nostalgia I wrote the long poem 'Buddy Afloat'. It is dedicated to an uncle who in the shadow of their torpedoed and slow-to-sink transport ship, the *Bliss*, kept a dead friend afloat a whole night in the autumn seas of 1942 off North Africa – and then kept him and that night buoyant with a lifetime of memory. Of this I wrote these closing lines:

> I keep the dead
> Together and afloat,
> In the dispersing seas of time.
> I do this
> With the buoying grace of memory
> And the treading kick of word and story.

So remembering is an ontological act. By it we enter into communion with the past and by bringing the past into the present we renew ourselves through our ties to the dead, the family, the community. Recollection elevates the mundane and ordinary into special times that enliven present communions.

The everyday – a mix of things and people, thought and actions, memory and imagination, work and habits – runs in and out of the heart and becomes the hearth of our meaning. And the everyday creates our sense of place, a brief discussion of which concludes this Introduction and sets the stage for Chapter One.

PLACE AND TIME

Life is lived out in a place. Any given place has a natural geography and belongs to a shaped landscape and a built environment of structures, buildings, homes, organized spaces and a multitude of objects, tools and machines. Also, a place, defined as a discrete locality or as an expanded region or state, embodies a stage of an economy. Commingling institutions, groups, communities and cultures, homes and the paths of migration, a place richly mixes unities and disunities. It can be known only by similarities, contrasts, juxtapositions, polarities and contradictions.

Woods, fields and rivers, walls, civil structures and buildings form the outer surface and boundaries of a stage for actions, rituals and experience. A place composed of ordinary and repeating phenomena also witnesses unique manifestations of movement, growth and forms. A place strikes our emotions and senses. It also holds the things, signs and signals by which we think, form images, launch metaphors and express dreams and hopes. In kaleidoscopic combinations, a place forms young minds and the roots of engrained habits in older citizens.

More concretely, we can say that structures, spaces, homes, neighbourhoods, villages and inhabitants, all of which change in various ways, define a place. Pavements, storefronts, alleys, fields, churches and schools host the rituals, ceremonies and celebrations by which individuals and generations experience and know, make and represent, their lives. Places are worlds as similar and diverse as humans can be.

As much as a place is rendered real by its geography, environment, demography, its social and built structures, material things and social forms, a place also belongs to time – to a multiplicity of days and seasons, lives and deaths, periods and stages of happenings and events. A place forever belongs to real and imagined temporalities. We see and know time by conditions, idealizations, expectations and occurrences – and the simple certitude that humans are born, age and die. On this count, I plead guilty to singing the historian's song: our lyrics of place as home, family, neighbourhood, town, village and region belong to stories of now, next and before. Narrative alone tells us of the place that unfolds in time.

Narratives record cycles of climate, flora and fauna and the stages by which humans took control of a place's waters, land and soils. They join singular and separate places to larger regional, national and even global histories. In *Rethinking Home* (2002) I showed how the introduction of new technologies, materials and civil engineering altered the material world in southwest Minnesota and furnished successive generations with a fresh sensual environment of new sights, smells, sounds, touch and contact.[5] Likewise the local narrative, with diverse methodologies, can understand a place over time as a stage for changing emotions and altered definitions and treatments of insanity or address altered sensibilities in matters of the beautiful, the criminal and the clandestine. In this way the local historian can find fresh perspectives and invigorating themes for constructing places in time.

Places, then, are about unique objects and things and material and social dimensions, and their changing combinations over time. They encompass and stage lives on a landscape, where everyday lives are played out through work and leisure, public and private institutions, ethnicities and cultures, planning and utopian thought. Embodying homes and community, places are where family, friends, neighbourhood and society meet harmoniously and along ragged edges. Over the past two centuries immigrants, always strangers, and memories of those who went away have increasingly defined places.

The most special places are where we learned to speak, gesture, play and work, where we passed through the first and formative stages of life. Places imprint fresh minds and form the deepest fountains of feelings and affections – senses of heart and soul deeper than sociology and politics. Places call up nostalgia, evoking the time of first loves, wounds and hurt; they are of heart and home.

Places, for these reasons, and others as well, are singular. They beacon from the past a more primordial time, when there were purer and more innocent hearts and more elemental and natural affinities. Such places, however mythic, forever haunt those of us – the great majority – who have migrated. They stand opposite, even contradict, the seemingly ever more organizing and controlling mass societies, which spread at accelerating rates with modern and contemporary times – and, if my argument holds, give birth to individuals who turn inward to self and outward to the world at large, living in ever mutating places. In this way, what seemed ordinary everyday life turns – metamorphoses – increasingly into the extraordinary.

I

Bodies and Things

The body is man's first and most natural instrument.
Marcel Mauss, 'Techniques of the Body'

The historian of the everyday must begin with the materiality of life.

Body, things and tools make human worlds. The body needs and uses things, and it is this need and use that shape individual and group lives. Things, bodies and habit tie the knot of everyday behaviour. Everyday life, even in its wishes, conjectures and dreams, grows out of and through ordinary, common, typical and repeating ways of body and things.

Everyday life is about the peasant and his land, the merchant and his goods and books, the desk and computer at which we sit and write. Our grandfather in life and memory was the garden he kept; our grandmother the kitchen in which she stirred and the living room she commanded. Historians of the quotidian must capture how the everyday is rooted in the substance and habits of things and must see body and things as igniting senses, giving rise to perceptions, affording thought and defining the state and mood of consciousness.

Beyond this, things and body, singularly and entangled, not only fill the world with variety, differences and juxtapositions, but are a primary source for analogy and metaphor. Organized by name, things and their movement as well as the parts and actions of body become symbols and icons. Momentarily, daily, across seasons and years, body and things plant our lives in time and cloak awareness in temporality and mortality.[1]

Individual historians must construct their own ideas of material culture and conceive how body as real – in its diverse parts and functions, movements and motions, as well as by senses, in habits and with speech and gestures – joins us to the social world, others and self.[2] The body enters us in the world and action, to paraphrase the anthropologist and sociologist Marcel Mauss.[3] As much as the body enacts individual will, the individual body depends for survival, affection and information on other bodies. Human life, not unlike its animal ancestors, rests on dependency and advances in collective mutuality. The individual is born into the cradle of mutual dependency and lives out his life through exchange, reciprocity and gift-giving, which afford the very social sinew of everyday life. The individual's first use of body, attunement of senses and development of emotions depend on imitation, repetition and support. He or she advances by instruction, discipline, education and cultural norms. In a word, we will fail miserably if we ignore that humans live by and with shared bodies, things and senses.[4]

IN CONVERSATION WITH THINGS

The twentieth-century French thinker Gabriel Marcel gave a metaphysical edge to the connection of body and things and existence in his published notebooks titled *Being and Having*. He sees humans incorporating things into their meaning and self-identification only to discover that they are not what they have, for things constitute one form of being and the self exists consciously and mortally in another order of being and temporality.[5]

Nevertheless, humans constantly identify and weave themselves into the things they possess and wish to possess. And groups and cultures, which encapsulate individuals, weave selves and things into one fabric. Things – both animate and inanimate – have voices that are heard. They speak to humans through the full array of their senses, and humans literally and metaphorically speak to them with voice, gesture, want, command, wish, dream or conjecture. An ongoing conversation between things and self establishes the context and consciousness of everyday life. The interconnection of social being and material occurs on a landscape and in a place that are a mix of bodies, things and minds. All this makes everyday life a heterogeneous and multiform state, condition and mind of existence.[6]

Twentieth-century French essayist and poet Francis Ponge (1899–1988) consciously privileged conversations with things in today's world when words turned brutally abstract and warring ideas and ideologies pervaded all quarters of life and overran the mind. In his seminal book *Le Parti pris des choses* (1942), which dwelled on the encounter of everyday objects and the body itself, which in interaction becomes 'a thing among things', Ponge wrote:

> Ideas are not my forte. I do not handle them with ease. They handle me instead. Give me queasy feeling, nausea. I don't like to find myself thrown in their midst. Objects in the external world, on the one hand, delight me, but seem in no way concerned about my approval, which they immediately acquire. I do not question them.[7]

Body and things enter into combination by surprise, adaptive use (as the carpenter with his planes) and the familiarity of long habit as the cook in his or her kitchen. With great variation – and admittedly a licence to figurative speech – thing and body assimilate each other; and they account for the habits and grudges that anchor everyday life in affections, resistance, repetition and consistency and make daily routines.[8] Thing and body relay messages of danger and satisfaction back and forth, evoke emotions, ideas and dreams and spawn curiosity, which distinguishes the very genesis of the human species and most recently, as argued by Philip Ball, proved a great interior spur to modern science.[9]

Things made into instruments form distinct landscapes, which define home and place. Things, in turn, call us to thinking and making – or in the words of the art critic Leo Stein, 'Things are what we encounter, ideas are what we project. Things provide the substance, which we turn into objects and symbols of our place in being and narrative in life.'[10] The interaction of body and things writes the main text of human evolution while making the substance and texture of daily life, which is lived out by learning the ways of things and fidelity to habits.

The anthropologist Tim Ingold follows this approach, anchoring his studies in a wider ecology of life, which he calls 'a dwelling perspective'.[11] The sentient body in movement – expressive of our biology – is fully interactive with a sentient environment from which the body learns and fashions skills.[12] Biology and learning, perception and imagination, do not form antitheses for Ingold.[13] As humans walk, see and act, they perceive and represent the world of experience with lines and traces, which connect things with maps, drawings, genealogies, stories and even music.

Over the ages the body places humans in situations and affords them experience. As human groups learned and made things and built environments, they transformed and defined their lives.[14] Body produces the kernel of everyday life. Body forms habits with and around a set of repeating individual and shared actions. Habits meet the needs of the body's own physiology and the community's survival. The way a group of humans eats, moves, rests and associates establishes relations with the animal and plant worlds and the state of surrounding waters and soils. Habits likewise establish conduct and define the normal measure of everyday lives in terms of what is immediate, mundane and subject to repeating social actions.

Body, also, has a poetry. It sings polyphonically of voices and dances, so to speak, with a variety of steps. It purrs with contentment and cries out with pain. Blatant or sly, the body with gesture and voice constantly signals across its quotidian intercourse with things; it induces and repels, insinuates comfort and warns of discomfort.[15] Sometimes body (like a telegrapher who has lost his code) sends out ambiguous and indecipherable signals from mute organs or incoherent phrases and nonsensical stares from misfiring neurons. Multifarious in its means of expression, body gives out a daily discourse with self and world.[16]

The idea that the body corporally, technologically and socially form an ongoing dialogue with the world has attracted a rush of thinkers. This includes French philosophers and object-directed museum designers intent on giving a more concrete face to understanding the world. They have – I offer a metaphor – shoved off in vessels without theoretical rudders, afloat on the evolving and complex human body into such open seas as 'stuff', 'thing' and 'things studies'. Anthropologists (far more enthusiasts for the concrete and common than historians, who are prone to focus on the great and official) have examined the role of bric-a-brac, paraphernalia, ephemera and kitsch in making and defining everyday life. Starting with stone tools and shells and objects made of grasses and mud, anthropologists and archaeologists (whose goals are the stuff and ways of everyday life) have named ages by materials and technologies and techniques.

The Pitt Rivers Museum in Oxford, England, which opened in 1884, uses the development and design of diverse tools and instruments of every kind to offer a portrait of the development of human cultures and thought – and the abiding human predilection for applying, designing and even aesthetically refining things of hand and craft. With the entire collection of the British Museum at his disposal, its director Neil MacGregor seeks in his volume *A History of the World in 100 Objects* (2010) to portray the two-million-year advance of humans by elucidating the historical place and function of one hundred select objects.[17]

Things please the local and everyday historian – especially when they deliver us back to the tangible and offer an escape from historical orthodoxies and the updraughts of ballooning ideologists. Things are manifest unto themselves, epiphanies of nature and marvels of invention. All importantly, they can be touched, taken up, tested and, size permitting, put under the custody of hands and arms. They call out for investigation and bodily energy. They offer chances for dexterity that few have with words and arguments. And then, with no *finally* possible, they set the table for good company with such journalists and photographers, philosophers and poets as James Agee and Walker Evans in their book *Let Us Now Praise Famous Men* (1941), a keen act of reporting in detail the material and family life of three tenant families in the Deep South in the 1930s; or, to skip to a most inventive philosopher, Gaston Bachelard in his 1958 classic *Poetics of Space*; or yet Georges Perec in his *Species of Spaces and Other Pieces* (1974), which offers a truly refined dissection of material living space – or the 'infra-ordinary' life of daily acts and common places.

Then, too, things provide a marked trail for ever-latent nostalgia in changing times. They lead memory and imagination towards past places, peoples and times, when hearts were thought to be more in play. Things of the past offer traction to one's inheritance as given and assumed, so reassuring in a time of relentless change and urgent projects. Offering 'a philosophy of everyday things', the critic and writer Brian Dillon suggests that we travel home to good old days and ways by conjuring its objects and technologies. And, after all, replied his correspondent, professor of literature Steven Connor, things are inexhaustible. They provide 'a whole lifetime of stuff to be investigated'. Furthermore, he adds, things are 'what humans do. It's our speciality: things.'[18]

Whether we are interested in old shipyard tools, turn-of-the-century photographic equipment or the smell and juice of old pipes, things track places and time. They make the ordinary concrete and declare the extraordinary in the case of a novel invention and revolutionizing creation; hence the popularity of the British television programme *Antiques Roadshow*, which delights with unearthed things, good deals made and evocation by sight and touch of objects and tools that were of and made the world that once was. The requirement is that everyday historians have an acute eye for what is handy.

Historians and writers have long used things (artefacts, structures, tools, machines, artworks and photographs) to supplement biographies and memoirs and tell the story of a time, culture and even civilization. However, recent generations of historians have amplified their notions of material culture with the enhancement of economic, social and cultural histories and the history of technology as a matter of theory and application. The work of anthropologists and archaeologists offers historians fresh quarries and tactics for constructing everyday life.[19]

Drawing on diverse methodologies and disciplines, the *Journal of Material Culture* – a journal initiated in the Department of Anthropology at the University of London in 1966 – generated Marxist materialism anew. It marched under the banner of needing to examine the dialectical role of body and things. Under the editorship of Daniel Miller and Christopher Tilley and the support of an international and interdisciplinary editorial board of directors, the journal defined – for all studies, be they local or global, past or present – the importance of the study of the material as made, used, distributed, consumed and lived and as the source of thought, representation, symbol and imagination.[20] Its opening manifesto, staking out the imperative of this new field, declared:

> An adequate understanding of any social actions and relations, we would maintain, demands an understanding of material culture and vice versa. The world is constituted through a continuous dynamism, a dialectic of object-subject relations that can only be more fully explored through developing theoretical perspectives, methodologies and empirical studies.[21]

In their vital and changing relation to social and creative man, things form the basis for material culture. Things shape landscapes, dictate work, frame living conditions, establish communities and, to use an idea advanced by Tilley elsewhere, provide metaphors for understanding and valuing life.[22] Every order of human life is, to use a favourite term of the British archaeologist Ian Hodder, *entangled* with things.[23] Things, objects, goods and tools occupy lives. They satisfy bodies and emotions, induce and guide plans, and even in the form of gifts, as we learned from Mauss, constitute recognition and reciprocity. Goods that acknowledge status and define abundance, they also celebrate occasions, persons and groups.

Things anchor humans in place. As tools and containers, decorative, ceremonial and entertainment objects, they create and structure everyday interactions.[24] Myriad things envelop us and define the ordinary and the quotidian. They frame situations and call for identical and recurring actions, feelings and thoughts. They tether life in a place and set daily and seasonal rhythms of work and play. In prosperous consumer democracies – 'whose cups runneth over in the wash of objects and goods' – everyday life belongs to capitalism's production and profits and design and advertisement. Just one push of a trolley (shopping cart) through a supermarket in the early evening or during the weekend reveals the degree to which consumption pervades society and culture.

Along the riverbanks of accumulating goods stand official and business structures and intangible and mutating 'home'. As permanent dwellings or stop-offs in our migrations, homes offer for the majority a secure and comfortable environment. They are heated, painted, and have running water from flowing taps. For the well off, houses, following the differentiation of the modern person and family, have multiple specialized rooms – to eat, sleep, entertain and lull. The pampered children of recent generations have a bedroom of their own, which just possibly has a television and an adjoined bathroom. The family kitchen, no longer the ancestral hearth, is endowed with efficient machines – ovens, refrigerators, freezers, mixers and blenders and dishwashers. Usually close to the kitchen door, which opens to the garage, there are racks and shelves holding school backpacks, recipe books, a telephone or two and car keys. From morning to night, the car defines for many a cockpit of daily individual and family life. It moves along miles of paved roads leading to and from work, shopping, schools and leisure activities. En route in comfortable seats, radio and phone keep us in contact and direct our travel; and, if the trip is of any length and alone, it allows us to catch up with ourselves and even plan and dream.

Movement and travel are arranged around organized space and artificial calendars.[25] Everyday life today in city and country towns belongs to partitioning and segmenting streets, which, lined by structures, homes and apartments, define neighbourhoods and cities and form an interlocking grid. Movements, goals and things habituate our bodies to places and times. Although locale was once anchored by direct and repeating ties to immediate spaces, things and places, locale today is penetrated by all sorts of distant connection, varied and alien parts, and is driven by more cerebral and abstract affinities and obligations. Places increasingly belong in part or near whole to interconnective tracks and paved highways and electronic communications. Local crafts and trades, now mainly a matter of hobby, habit

and art, have been largely overrun and superseded by distant industries and their synthetic materials, mass goods and strategic design.

Contemporary daily life everywhere increasingly turns on discoveries and inventions, and their design and popularization.[26] A
single book of a fleet of books, Charles Panati's *Extraordinary Origins
of Everyday Things* (1987), offers a long list of common objects and
altogether extraordinary things we live by and for. We incorporate
them into sociability; their names and brands shape our day-to-day
speech and action as well as defining who we are and how we value
ourselves. Off my puny bookshelves comes a small tower of books,
each revealing an aspect of the origins and history of our entanglement with what we consider 'common and useful things'.[27]

The things that shape human bodies and habits direct the larger
part of everyday energy and movement. They emotionally, mentally,
aesthetically and morally make humans who they are. They account
for and arise out of distinct technologies, work and cultures. Any
single thing – animal, product or tool – can drive and justify humans'
everyday actions and account for the organization of lives and entire
societies. The American anthropologist Sidney Mintz exemplarily
showed in the case of sugar how a single crop can define a labour
force and a landscape and spread across the world to form diets,
tastes and senses of satisfaction and celebration.[28]

Beyond acknowledging the power of individual goods over
nature, landscapes and societies, historians have richly described the
past with reference to systems of work (feudalism, slavery and so
on), stages of hand and machine technology and the production and
distribution of goods. They have accounted for material processes
and systems that form societies and drive civilization forward. This
is quintessentially exemplified by the spread of the world of industrialization and the premier steam engine of the nineteenth century,
the train, as elaborated in Chapter Five. Launched on rolling metal
wheels on level surfaces and flat steel tracks, it drove Europe and
America, then the world at large, with initial and accelerating interconnection of mine and factory with market, city, town and even
village into an unprecedented social order of speed, abundance, command and truly national and global exchange.

We might also point to the great transformation of everyday life in the nineteenth century by public waterworks and lighting. Histories of the national industrialization and administration of water and light allow us to grasp that profound transformation in everyday health and security which changed not just a sense of well-being but our touch and taste of the world around us. While light took away darkness and shadows, running water swept away dust and dirt and made the fresh, clean and bright stand forth. Aside from sanitation, abundant running public water, ultimately accessible to every household, brought forth renovated regimes of cleaning, drinking, cooking, washing and bathing. On wide, paved and clean streets, now, brightly dressed populations strolled and shopped. So the world became for all more healthy, pleasant and sensuous.[29]

BY OUR SKIN

As removed as the historian of everyday life is from scarcity and labour, he or she must remember, as no older person easily forgets, that humans, like other animals, belong to their body.[30] Daily existence is a corporal matter; the quotidian is never far from bread and pain. Body is our first tool and container.[31] Human incarnation equals immanence and entails the heterogeneity of experience and action. Body is a source of energy and conditions of well-being. A multiplex of sensations, perceptions and actions, body, so important to everyday life, is the vehicle of learning and the repository of habits and instincts. Other than mind, the body is the sole agency and a prime end of our actions. It guarantees connections and interactions with things and constitutes a condition and goal of our projects. The body anchors the individual in space and time, and it is the corporate guarantor of community. Body compares and classifies what we see, encounter, take up and ingest. It affords a binary measure of what is like and unlike and attractive and unattractive to us – and with heterogeneity of eyes, hands and other parts of the body tells us what fits and pleases. It constitutes the everyday judge of friendly or adverse, useful or obstructing. It makes the art in which we see and invest ourselves. Body in mutual relation with things forms the reservoir of analogies and metaphors by which we join and associate, conjecture, imagine and wish worlds.

Body places humans in action, thought and wish.[32] Bodies move about. They take us to the labour and gardens of our days – along the troughs and ruts and up onto the roads and highways of every-day life. Eating, sleeping and mating, humans take and assume their place. Habits, like walking, bowing to, shaking hands with or gently patting or rubbing one another, make us approachable, accommo-dating, trustworthy. Habits underpin settlements and communities across generations, while gestures, traditions and metaphors keep societies in orbit.

Body is a set of surfaces in a world of surfaces.[33] Skin – for us not feathers, scales or bark – is our first surface, the face of human being. Skin is the most visible aspect of the human phenotype – and it is the first face of everyday social life.[34] It defines us to eye and touch. It puts us in fleshy dress. Buffering, resistant to sun, heat and cold and also plastic and self-replacing, its condition marks us out by age, col-our, wear and injuries.[35] The outer face of our incarnation, skin sports burns, wounds, scars, blemishes, tumours, warts, infections and other irregularities that testify to life's tattoos, a particular condition and a fate. While biologically the boundary, mediator, transmitter, monitor and regulator of interior and exterior worlds, skin, science's studied integument, is culture's much-read book, in which the fair are free of calluses and enjoy privilege (including a life out of the sun) and those with tattoos and scarification express cosmic ties, tribal identities and allegiance to gangs. In the most mundane corners of life, skin professes man to the world. With blush, standing hair, shivers, goose pimples and sweat, skin confesses physical, emotional, moral and other inner states. Of blush, the most revealing face of all – Byron declared, 'So sweet the blush of bashfulness', while Keats wrote in a letter, 'There is a blush for won't, and blush for shan't, / And a blush for having done it'.[36]

WE ARE ALL EYES

'Primates are visual animals, and we think best in pictorial or geometric terms. Words', wrote the palaeontologist Stephen Jay

Gould, 'are an evolutionary afterthought.'[37] Daily life is first and in large part visual.

To give a poetic genesis to human eyes, they were mothered by skin and were fathered by the stimulation of light, which Apollo doles out day and night and across the seasons. Sun joins us to all the other species classified as phototropic, phototactic and heliotropic.[38] Contemporary theories of neurobiotaxis affirm that individual nerve cells grow in the direction of stimuli. Responding to light, the eye is older than the brain itself.[39]

Vision itself thrives on visual surfaces.[40] Lit surfaces are vision's nectar. Without denying the importance of the other senses – touch, smell, sound and taste – sight frames the context and content of everyday minds. We discern foreground and background, identify objects in context and movement, and set them in juxtaposition by contrasts of light and shadow, stillness and motion, proximity and distance and contrasting colours. All of this, which sounds so philosophical in elaboration, constitutes ordinary common life like the blinds and shades that open and shut to passing traffic.

Eyes deliver people to first encounters and the most elaborate and delicate sensual experiences. The very eyes that follow the flight of a dragonfly pick up the path of a flying hockey puck and distinguish the brushstroke of a Manet from that of a Monet. Ever blinking eyes frame and reframe all that comes to them, and classify and file some small part of that, of which yet a much smaller part might be turned into words. Visual acuity occupies one-third of our cerebral cortex; a million nerve cells are dedicated to vision – which forms a constantly rotating kaleidoscope of detailed richness in patterns, shapes, colours, brightness and movement.[41]

Confirming that everyday life is visual, Paul Shepard, in *Man in the Landscape*, conceives of sight as throwing up a constant barrage of changing and even opposing streams of images.[42] Contending that animal binocularity arose from the needs of predation and jumping, he extrapolated that the human eye (significantly similar to a monkey's) resulted from living early life in the crown of a tropical forest, where our primate ancestors jumped and grasped as they went from limb to limb. Predatory eyes are never at rest. They constantly focus and refocus around the arcs of a gyrating head and the glancing eye, explaining in measure the immediacy, texture and complexity of our ordinary experience – and its heightening punctuations, juxtapositions and dichotomies.[43]

THE REACH OF ARMS AND THE TOUCH OF HANDS

We must look to skin also for the genesis of hands, which plunge us body and brain into the juxtapositions of experience.[44] In conjunction with the formation of a muscular and skeletal structure, hands grew as appendages to skin. With skin forming thick palms and sensitive fingertips, and protecting and cutting and penetrating nails, hands became another primary guide to life. With a capacity to grip and grasp, pick, pry and pull apart, and even touch and unfold, as eyes cannot, hands enter humans into the world of things and community.

Hands make things, landscapes and communities as well as establish connections and carry out actions. It is hard to grasp everyday life without understanding human reliance on the strength of a push and a shove, the adroitness and caress of hands and the intricacy and delicacy of fingers' touch. Arms, hands and fingers point out things and express the wealth of interior and exterior worlds. They measure and indicate what is close and far, alien and intimate, what is to be cherished and what is to be cast out. Shaking, pounding and touching are the ordinary ways humans validate the substance and form of things. They also use their hands to gesture and enact their emotions, thoughts and relation to others.[45] Aside from exploring and confirming things, hands serve as primary instruments by which humans act out their wills and signal their intentions.

Hands confirm that the world is real – and they classify things, especially tools, as 'handy', and they make and shape things to be 'handy'.[46] Hands make humans dexterous – which in Latin and Old French meant right-handed and, thus, skilful. In another sense, humans are handy users of tools. Ultimately members of the crafty and inventive race of Daedalus, humans, which we who belong to the age of manufacture and design and the ready-made might overlook, are ever poking, picking and manipulating things and, thus, adjusting everyday life.

In *A Natural History of the Senses* Diane Ackerman specifies the powers of the hand: touch picks out, makes special and even heals.[47] With touch humans bless and designate the chosen one. Touch also is about the finest graceful movements. With gestures hands express reactions, conditions, situations and states of mind. They conduct private and intimate finger talks with bodies. They do this with varying types of touch and even the scratch of a scalp, the pick of a nose, the pull on an arthritic finger joint or the rub of feet. All this supplies the romance, drama and comedy of everyday life – and makes hands the enactors and commentators on everyday life.

Hands, which define all that humans do in common ways and days, from salting their pork to buttering and slicing their bread, also make them brainy. In *The Hand*, neurologist Frank Wilson argues that the brain's development followed the acting hand and its tool making. *Homo erectus* remodelled – articulated and specialized – his freed arms and hands and thereby opened 'the door to an enormously augmented range of movements and the possibility of an unprecedented extension of manual activity'. This activity led to the 'redesign, or reallocation, of the brain's circuitry'.[48] In the last 100,000 years or so, active and tasking human hands completed the reorganization of the brain of *Homo sapiens*. Manipulating and conceiving the world became interdependent. Outside and inside thought work in tandem. As humans made things, their activity and work were incorporated into will, knowledge and design. In effect, in making things, humans made for themselves new brains and minds, and a new consciousness dawned around fresh possibilities for self-definition through manipulating the world of things.[49] Man's very capacity to create symbols arguably resides in an ability to convert the hands' activities with things and tools into objects of the mind, descriptive words and even metaphoric language.

The freeing of hands and their coordination with eyes depended on bipedalism.[50] In conjunction with eyes and legs, arms underwrote hominid migrations across the world. En route in deep time, humans used eyes and hands and became the learning of their eyes and hands as they explored, searched, gathered and hunted. Rotating arms, moveable elbows, fully flexing and sensate fingers and opposable thumbs provided humans with a power and precision grip.[51] From the workshop of testing hands arose analytic, synthetic, aesthetic and fashioning minds and the material and bodily foundations of everyday culture. In the last 10,000 or so years – beginning with settlement and agriculture, towns and cities – *Homo sapiens* established unquestionable dominion over much of the world, which in recent times they came to consider largely their own – and an extension of their daily lives.

TOOLING THROUGH TIME

Tools, which were used by prehuman primates, supplemented humans along their journey from the deepest time. They accounted by definition for the birth of 'handy man', *Homo habilis*.[52] Tools increased early hominids' ability to explore the outsides and insides of plants and animals, earth and water. They permitted early man to hunt large mammals, and they allowed him to carry fire from site to site. (Many conjecture that fire itself was the first tool, the tool that made other first tools. Whether conforming to older chronologies 1.8 to 1.3 million years ago or having a more recent origin of 400,000 years ago, fire equipped humans to secure their daily life around a hearth.)

Tools defined human landscapes, cultures and power and existence in everyday life. They mediated and shaped relations with land and water, plant and animal. They gave definition to gathering, hunting, fishing, planting and harvesting. As hammers, chisels, saws, shovels and needles, as well as nets, clay mortars, pots and fabrics, tools made humans and their worlds. Drills, knives, gouges and files joined and smoothed the surfaces humans used and inhabited. Mediating the body's discourse with the world, tools distinguished the everyday life of groups and ages by differentiating hunter and farmer, extractor and producer, sailor and labourer, craftsperson and even architect, while dividing roles between male and female and young and old.

With tools, humans made landscapes, structures and objects in which they enwrapped themselves and set the premises for all facets of life, as we will see in particular in the next chapter on the

Middle Ages. Bridging one stage of technology to the next, tools permitted their evolving diets, complex shelters, specialized clothes and even a range of decorations and medicines. With tools furnishing a capacity to work with animal and human body parts, particularly bones, humans created whole tool chests for making their worlds. In the case of Plains Indians and their Alaskan and Asian forefathers, it was thanks to tools that slain animals served as more than their food. They worked hides into blankets and clothes; made tendons and muscles into cords and ropes; used organs as sacks, containers, clothing and bedding; crafted bone into hard and flexible struts and ribbing for cradles and boats and into weapons, knives, scrapers and needles, which permitted the use of decorative quills and beads and tailored impermeable exteriors and insulating interiors for coats, hats, mittens and footwear.

Other materials made human tools, containers, shelters and structures. Wood, so commonly available but, unless carbonized or scorched, lost as artefacts to the ages, was more versatile in its use than was bone – and could be worked with hand, stone, bone, shell and other harder woods. Wood, which came in all shapes, sizes and forms – from barks, branches, leaves and trunks – provided material varied in thickness, length, strength, smoothness, pliability, rigidity, weight and delicacy and thus served a host of common and inventive purposes. Shells, which came in diverse sizes and forms too, though more brittle and less workable than wood and bone, nevertheless served in the making of elemental hand tools like knives, punches, pinchers and drills, furnished ready-made scoops and containers and, singularly or joined as chains of beads, made the finest jewellery.

Stone, above all, furnished diverse and lasting tools. It has afforded anthropology and archaeology the most abundant and enduring evidence of who, what, where and when. The multipurpose biface hand axe was the star of early human tool making. It defined a group's work. It distinguished a high level of specialization, permitted types of hunting and farming and accounted for geographic movements and early trade routes. Made by handwork from the chips and wholes of highly crystalline rocks – quartz, agate, chert, flint, obsidian and fine-grained lava – stone tools, both strong and blunt and sharp, cutting and piercing, were instruments for rough exterior and fine interior work. As axes, adzes and sledges, they served to cut, smash and pound; as sharp knives and scrapers, they cut flesh, cleaned hides and shaped bone and wood; and as points, they made for deadly weapon tips, boring drills and needles. At the same time, they furnished troughs for washing, balls for milling and a variety of containers.

By extending the reach of arms and intricacies and manipulations of hands and fingers, tools advanced humans' perceptions and conceptions. They increased the human capacity to incorporate their wishes out of nature's materials and create meta-tools – tools for making tools. All this, however incrementally but nevertheless ultimately profoundly, initiated humans into changing the face of their place and power among things.[53] They helped make humans daily workers and dream makers.

Beyond this, tools were a great source of language. They equipped cultures to speak of the different ways they acted and were empowered in the world. Tools – a distinct category or type of thing – supplied workshops with metaphors to speak about the dwelling places of all being. The act of entombing, accomplished by tools, made 'tombs the metaphors of houses and landscapes of social systems'.[54] They provided, I suggest, 'the net' that snares hearts and groups; the 'stitch' that pulls people together and binds ideas; they unleashed and quickened tongues. The heating forge and sculpting wheel, whose origins lie near the beginnings of city and civilization 10,000 years ago, continued to underpin everyday life and evoked a skilled but mysterious transformation of materials. Tools etched metaphysical lines on the world. For human culture, they drew a line between natural and human-made, the wild and the tame, the ordinary and the decorated. Humans had tools and containers, which afford a grammar of distinct human actions.[55]

HOMES AND WALLS, CITIES AND CIVILIZATIONS

Thanks to the powers of fire, language, tools and building, everyday life belongs to the deepest quarters of human history. It is rooted in the interplay between exterior control of body and things and a corresponding increased capacity to feel, conceive, reason and imagine.

Humans took control of their bodies – brought them in some measure into the reach of their own diagnosis and therapy and cure and care by fashioning and experimenting with instruments and potions. They learned to soak in mud baths, take emetics and laxatives and even to scar and to patch their own wounds. They utilized tourniquets to stop bleeding and employed ropes and pegs to reset limbs, while fashioning canes and crutches to support impaired walking. Beyond this, they shaped tools to cut and penetrate their own skins into order to treat growths and infections. With wood then metal picks they probed aching teeth and skin and used a variety of straight and curved sticks as instruments for entering the body's orifices. (This was surgery, its sense coming from the Greek *kheirourgia*, 'a working done by hand', *kheir* and *ergon* meaning 'hand' and 'action'.) By the medical craft of trepanning, which dates from the Neolithic, humans bore holes in their skulls to relieve pressure.

As humans took control of their own bodies, so they fashioned landscapes and domesticated communities. With a place secured in nature, humans took a fresh measure of the world and themselves. With regularity and predictable control over daily needs and affairs, groups classified existence and made conjectures. And out of their tools – as instruments to work on the earth or contain it – sprang the metaphors and symbols they could use to understand themselves, sexual relations, the earth's energies and, by analogy, their own place in creation and nature.

From this perspective, everyday life is about self-making – the shaping of body, community, environment and mind. Expanding materials, diversifying technologies and increased production and building went with the organization of groups and the extension of a puzzling and conjuring intelligence. The roughest formula might suggest: as humans secured their quotidian place on the landscape they experienced an enhanced capacity to entertain and digest their experience. With an increased capacity to compare, classify and conjecture about themselves, objects and the world around them, they took up the world beyond them. With a vast range of analogies, a metaphorical intelligence and reaching myths they placed everyday life and its perimeters in the greater cosmos of space and time.

The bedrock of everyday life was laid by early development. With great variation of place and time, the British evolutionary psychologist Nicholas Humphrey conceives the mind and its functions as a historically generated multiplicity dependent on interactions between interior and exterior worlds.[56] In *A History of Mind: Evolution and the Birth of Consciousness*, he locates these interactions along the axis of the sensed and touched, and the perceived and conceived.[57]

WALLS AND HOUSES

The everyday was self-built. Since the late Neolithic, first in the Near East and then in China and the Mediterranean, humanity incorporated itself in dwellings and enclosed settlements. Within made spaces humans lived their lives and incubated new minds and hearts in established places and routines.

The house with walls – be it a refurbished cave, a heaping of clay, a gathering of brush or a mounding of snow – became a primary encapsulation of life, a first nest of security and intimacy, if one wishes. With made and designed mud, brick, wood, stone or plastered walls, homes became even more. They came to constitute organized small and interior worlds, which could be conceived as man's place in nature and a human nucleus in the cosmos. In *The Poetics of Space*, Bachelard wrote: 'Our house is our corner of the world . . . it is our first universe, a real cosmos in every sense of the word.'[58]

The archaeologist Ian Hodder sees *domus* as hearth and home. Beginning in the early Holocene (which began 12,000 years ago), it became prime ground for increasing human entanglement with things and literally a symbolic vessel for holding and treasuring self and things and a means of establishing a unique form of life.[59]

The centre of the ancient home, which the walls enclosed, was the hearth. In the hearth, fire lives – warms and cooks. The head of the house had his legitimacy as the keeper of the fire. For classical peoples the hearth, as articulated by the historian Numa Denis Fustel de Coulanges (1830–1889), was where the dead and the family spirits resided. From underneath the hearth the emissary of the dead, the snake, came forth.[60] As the parental bed biologically centred the living family, special corners and niches in the bedroom, if separate, and also in the main cooking room, furnished alcoves for powerful holy objects and saints. (I think of the 'Holy Corner' – the *krasnyi ugol* – in the Russian hut, *izba*; or the West Room in the Irish country home, where the old man and wife live out their last years among the family's heirlooms.)

Lewis Mumford, the American historian of technology and the city, pertinently wrote, 'House and village, eventually the town itself, are the woman writ large.' ('In Egyptian hieroglyphics,' he noted, 'house or town may stand as symbols for woman.')[61] As biological platform and spiritual agency, to borrow a phrase from archaeologist Colin Renfrew, the home allows us 'to appropriate the cosmos'; and this allows humans to centre and anchor the everyday rituals and their actions in the cosmos.[62] 'In many domesticated societies', as Peter Wilson wrote in *The Domestication of the Human Species*, 'the house is appropriated to mediate and synthesize the natural symbols of both the body and the landscape.'[63] The twentieth-century Welsh poet Glyn Jones did this in his poem 'Goodbye, What Were You?', making the kitchen the place where mother and fire are one. Her cooking, metaphoric and metamorphosing, is the cauldron of birth and sustenance.[64]

WALLS GO UP, OUT AND ALL AROUND

In the Near East, starting approximately 12,000 years ago, walls first flourished in the building of dwellings, other structures and as the protective and sheltering ring of settlements – and with pens for animals, sheds for crops and homes and temples of a sort for goods and sacrifices. The explosion in walls and their encapsulation of human bodies, things and groups, and the redefinition of everyday, marked a phenomenal revolution in human history. Growing populations went with settlements and the taming of space, the ordering of fields, the domestication of animals, the building of structures and the organization of community. 'The domestication of plants and animals, the domestication of man and the material landscape', for Mumford, 'all went hand and hand.'[65] Located principally in fertile river valleys, these enlarged settlements dwarfed the largest hunting settlements of the Neolithic. By size and scale nothing of the like had ever been dreamed of before in mankind's two- or three-million-year trek, which began when bipedal man, *Homo erectus*, came down out of the trees on the African steppe and began the long march to Central Asia, to China, Europe and beyond.[66]

As increasing populations drove developing agriculture, humans, with great security and abundance, incorporated themselves into place and the routines of fixed settlements. Therein, greater specialization and leisure encouraged human advances in discovering, making and trading objects. Multiplying objects wrote diverse narratives of their creation and place in everyday life.

Humans literally made themselves into different types of beings as groups mastered different crafts and advanced in canvassing the heavens, inventorying animals, harvests and goods, accounting transactions, interpreting the law and reading and writing. With differentiated statuses, royal and religious, classes and cultures, humans, largely one, increasingly made themselves into different beings.

Abstract social orders developed from the division of labour and specialized crafts. Writing and auguring priests advised sacred kings, whose agents and armies commanded cities that dominated their immediate landscape and reached towards distant lands where their merchants and armies went in search of materials, goods and slaves. Cities and civilizations influenced and even enfolded the countryside and everyday life into their needs and designs.

Within walls humans stored their harvests, protected their livestock, practised crafts, exchanged and stored treasured goods and accumulated their past. Defining home, community and landscape, walls delineated place in society and on the landscape; they were primary and indispensable in defining everyday life as a condition of body, movement and mind.

Humans became, by the force of town and yet the expansion of empire, intramural beings. The built world not only secured biological needs and embodied and protected social orders but ringed off the arenas in which humans lived out their daily minds and concentrated on their most advanced crafts, but honed their language, arts, philosophies and religions.[67] Summarizing the dimension of this revolution, Trevor Watkins contends that amid these first-built architectural frames and settled communities, humans established social orders and sovereignty, consolidated crafts and skills and formed 'symbolic orders of meaning'.[68]

Between the walls, cities and civilizations incubated human advancement in social order, technology, building, goods and decoration. In their confines and their extending reach by land and sea, humans more and more complexly and inwardly thought and expressed themselves. At the pinnacle of their thought, with their religious thinkers and philosophers, they sought not only to define man's place in being but the foundations and corridors of consciousness.

Cities defined the extraordinary for the great majority of humanity then, and for some vast variable number until recent times. Most people lived in isolated camps and villages. Actions and thoughts had their traditions, cultures and boundaries in distinct places. Place, indeed, defined everyday life for most as a continuity of actions and obligations. It doled out daily necessity and seasonally had its celebrations. Though outsiders were distant aliens, they were sought out and traded for wives and reproduction.

Cities, then, in all they represented, brought about, demanded and made manifest, were extraordinary. They threatened to split the atom of villages, countryside and places – with the lure of goods and different ways, the disciplines of money and imposing taxes, as well as conscription, armies and their laws. At their extremes, they overran places with changes that could be absorbed, localized and made moderate; at their worst they brought new souls and minds to tribes, country folks and rural and village inhabitants. With new institutions, ideas and religions, they threatened, as we will examine in later chapters, all autonomy, initiative and tradition. They took away local people's ways, lands, paths, crafts, customs, children and homes; everything, everyone, even the spirits and gods were knocked down and turned upside down. Whether a matter of despair or even hope, cities constituted the extraordinary in the countryside, perennially laden with body and labours, tied to long-practised technologies and harnessed to the cycle of life and seasons. Urban novelties, passions, compounding thoughts and enthusiastic beliefs simply did not fit in old bodies, skills, minds and hearts.

2

In a Place at a Time, with Changing Orders and Rising Spires

Behind the features of a landscape, or tool and machinery,
or the most formal written documents, or the institutions
that seem entirely remote from those who establish them,
are the men whom history seeks to grasp.

Marc Bloch, *Apologie pour l'histoire*

Only in dreams do people live in an empty landscape, free to be imagined, named and constructed. For the vast majority throughout time, landscapes have been given from childhood. With their heads stuffed with images, relations, concepts and stereotypes, people experience everyday life as a kaleidoscope where their feet carry them between home, work and bed. The four cardinal directions belong, beyond all choice and even the power of spirits, to the winds and seasons and where rivers gather, flow and empty themselves. Once men and women lived out their lives in lush valley flats and up and down the slopes of ascending rock and increasing scarcity; and in the ancien régime, as Malthus argued, population, which increased geometrically, forever outran food supply, which could at best be increased only mathematically.

Place is where humans are anchored. There, in a given environment, they experience first sights and sounds, smells and touches, and organize themselves, their roles and their place in and around constant needs, set habits and a small community. Within this world arises their thought, judgement and imagination, along with a sense of order and predictability. In turn, with groups, tools, social structures and cultures, they incorporate themselves into places they know as their own.

The human compass is also staked out by more abstract thought. It has its genesis in thoughts about the source of seasons, the origins of spring and autumn, birth and death, and looks upward to measure the course of the passing sun, moon and starry heavens. While priests chart the course of kingdoms by the movements of the heavens, the majority returns from daily work in the fields or on royal projects to their home, where they reproduce, store and secure food and sleep at night. The main difference between home and field, and forest, mountain and marshland, was the divide between the familiar and predictable and the wild and alien. The latter holds the surprise and magic of the unexpected, strange, monstrous and extraordinary.[1]

Everyday life for sedentary and agricultural people during the past 10,000–12,000 or more years had its hub in the village. Its circumference formed a ring of repeating expectations and significance. The shell of communal life, its walls were a group's defence and stables; and its structures held its harvests and tools.

The village, which held a handful of homes, was the plenum in which groups lived out their lives on a material and social landscape. Attuned to human wit, perception and everyday emotions, life was made constant by habits, manners, language, gesture and orders of respect and tradition. At the same time, the village assimilated rituals and religion into its everyday biological and communal life, by which it sought to assure the benevolence and abundance of nature and to connect the living and the dead.

Much comprised and made everyday lives single and distinct. There were repeating climates and reiterating topographies of hills, rivers, lakes, wetlands, fields and soils. With natural and made landscapes came available materials, adapted tools, made containers, objects and structures. Customs and habits provided ways to express emotions and values, as did food, games, dress, gender roles and rites of passage, while gifts and exchanges, always to be calculated, called for gratitude and equality in reciprocity and formed traditional and spontaneous relations within and outside community.[2]

Imagination, embedded in traditions of song, dance and myth, supplied metaphorical roots to ordinary life. Language and gestures both abridged and elevated actions and experience to communication, while decorations and symbols classified life in its immediacy and universality. Stories bound together experiences real and imagined, allowing them to be enacted and memorable. In this way, material life – hard, dull, detailed and redundant – had a profoundly mental side; or to make an argument out of Marc Bloch's section title for part II of his *Feudal Society* (1939), the environment was composed of both 'Conditions of Life and Mental Climate'. The latter, according to Bloch, was composed of feelings and thoughts, with attitudes to nature and time, expressions of culture and social classes and religious mentality, along with folk memory.[3]

Wherever everyday life existed in the traditional order, it had vitality and wholeness. In single villages or extended to region or kingdom, there was a sense of uniqueness and timelessness, and enduring persistence. In this way everyday life in small, local and traditional villages (the dominant mode of life from the agricultural revolution to modern times in Europe and recent decades across much of the world) stood as the model of the natural and God-given way for humans to dwell in nature and among one another. Only in the nineteenth century did historians and ethnographers systematically seek the common man in distinct places and typical everyday lives.

My shelves alone hold books on everyday life in ancient Egypt and Mesopotamia, biblical times, ancient Greece, Homeric times and ancient Rome.[4] They come with growing knowledge of the social and material lives of early civilizations, telling us about people and places, materials, objects, tools, works, crafts and popular beliefs and religions.

According to the Annales School historian and medievalist Jacques Le Goff, a major goal of history and modern anthropology, along with its sister inquiries folklore and ethnography, has been to capture the distinct essence of the lives of traditional places and peoples. Inspired by Romanticism and moved by nostalgia and a distinguishing genealogy, this quest for the uniqueness and organic, spiritual wholeness of traditional life sought to differentiate the past from the flux of artificial and fragmenting modern life. In contradistinction to emergent industrial and conflicted democratic society, anthropologists and historians idealized traditional folk society for its innocence, spontaneity and even cultural homogeneity. They found in early peoples a missing balance between man and nature and a coherence of material life and inclusive symbolic and mythic culture.

Twentieth-century anthropologists, often joined by sociologists, continued the pursuit for hidden communities and cultures even amid contemporary mass urban life. They found vital and integral daily lives in parishes, ethnic neighbourhoods and on street corners, in back alleys and lanes, and even in such out of the way places as tent cities and homeless shelters. They located the distinct social groups and cultures in apartments, workplaces and institutions – and even in prisons, asylums and army barracks. At the same time, anthropology, serving a critique as old as colonialism itself, spoke of the validity and integrity of the everyday lives of non-Western and indigenous peoples and agonized over distorting compromises and mutations that came from straddling old and new ways.[5]

FEUDALISM AND SOCIAL FOUNDATIONS

As much as successful technology defined the shaping of the landscapes on which daily life materially and symbolically operated, there had to be an underlying structure of authority and social relation to define the formation of human collective life across regions and over centuries. Medieval historians find that authority over land and people in feudalism. While feudalism, rich in forms and of varying definitions, did not take root in city-filled Italy, Scandinavia and the other European borderlands, it provided the foundation of political authority and an interlocking social order for most of Britain, some of Russia and Europe. Based on the exchange of land for the military service of specially mounted warriors (with their reciprocal vows of fidelity and promised terms and periods for grants of land, fiefs), feudalism lies at the foundation of the Middle Ages. It accounted for the partition and addition of new lands as well as the resolution of centuries-long internecine wars in Europe and the repulsion of invading tribes from the east, Vikings from the north and Islam, which swept across North Africa and, with the conquest of Spain in 710, went on to invade France from the southwest.[6]

Providing the frame of everyday life, feudalism offered a replicable mechanism of authority and ownership over a vast territory in Europe's embryonic stage first crystallized by Charlemagne at the start of the ninth century. Distributing land and military obligations among the powerful rivalling warriors, feudalism turned them into one another's lords and vassals, producing myriad and asymmetric relations. With land (fiefs) secured and peace prevailing, armed knights over centuries mutated from warriors to estate-owning lords and nobles. They became a second estate, clergy and Church officials forming the first and members of autonomous towns and cities developing later into the third. Peasants, rural by definition, found their place on the land through becoming indentured servants on a lord's land. Not without tensions and conflicts, serfs had claimed their place by belonging to the land of the lord and his manor. Though not slaves owned in body, serfs had gained their meaning in everyday life from their mutual place and work on the lord's estate.

Holy Roman Emperors – so the heirs of Charlemagne claimed, as kings later did – were the lord of all vassals. Adding to the hierarchy of power and control, bishops, official representatives of the Church, also claimed to be the lords of the land and collectively presumed to form the first estate of a kingdom. Formally invested by the power of the king and the authority of the Church in the early twelfth century, bishops filled in and extended the hierarchy of control, without subjugating Western Europe to the eastern tradition of Caesaropapism. All this convinced men and women that even the heavens had a hierarchical order, with God at the top and his son in command of the second order of Creation, which would last until the end of time when, in the words of Psalm 85, 'Truth shall spring out of the earth / and justice shall look down from heaven.' In this way, everyday order, encapsulated in a social order and crowned by a political order, belonged to a world view that organized heaven and earth and the beginning and end of time.

ON THE GROUND LEVEL

To understand place and daily life throughout time prior to the coming of the Industrial Revolution and the massive building of roads, tracks and cars, we must recognize that the majority lived out their lives on foot. They did this by necessity and habit; it was the condition of moving about – working, travel and social contact.[7]

When Europeans and Westerners look for their childhood (the youth of nation, race and spirits), they must first look to people who worked, travelled and danced on foot. Medieval peasants – those who worked the land and lived in small villages of two hundred or fewer inhabitants – measured out their work and had their social encounters on foot. To understand exactly how isolated and in turn how autonomous life was, we must grasp how – absent of roads and wheeled vehicles, except their heavy hauling oxen cart – life moved on foot and followed the paths least costly in energy through woods and mountains, wetlands and streams and rivers. Seasons forbade travel, which was ever travail. Darkness itself was a great wall to movements of any sort. No place except later parquet-wood palace floors permitted smooth and free ways for the lightly clad foot. Walking for the great majority, especially the peasant, was about the drudge of the trudge – trudging, stepping, climbing, bending and wading; anything but stylish gliding, which we identify with straight, even, level and smooth floors, sidewalks and paved surfaces. Each meeting with a passing horseman or a lord and lady in slippers reminded the trudging peasant of his inferiority.

The world was largely perceived and experienced by going on foot. The opposite of walking was sitting on scarce chairs, which were not comfortable, or lying in beds of hay and straw. In the day, any way to be off one's feet meant to be down on one's haunches, leaning against tree or wall or even testing the top of a cut log or sitting on a wooden bench. In truth, nearly all things humble, and almost all things great, were accomplished by going on foot. Even the army spear-headed by mounted warriors still depended on the slogging of infantries and the legs of grooms and porters. Ordinary life in all theatres of village and town took place on foot. Even dancing set peasants' feet stomping, not gliding and shuffling to refined rhythms.

Unlike us, for whom smooth wheels roll on pristine roads, medieval people lived and imagined around long and difficult foot travel. On foot, merchants travelled with packs on their back and saddlebags on their donkey; mendicants and robbers did their work; and pilgrims did penance and sought miracles. Medieval people had no trouble imagining Christ's three years of peregrination across the Holy Land. They easily incorporated into their folk stories strange travellers met at the crossroads and down long and twisting paths as well as 'the myth of the wandering Jew – who was condemned to travel afoot until the Second Coming for having taunted Christ on his way to Calvary'. The medieval mind found, as contemporary historians of everyday life should, meaningful metaphors with travel, legs and feet, shoes, footprints, walking sticks and crossroads, where people congregated, erected altars, chapels, shrines and gallows and buried those who committed suicide.[8]

Indeed, medieval life moved not on the straight, efficient and administrative Roman roads but on paths to local fields and lanes. Walking and carrying goods, the medieval merchant was first intent on local trade. He followed lanes and paths that connected such fixed points as towns, fairs, destinations of pilgrimage and the rare bridge, important fords and indispensable mountain passes. The wheeled cart, judged inferior to human and animal feet on rugged terrain, meant pack animals still carried the day in mountains well into modern times.

The medieval historian of everyday life must realize that life in the early centuries was lived in relatively isolated villages off the main paths of invasions, pillage and plague. Serfdom and walking bound the place by law and ease to place. However, starting in the eighth century, settlements sprang up in ports and along rivers as a consequence of the revival of European travel. Around the end of the eleventh century, travel began to flow into and out of valleys holding larger populations and fertile agricultural lands. Kings granted independence to nascent towns, to which landless beggars, soldiers, outlaws and ambitious peasants flocked to improve their condition. Their migrations were joined on the roads by swelling streams of students, scholars and pilgrims, and craftspeople, artists, herbalists, itinerant pedlars, jongleurs, minstrels and charlatans of every sort in search of work.

MEDIEVAL PEOPLES

In truth, we can depict as many varied everyday lives as we can name distinct medieval groups. In her classic text *Medieval People* (1924), Eileen Power chronicled the life of six medieval people; of her portraits, the daily life of Bodo, the typical peasant, catches attention. In a 1947 work, Chiara Frugoni surveys, as her title indicates, *A Day in a Medieval City*. Her topics include images of peoples and places, roads to and streets within, along with labour, 'childhood learning', 'adult reading' and 'indoors'.[9] In *Daily Life in the Middle Ages*, Paul B. Newman makes his topics, to cite his chapter titles, 'eating and cooking', 'building and housing', 'clothing and dressing', 'cleaning', 'relaxing and playing', 'fighting' and finally, appropriately, 'healing'.[10] Under the dichotomizing title of 'Man or Men', Jacques Le Goff as editor introduced his *Medieval World*, a volume of ten essays, each devoted to a distinct medieval life.[11] First come monks, warriors and knights, peasants and dwellers in cities and towns. Next come intellectuals, artists, merchants, women and families, the saints and marginal men – those who belong to the fringes of medieval society.

Throughout his long introductory essay, Le Goff concedes that his typology of ten, which does not truly capture any one individual life, does not cover the spectrum of distinct medieval lives. Where, for instance, are the pagans, charcoal burners, witches, non-believers, crusaders and pilgrims, who skirt the established trails and fixed life? How do we account for those whose outsider and eccentric lives are hidden in mountains, forests, marshes and the shores of rivers, seacoasts and small outer islands?

Variety defies any one typology of everyday life. Time itself, the subject of Chapter Three, illustrates how place and people must likewise be gauged by mutations, developments, transformations and the irregular course of events. Monks belonged to different periods. At different periods and places they formed and enrolled in different religious orders, each observing different daily regimes of work and prayer, and following different vocations and rules regulating their ability to travel and serve the world.

Different stages of warfare and land ownership and political control distinguished warriors. From the seventh to the eleventh to the thirteenth century they mutated from hardy bands of warriors into organized property owners and an established aristocracy.

City and town dwellers, too, followed and accounted for the development of an urban and commercial civilization. By the thirteenth century in Italy and the Lowlands, strong markets equalled autonomous towns, free of the hand of a lord and the hierarchy of the feudal order. Under the banner of 'city air makes free', the third estate claimed a place equivalent to the first estate of clergy and the second of landholding nobility. The third estate incorporated to itself a spectrum of wealth and power including merchants and bankers, differentiated guilds and craftsmen, and such undifferentiated city people as newly arrived immigrants from the countryside and the poor and unemployed.

Everyday life held worlds of different peasants. Proximity and ties to spreading markets characterized peasants of different places, times and notions of necessity and opportunity. In the aggregate, peasants saw increasing possibilities of owning land and having money. Likewise, there were profound divergences and contradictions in the everyday lots of intellectuals, artists, merchants and women and families. Even so-called marginal men and even saints proved that fantasy and myth, irrationality and holiness have histories. Not all beggars stand at equally productive crossroads.

In effect, Le Goff calls attention to altered places and times. Surveying lives over five hundred years, from AD 1000 to 1500, produces a dramatic temporal diptych

> whose first panel shows the prodigious development of Christianity [and a great growth in farming the land and city] between 1000 and the thirteenth century and whose second panel shows that turbid time called the later Middle Ages, when a world of the past in crisis and a New Middle Ages, the Renaissance, whirled in tandem.[12]

THE VILLAGE, THE LAND, THE PLOUGH AND THE MILL

In the medieval world, the peasant is the dominant type. While there were independent farmers in southern France, the majority of peasants across the greatest part of the Middle Ages belonged to communities of serfs. Not slaves owned in body but serfs attached to the land, they fell under the jurisdiction and authority of a lord (even in matters of marriage and, in certain places, the lord had the privilege of breaking the bride's virginity). Peasants depended on the lord's manors and mills, while being conscripted annually for so many days – *la corvée* – to the lord's work on his lands and the roads. Peasants were also subjected to the community's rotating assignment of fields, percentage of harvests and use of waters and woods. At the same time, peasants on certain ecclesiastical estates were subordinated to the bishop as ruling lord of the lands and the priest as administrator of sacraments and confessor.

With considerable national variations in types and stages of English, German, French, Polish, Russian and Italian feudalism, historians concur that the medieval peasant was rural. He belonged to geography – the valleys, marshes, mountains, woods, water, rivers and seas that surrounded him. His survival and abundance went with the climate, soil, vegetation and diseases and plagues that appeared. Mediterranean and Continental European environments formed a primary division of life in northern and southern Europe. Locations in turn varied by animal and plant resources, types of structures and applicable technologies, diverse concentrations of population and the desirability of lands and proximity or distance to nearby rivers, paths, market centres and command posts. Medieval man survived and thrived by what he harvested from the land, could cut and gather in the woods, fish from waters or, in Holland and elsewhere in northern Europe, win from the sea and wetlands by dam and drainage.

In the small and tight orb of a community of one or two hundred, people knew and met the changing conditions year in and year out. Cycles included extremes – flood or drought caused all to beseech the saints to provide, and when they did to say 'Enough!', 'Basta, San Antonio!' Spring brought late frosts and autumn rains and floods, which stole land and caused mudslides. In the worst times wolves came down hungry from the mountains and brigands scavenged the countryside and ambushed the routes of early merchants and travellers.

From the earliest stages of the Middle Ages, as Rome neared its ends, Europe was besieged by great and prolonged invasions. They started in the fourth century AD with mounted Huns coming from the East; and then from the eighth to the eleventh centuries seafaring Vikings came from homelands in the north. They poured down on Europe, ending as ruling Norman administrators in northwest France, Kiev in the east, and in southern Italy and Sicily. From the early eighth century Arab warriors from the Near East and North Africa began their invasions and took control of the Mediterranean, occupying Sicily and Spain. Simultaneously, as feudalism and agriculture in Europe took form, internal quarrels between lords and warriors and settled landlords abounded, culminating in battles between princes, kings and Holy Roman Emperors for vast territories and the peoples of Europe.

In a word, while the clock of everyday life was set regularly and predictably by the rising and setting sun, time did not beat a regular year in and out as material, economic, social, political and religious life developed and mutated.

Everyday medieval life, sharply differentiated and sharply divided in countless ways by place and time, lasted roughly a thousand years, from the eighth to the eighteenth century. With peasant and village the substance of place, the life-giving proteins were land, work and family and community, authority and belief. Depicting this is indispensable to any particular portrait of everyday life.

The land dictated everything during the five centuries from 800 to 1300. Individual survival itself was contingent on having a place on the land while the highest activity of civilization included taking hold of, protecting, allocating and developing the land for agriculture. Second, as land was consolidated, warriors and knights had to be tamed – which they were by stewardship of land, the civilizing refinement of court and chivalry, and the Church's teaching of morals and capacity to dispatch Christian soldiers on Holy Land crusades.

Third, and immensely transformative, were the rise and spread of markets from hill to valley, river to sea. With markets and merchants went the beginning and growth of towns, the commercial integration of Europe and extensive European trade in the Mediterranean and the beginning of true independent urban life. In addition to narratives tracing the material, economic, social and political development of medieval civilization, an entirely different set of developmental narratives – forming the conclusion of this chapter – focuses on the spread and influence of Christianity, which, while never total, nevertheless made the Middle Ages a Christian civilization from its most elaborate exterior forms and rituals to its inner systems of conscience, belief and hope.

Land clearance is the start of medieval Europe. It enabled agriculture, on which Europe built its population and around which it shaped its work, social life and villages. Rooting our portrait of everyday social life in geography, land and economics, Marc Bloch in his classic *French Rural History* (1931) ties village and everyday peasant life to human dependency on the fields he worked. Social life, work, ownership and distribution went with the size and shape of the fields. Crop rotation enhanced the fertility of fields and type and sequence of seasonal labours.

Such a material-social approach recognizes a primary role of technology in defining the nature and potential of human labour.[13] Accounting for human use of animals, with horses serving warfare and more sturdy and constant oxen ploughing and carting, machines determined which land could be worked and how a community collectively organized itself to work the land. A singularly important piece of technology in defining medieval farming was the wheeled plough. Pulled by a team of oxen, the wheeled plough proved key in opening the heavy, fertile soils of northern Europe. Its success had the consequence of subordinating all lands – gardens, woods and wetlands – to all-important fertile crop-lands for grains. The wheeled plough shaped the contour of the fields and the dead land that lay between fields and the path of field drainage. The harvest was doled out in shares according to the number of oxen a peasant contributed to the plough, and one share was given for ownership of the plough's steel tip. This made ploughing with the heavy-wheeled plough a communal affair. Ownership of ploughshares constituted claims to seasonal land allocation, share of harvested crops and, of course, made calculating and jealousy a characteristic of the community, which worked or starved together.

Wind and water were brought into the service of human energy by all-important mills, which profoundly supplemented human labour. The primary use of gears over centuries was refined into the elaborate mechanical movement of medieval clocks, which measured hours, days, years and even the movement of heavenly bodies. Located at crossings and forming ponds, mills were the churning heart of larger agricultural communities. Tapping an inexhaustible supply of energy and utilizing materials on new scales, abundant mills applied mechanics to grinding grain, sawing wood, pounding metals and fulling cloth. On the plains of Spain windmills did the work of watermills, and in Holland windmills, numbering in the thousands, stole back the land by pumping water into the invasive sea. Housed on polders, mills were structures for work and dwelling. Centring villages and their activities, they served agricultural and other production tasks, while pumping, raising and channelling water from the land. Further defying old stereotypes of being anti-mechanical, medieval men used machines to raise towering churches and cathedrals with delicate interiors.

Mills and mechanics defined everyday work. They played a crucial role in defining medieval Europe as a land of farmers, builders and workers. Increasingly adroit at working wood, stone and iron, Europe took on truly phenomenal building projects, with volume, height and beauty no peasant could imagine. Starting in the twelfth century, encircling walls were lengthened, thickened and given more elaborate gates. Roads ramified, bridges multiplied, monumental palaces and lordly residences increased and, as we will discuss later, cathedrals, the crown jewel of urban building, began to define the prominence and pride of towns and cities.

Technological innovations began to shape everyday labour and communities. They differentiated the role and value of crafts, adding additional layers of society to the hierarchical Middle Ages. Organized into a range of guilds, including production, commerce and banking, crafts formed the basis of complex medieval urban society, which bloomed in thirteenth-century Italy.

METAPHORS MAKE LIFE'S MEANINGS

Humans of all times transform the ordinary, material and common into the extraordinary.[14] They organize and project the world and their place and movement in it in lines, curves and circles and squares.[15] They do this with and because they live by mind, language and metaphor. They write their bodies and minds, their homes and things, into the world and they turn those real and imagined worlds into meanings for their own place and time. People use their metaphors of God, heaven and religion to give significance and meaning to their common ways and days.

Metaphors, the body and spirit of joining and comparing things, weave associations. Metaphors turn bread, homes and whole cities into the food and dwelling of animals and the halls of gods. Language furnishes the rooms and furniture of our lives, to use a metaphor by the philosopher Eva Feder Kittay.[16] Never completely tidy in use, given we live a life of ignorance, confusions and dilemmas in a world of change and tumult, metaphors nevertheless help us reach clarity. 'It is within a carefully conceived chaos', Kittay further contends, 'that metaphors attain an irreducible content and their special meaning.'[17]

Meaning belongs to where body is and where mind and language carry us. The historian Robert Evans conceives of meaning as the process whereby 'experience becomes language and thought'. With metonymy and metaphors, Evans adds, humans create 'the poetries of association by contiguity and association' and they join them 'in a plurality of worlds, mixing, in the striking phrase of Karl Bühler, *a cocktail of spheres*'.[18]

As seen in early artefacts and decorations, the human mind reaches and leaps beyond itself. It transports significance, values, ideas, suppositions and hopes across multiple dimensions of place and time. Whether the local historian chose his or her instructors to be Sigmund Freud, Ernst Cassirer, James Joyce or Mircea Eliade, everyday life irrepressibly registered, from the early cave paintings, psychoanalytic, symbolic, mythic and religious meaning. Humans seemed destined with tool and mind to try to account for their niche in things, and why they hurt, suffered and died.

Humans carried the dead and gods forward in time. Religions and priesthoods conducted and regulated primary transactions between domains of being. Walls that encircled places were built holy. They were set on consecrated land; earth and ashes of the dead were brought from the mother colony to place under the footing of a new colony. In classical times homes too had sacred foundations. As we learn from Numa Denis Fustel de Coulanges' classic *The Ancient City* (1864), the hearth of the household was its centre. Its fires joined the ancestral family and the sacred underground and its emissaries, snakes. Human landscapes have traditionally fashioned their landscapes around spots where underground and heavens meet.

IN THE SHADOW OF THE CATHEDRAL

Christianity planted metaphors across the Middle Ages. And through these metaphors people, in different ways, understood their fathers and mothers, bread and wine, the waters and the desert, and the screens of their tabernacles and the heavens.

Christ turned followers' lives with stories, proverbs and parables. With parables (so clearly expressed in Mark 4), he probed hearts about justice, fairness and generosity. With them he puzzled his own disciples, asking: Why does the Lord reward equally those who enter the field in the last hour of work? Who is it that invites strangers from the crossroads to his banquet and then evicts them when they come improperly dressed?

Christ, master poet, with the great and challenging reach of metaphor between the material and spiritual, described himself as the living waters of Jacob's Well and the bread he gave his disciples to eat at the Last Supper. With metaphors reaching from earth to heaven and an array of miracles, Christ metamorphosed the Father's first Creation to the Son's coming and return, laying the basis for a religion and culture and civilization in which body and person and the materiality of everyday life were sanctified by message and hope.

Christianity, like other great religions, did more than offer beliefs and hopes. It also shaped and transformed minds, society and the imagination where it spread. Its power was drawn from the words and miracles of Christ and the apostles and the experience, teachings, doctrine and theology of the early Church council and the Church Fathers. Its unique and singular symbols distinguished Christianity as a belief system.

The metaphors of Christianity made a fresh order of connections between the material and spiritual, the profane and holy, and present, past and times to come. Christianity made an invisible kingdom present. It formed moral conscience, extended the love of God and made the ordinary and humble godly. It constituted a revolution in the inner dimensions and consciousness of everyday life.

Christianity gave its believer distinct identities – and filled pools of metaphors and symbols from which to draw and value lives.[19] It also changed the very symbols of life and death. It redefined the powerful language of food and feast.[20] At the same time, it offered theological premises and imaginative visions of the afterlife, while the early and medieval Church elaborated the doctrine of the Communion of Saints, which joined the living and dead in prayer, sanctifying grace and everlasting and eternal communion.[21] Indeed, as the Church articulated and implemented its sacramental system of baptism, Eucharist, penance, marriage, priesthood and last rites, it afforded believers, communities and cultures a symbolic world and metaphors connecting grace and sin and individual present life and the everlasting life of saved souls and God.

Christianity, not a sect for the hour or a secret cult for a select community and single place, provided a Church with a structure and authority, which embraced regional bishop and local village priest. How far it penetrated into the everyday ways and mind, especially of remote villages and forest peoples, is questionable. Nevertheless, with waves of missionaries it converted peoples and kings. Monasteries and schools trained clergy, wrote and preserved writing and assimilated an inheritance (of Church and classics) to pass on and explore. With theology so prominent in the late and emergent medieval universities, Christianity stood confident in studying and absorbing the most refined thoughts of the Greeks and Arabs. And, combative over its own doctrines, Christian thinkers, with Paul and Augustine's confidence, dared even to reflect contemporary affairs, draw limits around royal sovereignty and analyse the conditions that have to be met to launch a just war.

Over a thousand-year period, through missionizing, teaching and preaching and the influence of politicizing bishops, practising priests and the sacraments, the Church formed the outer structure and some significant part of the inner substance of thoughts and values for the entire society. Or, to rely on the Catholic historian Christopher Dawson, every narrative of the Middle Ages, from highest Church culture to the formation and valuing of common life, must relate how Europe over the thousand-year period from AD 500 to 1500 became dominantly Christian and Catholic. Over a millennium Christianity engendered medieval culture (its beliefs, practices, morals and intellectual standards) and defined for Europeans who they first were and still, in a radically diminished measure, remain.[22]

Most to our purpose here, Christianity gave everyday medieval life a mind, so to speak – a substratum of thoughts, beliefs and values. It afforded peoples of all classes a disposition towards and a supposition about the nature, end and worth of things. It reconnected and energized relations between the living and the dead, declaring all souls eternal with a place in God's Creation through renewal and redemption in Christ.

Also, ministering to man's misery and hope, Christ's mother, Mary, central of all the saints that inspired medieval piety and prayers, sanctified body and woman. Mary, the bride of God and the vessel of the Holy Spirit, was graced and graceful flesh. She heard the human call for pity. She, who bore and witnessed her divine son's life and death, dispensed mercy to all but the proud and foolish. She was the heart of sympathy for all who suffered loss or were stalked by illness, accident and death. Who better to pray to than Mary, mother of God, the antithesis of the jealous and malicious goddesses of antiquity, such as Demeter at Enna in Sicily, who supposedly carried out the curses of the living against the dead.

Jesus Christ was the incarnation of spirit. His very first miracle in the New Testament was performed at the request of his mother, Mary, at the wedding celebration at Cana. He turned a little wine into a lot of the last and best wine. Another early miracle in the first days of his three-year mission was his cure of a paralytic. Unable to reach Christ, the paralytic was lowered on his pallet through a roof by his friends to secure Jesus' healing. Scandalizing the Pharisees, Christ first forgave the paralytic his sins, explaining that it is far easier to cure a body than cleanse a soul. Then to accent his words to the Pharisees, Jesus told the paralytic to take up his litter and walk. In another miraculous cure joining body and spirit, Christ drove the demons out of a man into a herd of pigs that, possessed, ran headlong and wildly off a cliff. With miracles Christ demonstrated how his grace works on the matter, body and mind of everyday life.

The Church appropriated Christ's healing power with its sacraments and celebrations. As if to bring miracles and enter the divine into ordinary daily life, the Church in the name of Christ blessed meals and feasts and honoured births, marriages and deaths, while turning abnegations and fasts into sacrifices and prayers. In this way, Christianity sublimated love songs and poetry into mysticism, turned renunciation of all and anything into humble prayer, and dubbed rough soldiers the blessed warriors of Christ.

The Church extended forgiveness and blessing to all. Sprinkling and showering water on society, it took up and superseded pagan rites in the perennial matters of blessing fields and animals, christening boat and bridge and consecrating buildings great and small. Likewise, being the only source of reading and writing, the priest was the village expert and authority on all matters except those of family, land and imaginary powers like fairies, werewolves and witches.

The spiritual power of the Church was profoundly enhanced by its capacity to analogize between God and man, eternal and earthly time. Theologians of highest brow and preachers of common rout could read Old and New Testament stories and parables into all ordinary things, acts and situations. With an extraordinary richness of symbols the Church was the prime instructor of both literate and popular cultures. The Church's power to transform with symbols and icons showed at every local church and was on absolute and full display in the medieval Church's magnum opus, the cathedral.[23]

A cathedral was a century-long project. It was the pride of a community and even an entire region. It was a treasury of sacred knowledge, precious objects and the inheritance of the faith. Requiring the support of a powerful bishop, a steady run of funds, architects and craftsmen from far off and in general a variety of local and distant material sources, the building of a house of God outstripped all civil projects in size and complexity, including the construction of city walls. Dedicated commonly to Mary, another saint, the mystery of Christ or the Trinity itself, a cathedral proved at one and the same time that the Church was materially, spiritually and even politically paramount. Towering over all other structures in volume and height, unrivalled as a creation until the cavernous nineteenth-century metropolitan train station and century's-end department store and skyscraper, the cathedral was the centre of a place; its towers and spires defined the horizon.

The cathedral was the premier project of the architect, craftsmen of stone, wood and metal, glassworkers and myriad other artists. The most elevated work of beauty and constructed with the symmetries of classical geometry and plumb line and protractor, it sought to fill with awe all who entered. Raised and conceived with analogies understood between earth and heaven, cathedrals, the catechism of all, sought to incorporate Old and New Testaments and the stories of saints, kings, nobles and bishops. God was great, vast and overwhelming. His grace and Creation belonged to light radiant. In unity with God's being three, the cathedral celebrated the Trinity. Facades featured Old and New Testament authorities and prophets. Inner walls of halls and apses bore painted and sculpted narratives of Old and New Testaments. They paid particular attention to the birth, miracle, Way of the Cross, Resurrection, Second Coming and Final Judgement of Christ. Interiors illustrated Christian belief for the illiterate.

Cathedrals served other ends too. With intricacy of design, miniatures, flashes of colour, exotic materials and stained glass portraits of everyday crafts and life, cathedrals offered a panorama of knowledge, wealth and technology. In the closing centuries of the Middles Ages clocks ticked time – not just hours and days but ages and the movements of the heavens.

The altar was the epicentre of the church. Here was the priest's stage and the Eucharist. The altar, under the elevated dome and encircled by panels of glass, was the exact point where nave and apses, earth and heaven and Christ crucified and resurrected intersected. Above ascending front and side stairs was the altar itself. With a marble or rich stone top, the altar was embellished with the bones of saints, assuring the continuity of faith and the Communion of Saints. It displayed the most precious objects of gold, silver and ivory to celebrate the Eucharist: literally the consecration and transubstantiation of bread and wine into the body and blood of Christ. The consecrated chalices of body and blood were stored most often in the centre of the altar in the precious tabernacle, whose sculpted inner doors and gates opened to the Lord. Present in the smallest early Romanesque church, the altar was the anvil on which the Church as inheritor and dispenser of truth and grace forged the Middle Ages materially and spiritually, aesthetically and mystically.

In this way, Christian faith formed a culture that both permeated and created everyday life in the Middle Ages. It baptized and infused body with vision, conscience and hope. It declared the most ordinary and common lives worthy of God's eternal kingdom. On the wings of analogy, metaphors and poetry it flew ordinary bodies on ever so deep and lifting flights into being. It declared extraordinary grace at work within the most common and humble days.

3

Many Times Make Many Minds

Historical, contingent truths can never be proofs of rational, necessary truths.

Gotthold Ephraim Lessing

Times are plural, and they multiply things, places and peoples. Whether comprehensible or not, happenings take place and events occur. Change measures the length of earth's history and the course and seasons of everyday life. Whether time is linear or cyclical, whether past and future and fate and freedom exist together and whether cause and effect can or cannot be clearly identified, now and then make this and that mark differences in days, years, lives, aeons.[1] The only known self and community are the narrated self and community.

Time comes with motions and movements, transformations, metamorphoses and revolutions. They define perceptions, organize experience, give substance to our thought and animate our language. Seasons and successions, births and deaths, and the maturation and decadence of institutions are chronometers of human experience and consciousness. The social sciences – economics, sociology, anthropology, political science and even psychology – are predicated on happenings and events and their construction.[2]

When we do history we think time. We allot our stages and form our plots by the parcelling of time. Diachronically, we know body and landscape. We live in the instantaneity of time – its unifications, divisions and leaps. Mind goes from being captive of the present, prophet of the future, prisoner of nostalgia and conjurer of and speculator on other times. Time enwraps consciousness. Mind lives by an array of inner and exterior clocks. They tick with the resonance of all that is, was, will, might and should be. Memory persists in moments of failure and victory, speculating on fates and fortunes and hoping that things will be different. So time in all its forms changes, divides, dichotomizes and distinguishes things separate and together, creating what can be called the 'thenness of being'.[3]

Cultures, as historians are keenly aware, are timekeepers. They indicate calendars for planting, hunting, harvesting and worship; designate periods of mourning and celebration; and mark out auspicious occasions for undertakings. They give meaning to life by dividing and subdividing humankind into the young, mature, old, fey – those doomed to die – and the dead themselves. The professor of literature Robert Pogue Harrison, in his *Dominion of the Dead* (2003), considers the dead as a central axis of a culture's construction of world and time.[4] To the old the dead can seem more alive than the living. To people of all ages indebtedness to the dead is part of the planking of individual and common memory. Rituals are often based on the recognition of the primogeniture and authority of the dead. Authors of our most enduring institutions, conventions and traditions, the dead claim first gratitude. Drawing on the works of the seventeenth-century Italian historicist Giambattista Vico and the twentieth-century German philosopher Martin Heidegger, Harrison concludes that the notion of the dominion of the dead is the primary dimension of human self-making.[5]

TIME DOES RULES

In Chapter One I affirmed that body, materiality, geography and landscape define place and everyday life. In Chapter Two I argued that symbols and myths structure place, society and the routines of everyday life. Here I assert that change, in all its variety, forever mutates places and daily life. Lives embedded in place – its geography, geology and landscape – are also encapsulated in time and must be narrated.

The duty that historians of local and daily life owe their subject is temporal precision. By virtue of being historians they must distinguish and assess the significance of times and types of change.

They must define life at a given point or over a prolonged period with reference to abiding and transitory structures and the significant changes they cause and undergo. They must recognize the fundamental division that exists between faster-changing civilizations and societies – with greater specializations and trade and wider interactions – and the relatively slower pace of remote, distant and autonomous local and regional life.

Of course, historians of the everyday, like all historians, must wrestle with their conception of a proper time frame for their work. Are they disposed to cast change as steady and incremental, a type of evolution or decline occurring over a long arc of time; or do they wish to narrate their subject in terms of dramatic, precipitous and consequential change? Do they depict everyday life in terms of models of constant change or do they depict it as a course of unpredictable events? And, to stack question on question, do they conceive of time and its passing as naturalistic, material and secular or as revelatory and even religious in its import? And, finally, is their view of time more in conformity with laws and supporting generalizations or do they conceive of time as radical, unique and decisive turning points (*kairoi*) culminating in some unifying end (*telos*).

Local, micro- and everyday historians face a particular dilemma in structuring their narrative. They can utilize such a great stage and fill it with such immense figures in overarching plots and denouements that there is no room for the rich details and diversity of common ordinary life. Conversely, they can slice their bread so thin that it will not make a sandwich of any significant meaning. Or, if our temporal cross-sections are too many (we distinguish not just the decade but the year, the hour, the moment), there comes an unbearable infinity of 'thens and nexts' such that, referring to Zeno's paradox, Achilles never catches the tortoise, for he invariably can arrive at only one of infinite discrete points where the turtle has just been.

Enlightenment historians and their secular progressive heirs commonly impeached medieval historians on two counts. Their chronologies were mindless collections of happenings. They were composed of uncritical recording of 'one darn thing after another'. Dismissing medieval history as unbearably detailed and random, on the one hand, they charged it with a gullible universality on the other. Starting their narrative with Creation and the Divine Covenant, medieval historians ordered the universal story of Jews and empires to lead directly to their monarch and his villages and ultimately to the final return of Christ. Neither side of their history squared with the rational and general story of mankind making itself over time for its own ends and purposes.

Early nineteenth-century historians, with roots in the Neapolitan Giambattista Vico (1668–1744) and Prussian Johann Herder (1744–1803), affirmed the need for historians to write their narrative in terms of the birth, growth and maturation of distinct peoples and times. Romantic historians of the early decades of the century would have historians connect the story of a people's genesis and development with sweeping and dramatic contemporary struggles for democracy, liberty and nation.[6] Ever the realm of the surprising and erratic, the intrusive and tentative, politics proves a thorn in schemes of the progressive and developmental historians. In the nineteenth century, politics arose out of freedom and passion. In mid-century there were the spontaneous, near universal, short-lived, yet profoundly consequential and irreversible, revolutions of 1848. Sweeping across much of Western Europe, the revolutions were born out of democratic and utopian hopes and universally collapsed in the following three years, teaching all the powers of reactionary armies, dictatorship, the divisiveness of nationalism and the pitfall of popular plebiscites. Politics not of the people reappeared within less than a decade. It came in the dual-headed form of the genius of Italian unification, Piedmont's Cavour, and the ruthless and calculated cunning of Prussia's Bismarck. Politics simultaneously raised and cast in doubt the unifying narratives of peoples and nations. Political institutions, rarely synchronized, ingeniously created and tenaciously reactionary, offered wishes and taught limits. War, one of politics' primary instruments, forever produces unexpected, unwanted and even uncontestable results. Defiant of static local and everyday history, political action drags all – villages, regions, whole peoples and entire nations – down unexpected alleys, undermining the historian's role as teacher of great causes, definite trends and uplifting ends. Politics does not vouch that the past offers lessons for the present and future.

I suspect that this as much as anything accounts for why global, social and everyday-life European historians turned to Marxism. Offering a universal view of inevitable history in which those at the bottom end up on the top of a progressing humanity, Marxism promised the defeat of the vicissitudes and eccentricities of political history. It rooted human history in man's material needs and work and the common aspiration for equality and wealth. Marxism differentiated historical periods in terms of elemental antagonistic social classes with reference to their differentiation by stages of advancing means of production and the place of workers in a society commanded by owners, their machines, institutions and beliefs. In accord with advancing industrial society and the revolutionary impulses of France and the rest of Europe, Marxism placed economics – production, commodities, trade, labour and wages – at the centre of human narrative. It proposed present times as belonging to a great and escalating moral drama focused around the struggle and eventual victory of the have-nots against the haves. Marx and his immediate followers in the last decades of the nineteenth century cast the showdown at the barricades or eventually at the ballot box as between the ever fewer capitalists and an ever exploited and alienated greater many, the proletariat. Emptied of all traditional ways and beliefs, the proletariat, giving order and end to all past history, was seen marching toward an ultimate European and world revolution.

With and without a formal subscription to one or another brand of Marxism, materialism and economic history were increasingly viewed as an alternative way to narrate the past and the development of the present order. In turn, events of the first half of the twentieth century – the First World War, the Depression and the Second World War – which denied European supremacy turned historians away from traditional political history towards a global history of the rise and fall of civilization and the formation of world markets. Additional global themes were found in man's relation to nature, the growth of population, the use of physical resources and ultimate interconnection and interdependency of all peoples of the world. To take one example, in 1962 Carlo Cipolla wrote *The Economic History of World Population*, as the story of 'the two revolutions . . . the agricultural and industrial'; 'sources of energy' from plants, animals, inventions and the steam engine; 'production and consumption'; births and deaths and how many people; and our age of transition.[7]

The American historian William H. McNeill offered another global approach. He presented a biological and ecological view of world history in his *Plagues and Peoples* (1976). In *Human Condition* (1980) he discussed the urban and commercial transmutation of parasitism and macroparasitism – the former indicated the parasitic germs human pass about, while the latter metaphorically called attention to human rulers and exploiters who consume the productive activity of others. A third example of writing European history in conjunction with the rest of the world came with Eric R. Wolf's *Europe and the People without History*.[8]

An anthropologist working in the spirit of Marxism, Wolf in this book introduces Europe in 1400 on the eve of its expansion into the world. In following sections he takes up the 'Iberians in America', 'The Fur Trade', 'The Slave Trade' and 'Trade and Conquest in the Orient'. In the last section, 'Capitalism', he explores how the Industrial Revolution and the outward flow of commodities annex the entire world to capitalism. He writes there:

> It has been an argument of this book that we can no longer think of societies as isolated and self-maintaining systems. Nor can we imagine cultures as integrated totalities in which each part contributes to the maintenance of an organized, autonomous, and enduring whole. There are only cultural sets of practices and ideas, put into play by determinate human actors under determinate circumstances. In the course of action, these cultural sets are forever assembled, dismantled, and reassembled, conveying in variable accents the divergent paths of groups and classes. These paths do not find their explanation in the self-interested decisions of

interacting individuals. They grow out of the deployment of social labor, mobilized to engage the world of nature. The manner of that mobilization sets the terms of history, and in these terms the peoples who have asserted a privileged relation with history and the people to whom history has been denied encounter a common history.[9]

ALL OVER THE LOT

In a counter direction to global history and of special importance for everyday historians, along with local, regional and micro-historians, was the concerted move in the post-Second World War West to abandon traditional political history, often accompanied by histories of great men, for social history. Often rooted in Marxism and socialism, and borrowing theory from sociology and anthropology, social history exploded in varieties. This was not unlike earlier everyday histories of the people looked on as common and ordinary folk in their daily ways and routines, their work and leisure.

Well- and long-known groups were subjects of penetrating glances. The bourgeoisie and industrial workers received increased, more prying attention – as well as pre-industrial groups like peasants, clergy, intellectuals, artists, craftsmen and guildsmen, who could be found in any medieval or Renaissance text. In turn, with doctoral dissertations to be written and novel theories to be established, historians took up the dangerous crowds and mobs of eighteenth- and nineteenth-century France and the dark lanes and back alleys of early modern and modern England with studies of prostitution, gambling, con men, drugs, begging and whole underworld populations. Imitating and analysing what nineteenth-century novelists, realists and naturalists offered, historians filled their works with irrational crowds and mad times. They drew vignettes of what people ate, where they slept and defecated, how sickly, smelly and lethal ordinary places were. While there were tempering portraits of how the masses played (in beer and dance halls, at the beach and new seaside amusement parks), mortality completed shocking accounts of the underside of industrial cities, where more died than were born in these times before police departments took form, public water systems flushed dirt and disease out of the life of many and lighting lit up a world once impossibly dark and dangerous to comprehend.

Everyday historians of early modern Europe can chapter their works with abundant lines of enquiry into places, groups and inter-actions with one another and emerging political processes. In *Shaping History* (1998), Wayne te Brake took up the complex subject of the entrance of ordinary people into European politics in the period 1500–1700. Starting with the proposition that modern man is an inven-tion of modern history, or yet himself, it is possible to trace the history of sensibilities and cultures from the fifteenth century through to the eighteenth.[10] In his telling of 'the invention of modern man', the pro-lific historian Robert Muchembled takes up themes found in his books on popular culture, violence and magic. In this book he devotes chap-ters to 'the violent, the filthy, and evil' and 'savage and beastly men and women' and, following a chapter on the mediators between culture and people, he discusses 'the criminalization of modern man'; the ways we represent, educate and discipline our bodies; the changing relation of fathers and sons and the birth of adolescence; and finally the honing of taste and disgust in city and countryside.[11]

Individual studies pepper our understanding of social and every-day history with discussions of trade and goods and lives in town, court and countryside. Micro-institutions, like the coffee house and tavern, help explain how ordinary people put tracks and ruts in their everyday life; historians explain the beginnings and role of the coffee house, tavern and saloon. With daily lives hinged up and down the import, transport and consumption ladder, new groups can be seen to organize their lives around such select commodities as crops, cloth, furs, foods, spices and sugar. Daily lives were written of suppliers, users and entire communities linked from production to consump-tion. Stories of goods already join continents.

Eric Hobsbawm (1917–2012), the prominent British Marxist historian, attacked the splintering particularization and trivialization of history.[12] Social historians evaded 'small and eccentric qualitative histories' by giving their works a long-term trajectory, attaching them to decade- and century-long demographic and economic trends and tracking the movement of family structure, which held one key to everyday life.[13]

Quantitative studies allowed precision in documenting a changing and redistributed population by place, age and size of household. They examined trade statistics of towns, companies and ports and tracked prices, wages, distribution of materials and even books. The last proved an interesting gauge of the spread of literacy and religious and popular culture.[14] Identified as the mob, in French as *la rue* (the street), or, filling in Marx's *Lumpenproletariat*, as the suppressed, the downtrodden, the hidden, the criminal, the people of the night, the underclass offered a persistent substratum below emerging modern society and its workings. At the same time, the nature of the enduring countryside and its peasant serves as a measure of the changing town and city and changing and self-inventing modern man.

FERNAND BRAUDEL: A GUIDE TO MATERIAL AND GLOBAL HISTORY

For the sake of framing a history of everyday life, the historian must thread his way between detail and generalization, short- and long-term changes and analytic and descriptive history. He or she must watch against making places and peoples the marionettes of great outside forces and agencies. At the same time, the historian must avoid turning the past over to the play of politics, personalities and events. Likewise, he must ward off the encroachment of intellectual history, which can turn everyday people into robots of abstract ideas and symbolic world views.

In his desire to give the daily past a footing in body, things and community, the historian of the everyday must not be seduced by a romance with the laws drawn from the social sciences. A Ulysses on a journey to the sensual, ordinary and common, the historian must sail the Charybdis and Scylla of the century-old sirens of geography and economic history and yield to the allure of fresh materials drawn from biology (especially energy and food supply), ecology and environmental history. Surely singularly and in combination, they are attractive springboards into people's everyday lives. And more, they offer bridges from modern Europe and the West to emerging societies. They even promise connections between medieval and early modern Europe and what anthropologists have labelled deep history, which takes up early human migrations, settlements and languages in Europe; the Neolithic Revolution and the beginning of agriculture; increased population and the formation of urban life, with new technologies and energy sources, centralized control, systematized religion and thought, and the increasing role and influence of distant markets and urban centres.[15]

One way for an everyday historian to examine the usefulness of the new material and global approaches to history, which came to full bloom after the Second World War, is to examine the works of the French historian Fernand Braudel (1902–1985), the most distinguished of the second-generation scholars of the Annales School, the movement and journal (*Annales d'histoire économique et sociale*) founded by Lucien Febvre and Marc Bloch.[16] Braudel from the start of his career wrote global histories of ages, societies and civilizations. Relying on the new work from both the social and natural sciences, and a standing interest in geography, as did Bloch, Braudel sought to write everyday history in light of the material and economic conditions and directions of whole societies and civilizations. Laws and generalizations on the formation and development of society's basic structure framed his view of local and political history. Admittedly, he continued Marx's intellectual enterprise in having the material, the biological and economic captain the ship of changing humanity.

Braudel specifically declared himself to have been on a separate path from Febvre, whose 1942 masterwork *Le Problème de l'incroyance au xvie siècle: la religion de Rabelais* – dedicated to Braudel, who was imprisoned in Germany – was a study in religious sensibility and sixteenth-century culture. Braudel's historiography, conversely, rested on and was prejudiced towards identifying the primary material determinants and the overarching economic influence of markets and cities. This choice organized his two-volume *The Mediterranean and the Mediterranean World in the Age of Philip ii*, his three-volume *Civilization and Capitalism, 15th–18th Century* and his final work, his projected three-volume *The Identity of France*, which he was midway through writing when he died. He initiated the last work with lengthy descriptions of France's geography, climate and its immense variety as a country of many distinct places.

In *Afterthoughts on Material Civilization and Capitalism*, delivered as a set of lectures at Johns Hopkins University in 1976,[17] Braudel offered this overall description of the intent of his work:

> I chose to deal with long-term equilibriums and disequilibriums. To my mind the fundamental characteristic of the preindustrial economy is the co-existence of the inflexibility, inertia, and slow motion characteristic of an economy that was still primitive, alongside trends – limited and still in the minority, yet active and powerful – that were characteristic of modern growth.[18]

His dichotomous approach to modern history involved the changing lives of merchants and the nearly unchanging lives of rural peasants and villages that lasted well after the Second World War in France and the world at large. He writes of these two tracks as having entirely different lives lived at different speeds, the first with accelerating changes in environments and routines and the second with enduring and repeating ways in relatively static places:

> On the one hand, peasants lived in their villages in an almost autonomous way, virtually in autarky; on the other hand, a market-oriented economy and an expanding capitalism began to spread out, gradually creating the very world in which we live, and, at that early date, prefiguring our world.[19]

For Braudel, the history that was monumental, most determining and important, was, to choose his favourite term, of *longue durée*. He spent his life, so to speak, in state, city and business archives – shifting through business, personal and regional records. For him they revealed the formation and long-term changes of civilizations. They were the basis of his mega-narrative. He started his career with his 25-year, two-volume, 1,400-page study of *The Mediterranean and*

the Mediterranean World in the Age of Philip II. (The first edition, to
be revised several times in the future, was completed in 1946.) In it
he singularly plunged deep into geography, economic data (production, prices, shipping records and so on) and city and state archives,
in order to offer a full material history, which he begins by delin-
eating borders of peoples, places, cultures and civilizations and by
depicting geographies, landscapes and climates. He concludes the
first part of volume One by taking up the Mediterranean as 'a human
unit', made interactive by its land and sea routes and the functions
of its concentrated populations in its diverse cities. Part Two takes
up the measures of the sixteenth-century Mediterranean by population, distance between places and the interchange of its economies
in terms of its currencies, the rise of prices and the production and
trade of grain and spices. It concludes with a history and survey of
the entrance into the Mediterranean of the Atlantic powers, which
starts with the Spanish and Portuguese, the Normans and Flemish,
and finally welcomes the British and the Dutch.

Braudel directly approached daily life in *The Structures of Everyday Life*, the first volume of his *Civilization and Capitalism* (published
in 1967). Geography, landscape and climate determined the primary
activities of human life. Until the coming of the Industrial Revolution
a Malthusian equilibrium determined population size and condition
in the countryside. In a first chapter, 'The Weight of Numbers', he
showed how climate and food supply dictated population and the
range of daily needs and wants until the eighteenth century, when
the tyranny of famine and plague began to be lifted and fields were
expanded and more carefully tilled and fertilized. In 'Daily Bread', he
examined wheat and its yields, prices and trade in local and international markets. He then proceeded to explore 'The Spread of
Technology, Revolutions, and Delays', associated with rice, maize and
the potato – the protein ships for the great human voyage on the way
to greater numbers and abundance shown in the dietary revolution
in the eighteenth-century West. In following sections he addressed
what abundance means. 'Superfluity and Sufficiency of Food and
Drink', the 'Superfluity and Sufficiency [of] Houses, Clothes, and
Fashion'. He subsequently considered the influence on everyday life

of 'Houses throughout the World', their 'Interiors' and 'Costume and Fashion', which became a craze in the upper classes in the seventeenth and eighteenth centuries.

In separate sections, he next considered more dynamic and dramatic factors: 'The Spread of Technology', with early utilization of animals, wind and water, the use of wood and coal and the all-important poor relation of copper and bronze, iron. He weighed the consequences of innovation and invention in artillery and gunpowder, paper and printing and ships and navigation. He discussed the limited means, speeds and capacities of transport, truly limited as ensemble, I would note, until the Industrial Revolution and the railway and steamship. A last section deals with potent and penetrating worldwide forces and agencies such as 'Money', 'Towns', 'The Originality of Western Towns' and the emergence of 'Big Cities' in eighteenth-century Europe. In this way, Braudel's *Structures of Everyday Life* culminates a global material narrative with a consideration of the innovative economic forces and the beginnings of the Industrial Revolution that transform what to that point was rural France and Europe: the enduring material, biological and social order of the peasantry.

This framework served Braudel's histories of the Mediterranean, civilizations, France and Europe, especially in the period from 1400 to 1800, the time of the incubation of capitalism, urbanity, industry and the modern world. No doubt Marxist in inspiration, Braudel's approach to everyday life was global and social scientific. His preference is ever for the structures of long-term cycles at the expense of events. His countryside moves as a matter of predictable routines and equilibriums, despite interruptions of famine and plague and even intermittent wars and political interventions. Market and town drive everyday life at a heightened rhythm of control, while affording a new superfluity of goods and possibilities for everyday rural life. Braudel ultimately left it for other historians to wrestle the dramatic and cataclysmic events of contemporary history into long-term patterns.

Local historians, the orphans of the profession, recognize that Braudel's global approach crushes their narrative of unique places and peoples. Aside from the criticism that Braudel was reliant on a genre of Marxist determinism – a criticism levelled for one by the French local historian Guy Thuillier – they argued that the Annales School's generalizing themes and *longue durée* crowd out singular local and regional narratives.[20]

Braudel essentially excludes the Renaissance and Reformation from his treatment of Europe, 1400 to 1800, and their role in the birth of modernity. He does not find place in his work for Jacob Burckhardt's classic *Civilization of the Renaissance* (1878), a book that rests on the premise that the Renaissance was the microcosm and birthing ground of the modern world and mind. Conversely, Braudel's interest in this period turned on the great 150-year downturn in fourteenth- and early fifteenth-century European biological and economic life as initiated by the Black Death (1348–53), with the death of between 70 million and 200 million people in town and countryside alike. For Braudel, the downturn caused by the Black Death helps explain the ferocity and extent of the Hundred Year dynastic war carried on between the French and English.[21]

Likewise, Braudel did not have room for the Dutch historian and philosopher of culture Johan Huizinga. A fan of Burckhardt's and arguably the second great cultural historian of early modern Europe, Huizinga – author of *Erasmus and the Reformation* (1924), *Homo Ludens: A Study of the Play-element in Culture* (1938) and especially *The Waning of the Middle Ages* (1919) – conceived of the late Middle Ages as an immensely creative period: the great cultural watershed between medieval spirituality and modern aesthetics. It was then not in the Renaissance city-states, Huizinga contradicts Burckhardt, that men and women of the upper classes recreated themselves but out of the ideas, feelings, passion, poetry, sensibility and court rituals of the late Middle Ages. Art fashions new souls; it indulged and shaped the inner world as religion had earlier.[22]

Braudel defined as his polar opposites not just Burckhardt and Huizinga but those twentieth-century cultural historians (including many Annalistes themselves) who constructed the world around mind – symbols, religion and mentality. This explains why at the very outset of his study Braudel excluded the Renaissance, and Reformation as well, from his chosen period of 1400 to 1800. He did not explore the Renaissance as the source of a new and transformative culture; nor did he take up the Reformation – all those consequential questions of how its revolutions in faith and Church transformed communities, whole lands and even economics – or trace the dramatic interplay of religion in wars and rebellions across Europe until the middle of the seventeenth century. He did not seek to fathom the Reformation's social radicalism, radical iconoclasm, an anti-sacramental view of man and nature, and the permanent alteration of the boundaries of the religious and secular in mind and community. All this explains why he judged cultural matters as ultimately ephemeral and accounts for the short shrift given the Renaissance and Reformation at the close of the third volume of *Civilization and Capitalism, 15th–18th Century*.

THE CULTURAL HISTORIANS

Though prince of the second generation, Braudel did not command the flight of his and following generations at *Annales*. Representative of the third generation, the medievalist Philippe Ariès (1914–1984) pursued mentalities over the long term. Reaching sociologically into all classes, Ariès offered long-trajectory studies over centuries of childhood and changing attitudes towards death. (He was also an original editor of a five-volume *History of Private Life*, 1987–94.) Emmanuel Le Roy Ladurie (1929–), borrowing from anthropology, sought revelatory investigative histories. In *The Peasants of Languedoc* (1966) he took up, body and soul, the life of Languedoc peasantry. Studying a 400-year period, 1400–1800, he followed the interrelated cycles of demographic, agricultural and economic history. He observed the land and humans, in conjunction with each other, breathing in and out. He melded together long-term patterns of land use and population growth and retreat with interrelated vacillating prices, wages, rents and profits, and connected them with 'new states of consciousness and social struggles' that feature Catholics and

Huguenots in contest, lower classes undertaking protest actions and witches, off to the side, holding their sabbaths. He examined how intensifying economic depression bred savage struggles.

From his many works, which ranged from a thousand-year history of climate to an everyday examination of a town's life as revealed by the celebration of carnival in a town in southeastern France, Roman-sur-Isère, there emerged a second classic in our times, *Montaillou: Cathars and Catholics in a French Village* (1978). In this work his bull's eye, which might be that of the keen everyday micro- or local historian, was a small community and its most intimate actions. As if moving into a village in 1300, to become a type of historic field anthropologist, Le Roy Ladurie sought to get a grip on love and marriage, gestures and emotions, clans and factions and crime and violence. He took up concepts of time and space, attitudes to the past, animals, magic and beliefs about death and other worlds.

Braudel's materialism, of course, met strong counter-currents outside the Annales. Aside from historians of events, who wished to speak of decisive turning points for societies and nations, other historians adhered to the primacy of histories of ideas and cultures. With deep roots in Vico and Herder, an assemblage of social thinkers from classical studies, the study of philology, jurisprudence, history of law and folklore formed the underlying principles of Romantic history, which equated all peoples with an underlying spirit and mind, a way of thinking and being.

Drawing on maturing anthropology and nascent psychology, early twentieth-century historians of culture further probed daily life and common ways, what some would call the underside of everyday life. They found that ordinary acts and thoughts harboured the abiding power of collective rituals and myths and sometimes held passageways to the strange, the irrational and the clandestine. Adopting the proposition that at least half of life belongs to mind, they also asserted that the mind is a mansion of many kingdoms of the individual and collective unconscious.

Sigmund Freud proved influential in innovative approaches to exploring the hidden side of daily life. Already in 1901 he had written *The Psychopathology of Everyday Life*, in which, along with his later studies of dreams and jokes, he found a road to the ever present and insistent unconscious. Devoted to *parapraxis* – those famous revealing slips of the tongue, memory or physical action occasioned by the interference of an unconscious ('dynamically repressed') wish, conflict or train of thought guided by the ego and the rules of correct behaviour – *The Psychopathology* gained traction with the intuition that the maladies (guilt, fears, phobias, fixations and neuroses) that swarmed around his patients' minds actually had their source in the depths and formation of human minds, which underlay whole cultures of all times. Under hypnosis, and then the act of relaxed free association, Freud found hidden in his patients' stories, dreams, phobias, fixations and tongue slips clues to their unresolved frustrations, guilt, fear, anger, desires and repressions, their failed development and broken lives. But more than that, he found the dynamic, tension-filled and even crisis-laden genesis and maturation of human minds everywhere. From this came a second intuition. All cultures derived from and bore the universal burden suppressing incest, sexual rivalry and contests among the sons, and with the father, for the mother, harboured repression, taboos and unresolved conflicts.

With Freud's actual language or simply the spirit of his imaginative investigations, cultural historians turned their attention to the place of the unconscious, irrational and myth of everyday life, which offered an understanding of the mass politics and ideologies of the first half of the twentieth century. Ever influenced by folklore, ethnography and anthropology as well as experiments in the visual arts, historians too sought what was below the surface of the ordinary mind and daily culture. As superstition, proverbs, legends and folk tales revealed origins in archaic Greece and Egypt, so contemporaries were retainers and vessels of deepest memories, urges and needs. The irrational side of history played out in most common rituals and ordinary thoughts.

In the post-Second World War period, cultural history flourished in conjunction with and at odds with social history. They crossbred, and in differing but complementary ways gave inner and even subconscious substance to the history of peoples, classes, conditions and situations. They offered sympathetic portraits of the lives of the masses and everyday person, and even provided an ideological antidote to failed progressive, national and middle-class histories. Though far from twins, with social history born of material and economic history and cultural history parented by anthropology, psychology and intellectual histories of world views, together they shaped what was called people's history, folk history, everyday history and German *Alltagsgeschichte*. Each accented a turning away from official and national history, writing what the prominent English Marxist historian E. P. Thompson dubbed in 1966 'a history from below' and far earlier, in 1932, Febvre, praising Albert Mathiez for writing of the masses rather than the starlets, described as writing 'a history seen from below and not from above'.[23]

Historians of daily life can find multiple guides to cultural history to inspire the range and aperture of their work. Annaliste and intellectual historian Robert Mandrou presents *De la culture populaire aux 17e et 18e siècles* (1964), which is dedicated to a study of the *Bibliothèque bleue* of Troyes. Representing a tradition in popular French print culture of 250 years and involving the publication of inexpensive books that were sold to peasants for pennies by *colporteurs* (pedlars), the *Bibliothèque bleue* was comprised of texts ranging from the world of fairies and magic to practical recipes, almanacs and how-to books to books of piety, devotion hagiographies, prayer books and other religious instruction to the entertaining *romans de chevalerie*, songbooks and burlesque. All this provides unique insight into the popular culture of seventeenth- to mid-nineteenth-century France. Also devoted to early modern France is American historian Natalie Zemon Davis's *Society and Culture in Early Modern France* (1975). In eight essays she explores 'strikes and salvation at Lyon', 'poor relief, humanism, and heresy' and 'city women and religious change', along with such matters as 'the reasons of misrule', 'women on top', 'the rites of violence', 'printing and the people' and 'proverbial wisdom and popular errors'. Davis followed that book with the highly popularized *The Return of Martin Guerre* (1983), which takes up the provocative and intriguing issue of a town divided over the identity of a returning veteran and his claims to a village wife, family and land. Approximately thirty years separated the disappearance of the real Martin Guerre and the imposter and former military colleague, Arnaud du Tilh. At issue in the book and in a popular film based on the story are the memory and reasoning of villagers, and the procedures, evidence and findings of justice in a sixteenth-century court.

The English historian Peter Burke charts contemporary cultural history's shift inwardly to mind and downwardly to everyday people away from traditional political history.[24] In *Popular Culture in Early Modern Europe* (1978) Burke talks about defining who the people were and the integrity and variety of popular culture. He takes up the matters of popular culture's transmission; representation and featured heroes, villains and fools; and the world turned upside down by carnival. Looking at the period 1550 to 1650, he concludes his work studying the changes associated with reform and counter-reform, revolutions in commerce and literacy, and the people's entrance into politics. In a subsequent work, *History and Social Theory* (1992), he addresses standard sociological terms, including communications, orality and textuality and myth, before taking on central problems surrounding function, structure, psychology, culture and facts and fictions and also examining the limits of Karl Marx's and Herbert Spencer's models as well as those, following in the spirit of Max Weber, that philosophize diversely on the uniqueness of the West vis-à-vis China and India. He contends that in addition to theory, social theorists should consider narrative, facts, people and events. In the course of taking up a series of questions that divide and even fragment cultural history in *Varieties of Cultural History* (1997), Burke continues to remind that Burckhardt and Huizinga have not lost their power as models of cultural history and cautions that the downside of theory is that it forever seeks to simplify. Ultimately taking sides with the eclectic, Burke chooses heterogeneity over imperial and homogenizing theory, writing at the end of his work:

> For the outsider, whether historians or anthropologist, . . . similarities appear to outweigh differences. To insiders, however, the differences probably outweigh the similarities . . . In the words of Russian Mikhail Bakhtin . . . history has

to be 'polyphonic.' In other words, it has to contain within itself a variety of tongues and points of view, including those of victors and vanquished, men and women, insiders and outsiders, contemporaries and historians.[25]

LOCALITY AND TEMPORALITY EVER DIFFERENTIATE MIND

In my own work on the local and regional history of southwestern Minnesota, I took the side of local and regional history, finding worlds within worlds in a single place, using local, county and state historical records and oral history, select social sciences and the wealth of ideas and approaches to be derived from a single place's social and cultural history. I teamed with fellow historian Carl Pansaerts from Flemish Belgium to study how the Belgian and related Dutch Catholic farmers of a single county, Lyon County, in southwest Minnesota, in the course of less than a century came to take over the majority of the land in the county. In *Servants of the Land: God, Family, and Farm; The Economic Folkways of Belgian American Farmers*, we showed that sharp pencils, communitarian practices and a desire to stay and pray on their own land accounted for their success more than simply the demography of large Catholic families in contrast to dwindling Protestant families.

In another book, *The Decline of Rural Minnesota*, I worked with a demographer, John Meyer, and we showed on the basis of analysis of the 1990 census and the five previous censuses how throughout our region rural populations dwindled and small towns had declined since 1950 as farm size increased and the size of farm families correspondingly diminished. Equally provocatively, John Meyer, John Radzilowski and I titled another book on my hometown, Marshall, Minnesota, *Community of Strangers*. Again to the displeasure of the local town promoters we showed that a large and accelerating turnover rate in residents and a university, chain stores and regional companies transformed the town's sense of community and disrupted the continuity of leadership, as the business class of Main Street gave way to public employees and outsiders. In another co-edited book, *The Draining of the Great Oasis*, members and friends of the Center for the Study of Local and Regional History and Crossings Press took up the task of writing a nearly complete environmental history of nearby Murray County, with topics ranging from lakes, wetlands and drainage and early farming and barns to nitrogen use, hog operations, gravel pits and road building. Finally, another friend, writer and photographer David Pichaske, and I produced the work *A Place of Many Places*. In it our intention was to argue the side of the plurality and variety of things, showing how our villages, towns and farms, their residents and physical structures, reflect different minds, traditions and goals.

Following my own bent of mind for the power and place of telling, influentially, extraordinary events on the local level, I puzzled on a stunning and dramatic 'farm murder' here, in the hills fifty or so kilometres west of Marshall, at the outset of a significant crisis in farming in 1983 – a father and son killed two bankers. In *When Father and Son Conspire: A Minnesota Farm Murder*, I sought to put to rest the popular interpretation, which synchronized the murders as a matter of cause and effect resulting from the farming crisis and unsettling national economic conditions. I suggested instead that the migrant local and divorced father and the lone and militarized son, only putatively typical farmers, had gone crazy on their own irrational lives. They consumed violent ideas about evil and oppressive bankers and put them into the service of their own isolation, frustration, anger and sense they would avenge wrong done to them. Then one autumn day in September 1983, they returned to the farm they had surrendered to the bank years before, murdered two local bankers and fled to Texas, where the father committed suicide and the son turned himself in to the authorities. In a fourth book, *The Great Jerusalem Artichoke*, I traced the history of a local company, which in bad times in the early 1980s and with the stir of evangelical religion, the need to make a quick buck, the hate of Arab oil tyranny, belief in the sanctity of the American heartland and the promise of a magic crop, sold 30 million dollars' worth of Jerusalem artichokes in eighteen months to 2,500 takers across America and Canada. My conclusion, ever so fitting for the American countryside, was that ultimately there is not a single Midwestern rural history that mixes its narrative of local characters and places without the full inclusion of outside agencies, money and myths.

In *Rethinking Home: A Case for Writing Local History* (2002), I fused my long-standing interest in intellectual history with my growing interest in social, cultural and micro-histories. I contested there on behalf of local and micro-regional history that every place and time, especially those we call home, deserve a full history, one that ties a place in condition and mind to government, nationality and a changing world. Believing we were in need of histories that revitalize the past – in light of the stultifying and redundant modes of local history and the growing encroachments of outside forces and agencies – I sought histories that would awaken minds to our place and time. From what I took as new forms of social, cultural and micro-history, I included the history of cleanliness, sound, anger, madness, the clandestine and the natural in what I wrote, while concluding with business and economic history and the overarching demographic patterns of our region.

At this point I realized my thought had converged with the micro- and cultural histories abundantly offered by historians of the Middle Ages and early modern Europe. In that literature I encountered groups and individuals defiant of all ordinary norms of reasoning. Madness and folly, yet to be defined and made a matter of therapy, were bountiful. There existed a plethora of magic, witchcraft, pagan beliefs and rites.[26] Also, as documented by records kept by religious inquisitions, heretical, satanic and eclectic world views thrived (as influentially shown by Italian historian Carlo Ginzburg and especially his study of a sixteenth-century miller who had conjured an organic and celestial cosmos of his own invention).[27]

The sixteenth and early seventeenth centuries were profoundly rich in popular culture. Rabelais, Shakespeare and Cervantes offer unimpeachable testimony to this. Mind and tongue were untethered from a prevailing orthodoxy and uncertain and contentious in belief; and the orthodoxies of religion and rationalism were in a state of uncertainty and conflict. Religiously, community, regions and kingdoms were in freedom and travail. Town and countryside, responding to new levels of abundance and superfluities, were differentiated by size, wealth and decorative and entertainment variety. There were those of improved and prospering condition and those who still lived in relative isolation and autonomy under the harsh laws of Malthus and the rule of necessity; division seemed the law of the era's perception. With curiosity unbounded and science crescent, magic flourished, and the border between it and science was blurred, especially when questions about the genesis, growth and transformation of things, and the domain of the invisible, were in play.[28]

True to the underlying human tendency to represent things in opposition, the Reformation and the Counter-Reformation multiplied the divisions between high and low culture, heaven and earth, surface and underground world.[29] There were counter-cultures and distinctions to be made everywhere, in city, countryside and even monasteries.[30] With every surface having in fact or by mind an inner, exposed or hidden face, everyday life, as depicted by a drawing and painting style of the North, was composed equally of light and shadows, lines and snarls. Magic, cults, sects, witches' sabbaths, dissent and even proto-ideologies of mass rebellion were the forest floor of the sixteenth and seventeenth centuries.

At the same time, bathed in the sophistication of classical culture and yearly absorbing the discoveries of world voyages, learned people adopted more cosmopolitan attitudes, which permitted mixed and relative views. Relativism fed scepticism; and pyrrhonism, which nursed doubt and utilized scepticism, as seen in the *Essais* of Michel de Montaigne (1533–1592), produced arguments for policies of tolerance and for doubt's benefaction in reining in beliefs and passions. With piety and devotion diversifying, as people turned inwards and away from an outer world in contest, mystics called on theology, imagination and even tearful devotion, to know the unknowable God and represent and share what exceeded human understanding.[31] Thought, emotions and feelings modified the power of everyday life. Mind refracted war, conflict and plague onto ordinary life. Ideas, images, fantasies and illusions made minds volatile, especially when turned to death, coming days and salvation schemes.

Nervous, precarious, easily knocked out of balance, the mind is, especially in shaky times, the most sensitive seismograph. Humans are alert with fears of the real and the imagined. There were not only pie-in-the-sky illusions – such as those depicted by Pieter Brueghel the Elder in *The Land of Cockaigne*, where one could eat his fill and not do a stitch of work – but there was also the forest of dark fears and terrors. There were rumours and gossip about a new landlord, the appearance of bandits and marauding armies. An ageing and failing body, be it one's own or another's, reminded each individual of the inevitability of old age and death, long and certain, quick and sudden. In *Bread of Dreams: Food and Fantasy in Early Modern Europe*, Piero Camporesi explores *il pane selvaggio*, 'the wild bread', whose mould causes us to hallucinate and fantasize and whose abundance leads us to dream. Camporesi also explores the effects of famines and 'fears of hell', the world turned upside down – and blood magically and symbolically conceived as the sauce of life.[32]

Daily life receives its definition around what first arises in mind – what surfaces, motions, forms, colours and flesh present and insist on reactions.[33] Historians take up times and landscapes of 'the foul and fragrant' and the disgusting as integral to studying the power of the senses to define life.[34] With the aid of anthropologists, psychologists and traditional historians of ideas and sciences, medieval and early modern everyday life turns into a phenomenology of mind. Sensations and senses – sight, sound, smell and touch, which an author has recently called 'the deepest sense' – explain the mind's alchemy of life.[35]

In concert with histories of sensations and senses, historians, with use of visual art and long-standing literary traditions, have written histories of emotions, fear, pity, sympathy, sorrow and joy as cultural realities.[36] Tears not only pour out emotions, but they cry out for emotions to hear.[37] The eye, to paraphrase David Morgan's *The Embodied Eye: Religious Visual Culture and the Social Life of Feelings*, is always embodied; sight, like the other senses, forever carries with it a world of social feelings. The invisible is married to the seen and the shown.[38]

Beyond this, anthropologists and historians, as if to puzzle everyday historians with the unusual and abnormal, have taken up states of mind, stupors, trances and ecstasies that jump people out of their ordinary, daily, regular life. With them come questions about occasions, agents and effects attributed to these states – as well as questions about whether are they induced, on what occasions, and whether bestowal brings special powers. Do they go with certain characteristics of birth – the seventh child of the seventh child, born blind or with a cowl – rites of passage, select initiations to priesthood or sect, and do they confer powers to divine or augur? In any case, the historian of the everyday must be on the lookout for a group's unusual states of mind – times of repentance, frenzies of hate, states of exhilaration and even organized Mardi Gras celebrations. At the same time, the historian must seek to identify what for a given people compels and reveals, while designating those moments and individuals that offer extraordinary sight into this life or next.

Mind, then, shapes and multiplies experience and expression. With variations of time, place and culture and by difference of individual and group and spontaneity and plan, mind reacts, expresses, thinks about and represents all things. Humans sing in all keys – they intone pleasure and pain, love and death, and what is, has gone, and may come.

However, minds do not rule everyday history with a common and orderly consciousness, and even less a rational, articulate and chosen frame of comprehension. Cultures themselves grow out of the repetition of things done and seen, repeated words, relied-on gestures, select manners, limited and scarce material goods and, on higher levels of culture, traditions of rhetoric, decoration and art. Prayers have common chants and repeated hopes. By the eighteenth century, to move in the direction of our next chapter, aristocratic and upper bourgeois customs, styles, manners and comportment dictated outward appearance – and gave prime importance to seeing and being seen. In that world the gravity of need – that is, the first and overbearing necessity of food, drink and shelter – was overcome for the privileged few. In palace, garden and ballroom, nobles and the *haute bourgeoisie* performed for themselves and others, both to see and be seen, in an orchestrated, decorated and luxuriant society. And largely thanks, I say in conformity with Braudel, to early modern and nineteenth-century history, with immense variation, it is possible to trace the genesis of these refined individuals to the emergence of the interior and subjective person, a historical creature who thinks of his own happiness first and has sufficient space, goods, leisure and education to cherish and value self.

Writing a global history of the period 1400 to 1800 under the theme of the gestation of modernity is complex. Surely, the historian cannot deny events – wars, revolutions and ideas – in the name of a material and economic history of different cycles of population, prices and wages, any more than he can subordinate daily history to the formation and development of a single culture. In a word, the historian of everyday must be true to human nature and experience.

Beyond the theories and bibliographies that bristle the body of this chapter, the argument I make is simple. Historians must tell time. Time's courses, divisions and consequences are not one. Seasons and calendars repeat, but fates, fortunes and happenings do not. Loyalties to the past and plans and hopes in the present are not congruent. Time, in effect, slices all things differently. Narratives ultimately can tell but not encompass and own the world they describe. Events and minds make subjects and their narratives plural and heterogeneous. The craft of the everyday historian rests on the artful merger of place and time, matter and body, mind and freedom, and materiality and culture. The historian of everyday life, like local, social, cultural and micro-historians, is not called to writing theory. Rather, conceding that contrasts, opposites and ambiguities, as well as stunning syntheses and surprising unities, are inexhaustible, the historian's first duty is to honour the richness of human life in all its variety past and present. Yet the stars of night's observed skies do not absolve him from seeing by plain daylight.

4

Of Things and Selves I Sing

> I think mankind is more than waist-deep in daily routine.
> Countless inherited acts, accumulated pell-mell and repeated
> time after time to this very day, become habits that help us
> live, imprison us, and make decisions for us throughout
> our lives.
>
> Fernand Braudel, *Afterthoughts on Material Civilization and Capitalism*

Historians of everyday life in the modern world choose between two poles. They construct their work around a daily and repeating regime – a vortex that pulls down the uncommon to fit into its regime of habits of action and thought – or, conversely, they can conceive of everyday life as a plastic fabric ever moulding itself to disrupting and revolutionary change.

This polarity rests on another. One can conceive of daily life as belonging to the orbs of tenacious enduring peasants and resilient ethnic peoples or conceive of it as belonging to the modern and contemporary person's ardent pursuit of choice and happiness. Born in near autonomous and autarkic villages, the peasant was collective and communal. Fixed in place, the peasant belonged to the rule of group and nature. He or she did not have grounds to develop their individuality or space within which to cultivate emotions and subjectivity. Even in their dreams the inner self and imagination were harnessed by necessity, traditions and habits.

It is my argument in this chapter and the next that the great transformation from peasant to contemporary person, as incremental and incomplete or radical and total, is in large measure about an increment in things. Food, space and abundance of goods and things brought choices, rights and the possibility of alternative lives. Historians of everyday life must come to terms with the place and power of things in determining people's bodily functions, work and thought. Things shape diets, travel, communication, worship and daydreams.[1]

Humans make things and things make humans.[2] Things extend bodies in space and profoundly enhance human use of nature's materials and energies. They increase human imagination and potentiality. Things afford humble dwellings and decorate palaces and temples. As the historian of the everyday must grasp, things, often presumed and ignored, are also the most sophisticated, crafted, displayed and reverenced goods.

Things by variety, abundance and allocation measure conditions. They also express craft and knowledge, power and prominence. Surely, as the everyday historian must know, things in great variation are the spine of a people's daily regime, which, after all, often turns on making, acquiring, utilizing and consuming goods. Additional information about the course of ordinary life can be gathered by exploring the repair, collecting and display of goods, in addition to grasping their value as possessions and items for exchange and gifts.

Starting in this chapter and continuing into the next, in which we examine the Industrial Revolution, I will suggest that as scarcity was the principal definer of traditional peasant life, so has abundance, which began in the late fifteenth century and the sixteenth century, anticipated the modern: abundance of food and goods, and private and public space, gave birth to the modern individual endowed with rights and empowered with choices, and transformed him into the private, subjective and intimate self. Abundance not only endorsed comfort and leisure, it incubated choice, romantic love and the pursuit of personal happiness.

Surely the attentive reader will recognize that this characterization of two distinct, even diametrically opposed ways of life – that of the enduring, isolated and autarkic peasant and that of the modern protean and globally connected self – rephrases a polarity found in Braudel's description of everyday life. In his *Structures of Everyday Life*, Braudel judged court and middle-class life to be born of a superfluity of goods, elaborating itself around ample space. Baroque court life of the seventeenth and eighteenth centuries crowned itself in gold canopies, used manners to tell the world what it was and offered full-length mirrors to decorate place and show self. Dressed in embroidered silk, society then was on parade. It went up and down curving staircases, putting delicate feet forward on parqueted floors at court balls.

A WORLD WITHOUT INTIMACY

Let us begin with peasants, those beings of land and locality, who lived under the laws of Malthus and what we moderns would describe as a world without intimacy. Everyday life in the not-too-distant past tests the imagination of the contemporary historian. With a study, books, health, leisure and a clean and supporting community, the modern writer eats cake while the world he intends to describe daily suffered having its bread.[3]

The balance of the peasant world teetered on tiny grains. Peasants literally measured life by it. Grain meant food for today and seed for tomorrow. In good times, French peasants would respond to an enquiry about how they fared by saying, *J'ai du pain* (I've got bread). In bad times they dug up roots, ate bark, hunted nuts and ate rats and insects. Nothing was too small to be considered as food. During famines, which stalked European peasants until the nineteenth century, the smallest things could sway lives and fortunes.

Peasants who lost their place on the land became wanderers. They scavenged the countryside for food, sought refuge in the woods and flocked to the cities, where they lived under bridges, in piles of straw or even in manure heaps. Beggars in tattered rags were everywhere – at the door, outside churches, in the marketplace – and come bad times they died like the flies. Although their macrocosm, fleshed in by Church, magic and the most ancient metaphors and fantasies, reached to the stars, peasants' lives and hopes revolved around small things. Without photographs or heirloom objects, medieval people saved fingernail clippings and locks of hair from the head of a deceased family patriarch in hopes of preserving the *domus'* good fortune.

Lucien Febvre offers a perspective on the world without intimacy in *The Silhouette of a Civilization*. 'Concrete man, living man, man in flesh and blood living in the sixteenth century and modern man do not much resemble each other. He was a country man, a rustic; in all this we are far from him.'[4] He could not afford modern sensitivities. 'Life [for him]', Febvre wrote, 'was a perpetual combat to be waged against man, the seasons, and hostile and ill-controlled nature.' A person who was victorious in combat against a tough life, was hardened by toil and knew misfortune was always nearby, Febvre continues, was the contemporary person's opposite: 'The things which are nearest and dearest to us today – home, hearth, wife, and children – seem to have been', Febvre writes with some exaggeration, 'regarded by the man of the sixteenth century as merely transitory goods, which he was always prepared to renounce.'[5]

Medieval European peasants lived mired in muck. Even the medieval city, according to Febvre, wallowed in mud:

> The sunken road leading to the gate was muddy. Past the gate the street widened as it followed a capricious route through the town. A filthy stream ran down its center, fed by rivulets of liquid manure seeping from nearby manure heaps. It was a muddy slough in the rain, a desert of choking dust in the heat of the sun, in which urchins, ducks, chickens, and dogs, even pigs in spite of repeated edicts to control them, all wallowed together.[6]

For Febvre the person of the sixteenth century was of a different mind. His world was not of leisure, relaxation and education. Travel was, as it etymologically is, a matter of travail – as well as likely dangers and one-way finality. Goodbyes were taken to be once and for all. In a word, for Febvre, life then was not secure and not dressed in health, running water, light, love and happiness. Life, indeed, as the everyday historian can elaborate in a multitude of ways, was barren.

Houses, if not cottages, shacks, huts and caves, offered a material measure of normal life. They were composed of few rooms, often two; one with an attic room and the backroom, which wintered the animals, which helped heat the dwellings, and which forced individuals to live elbow to elbow and hip to hip. As in ancient and primitive times the hearth, and later the oven (stove and furnace), commanded the house and made gathering wood the first of chores.

There was minimal space for privacy for all except parents, while children slept several to a bed. Aside from a kitchen table, at which the wife rarely sat for a meal, a bench and just possibly a chair, furniture was scarce.[7] People leaned against walls and trees and mastered sitting on their haunches. Their dwellings were devoid of rugs, chests, religious keepsakes or any sort of art.

What intimacy existed was associated with primary biological senses of familiarity and parenthood. Conditions suppressed tenderness and care; circumstances fostered harshness and indifference. Little in their environment counselled individuals with claims to private happiness. Misery, hurt, hunger, illness, accident and death tramped emotional claims and individual rights.

Outside their dwellings peasants did not find individuality or privacy. Communities were small, and though each historian must run his own calculations for his place and time, most medieval and early modern communities numbered fewer than two hundred inhabitants. Rival river communities even on occasion stood on their banks for hours cursing, signing and mooning each other.

Everybody's affairs belonged to everyone else. Families, headed by patriarchs, commanded the order of necessity, while lords and landlords ruled the landscape. Fortunes distinguished, suspicions scrutinized. Little could be disguised in a village of fifty souls, and whatever good came someone's way was subject to jealousy and envy. A blanket of superstition covered wishes and fears. It falls to the historian of a particular place and time to divine how religion and magic cavorted in minds and rituals.

Magic furnished diagnosis and, along with home cures, served therapy. No end of proverbs and folk stories reveal legions of invisible helpers. The devil too, supposedly, had many nearby abodes and workshops. While demons and troublemakers spitefully messed up the world, saints answered prayers of all kinds. Grace made bread and the devil shat on it.

In this world women were reduced to being *une machine à l'enfantement*, and children were often too plentiful in number to be sheltered and fed. A woman's touch healed only so much, and children quickly died; those who didn't were needed at an early age, as early as four, for work and had no hallowed childhood.[8] Necessity spared nobody. Women and men were meant for reproduction and work. The mother, truly the heart of the family, was scrutinized for disloyalty; and the village examined the father for flaws of laziness, stupidity and serious breaks in character.

Friendships were rare and not long-lasting. Friends had few gifts to give and private moments to share. Relations were broken by death in a world of finite things and scarce advantages. To take a mate was to lose a friend; to enter a field of one's own was to leave a friend behind.

Getting old instructed all in their expendability. Survival for the old meant keeping one's place on the land and in the family, which determined all else. The old knew that to lose their ability to work and their grip on things made them vulnerable – to starvation and a last trip to the woods.

Romance was not banished in the world of yesterday. Its infatuation and cunning belonged to youth for a year or two in a lifetime. The poorest knew that their children married out of chance or necessity, possibly a pure heart but almost never to long-term advantage. All parents knew and dreaded that when marriage was left to their children much was risked. After all, to cite an old French proverb, 'A good-looking face is a fool's mirror!' – and youth was prone to choose appearance over solidity of body and earnestness of heart. Love's infatuation forsook cunning about wealth. Marriage, when calculated, counted such important goods as a new set of clothes, bedding, a good animal or two, or even a little money in order to procure a good match.

The poorest, who were many, barely clung to their place in society. Like my Sicilian great-grandparents, they were without land for tillage and a donkey for mortgage. In traditional society, many were without work. Beggars were everywhere – at doors, in the market, at the top of the stairs of a church and at the crossroads. Also at the crossroads, bandits lurked and lepers and the abandoned gathered. As cities grew, so too did the crowds of homeless and insane. Whores, thieves and con men made the night dangerous. Punishment and hangings provided entertainment. Expulsion was the regular civil broom, while the Church's charity, showing the other side of the human hand, welcomed orphans, the sick and the insane into its care. In bad times people envied well-fed pigs and successfully scrounging dogs; and in the worst of times people ate bark and rats and dreamed about cannibalism to assuage their hunger.

Peasant stories, a great source for everyday historians, told the tale of this world without intimacy. Folk tales reveal this terrible world, a world not invented by subconscious fears and desires but lived and learned by everyday experience. In the early nineteenth century, the Brothers Grimm collected folk tales that are truly 'grim'. Hunger, poverty, death, danger, fear and chance lurked all around. 'There are', according to the historian of Europe Eugen Weber,

> many orphans; there are wicked stepmothers, stepsisters, and mothers-in-law; there are poor children who have to go out into the world; there are forests inhabited by woodcutters and charcoal burners but also wild animals and outlaws and frightening spirits – forests that provide a refuge, but whose darkness breathes dangers, where it was easy to lose one's way or to run into trouble.[9]

Wolves prowl in this world and witches lure children to their ovens. In the words of Robert Darnton, folk tales voiced a Malthusian world:

> Most Frenchmen lived in or near a state of chronic mal-nutrition and offered little resistance when plague and famine sliced through the population. Of every ten babies born, two or three died before their first birthday and four or five died before the age of ten. Marriages usually lasted only about fifteen years, terminated by early death rather

than divorce. The old regime was a society of widows and orphans, of stepmothers and Cinderellas.[10]

Folk tales left 'the happy ever after' undefined. Certainly happiness could not be enacted in village or family, except on the occasion of feasting. Families fell under the rule of the father. Women and children were subordinate to survival, reproduction and work. The old clung to the land and goods lest they be abandoned. However we judge everyday family life, the personal and intimate side of life had no or little place. Again, to rely on Weber, that world mirrors the opposite of modern dreams:

> These stories are full of greed, envy, and exploitation: stepmothers are terrible, of course, and stepsisters are pretty awful, but you cannot really trust your friends either or your spouse. Husbands beat their wives or condemn them to horrid ends, wives betray husbands, and blood relations are no better: it is brother against brother, sister against sister, parents against their children.[11]

A BIOLOGICAL STORY

Even though historians, unable to tell all, need to group and gather in order to generalize, they violate the variety of everyday life prior to the French and Industrial Revolutions when they reduce any ho-hum story to biology or make it a single enduring mentality. Life cannot ever be entirely frozen in a classification of body and mind.[12] Historians routinely postulate an abiding and unchanging traditional peasant mind (as I have so far done in this chapter) at the cost of ignoring forever differentiating local and regional changes and the power of local events. And even a hypothesized uniform and universal mentality does not dispose of the problem of writing a narrative composed of diverse and mixed causes. No more than generalizations about geography, society and class do 'mentalities' encapsulate the whole of lives and thoughts. Humans are not perfectly tucked in groups, nor do groups fit into the containers of places, classes and times; they forever commit to a world of heterogeneity. Such a singular creature as man, ever of body and mind, so like and different from every other animal.

In the end historians must recognize that, beyond all their intelligence, they only probe the real. Their work is an activity. Their writing serves understanding. The smallest and most common subjects must ever be discerned in detail and context. Ever dependent on thinking about opposites such as high and low, light and dark, man and woman, understanding and exposition, historians rely on juxtapositions and polarities to think and explain.[13]

Piero Camporesi, the Italian historian of mind and class, puts readers in the skin and gut of the past. He probes in the largest sense the biological condition of everyday life, along with its bugs, itches, scratches, diarrhoea, maladies and warming piles of manure. Placing his work at the opposite pole of commanding ideas and high metaphors or the predictable rhythms and movements of peoples and classes across time, he directs us towards minute things and biological conditions that go with having a body and being human. His narrative turns on anecdotes about a time before indoor water and light and public sanitation and health.

Camporesi writes of peasants:

> [They were] dirty, almost always barefooted, legs ulcerated, varicose and scarred, badly protected by meager and monotonous diets, living in humid and badly ventilated hovels, in continuous, promiscuous contact with pigs and goats, obstinate in their beliefs, with dung heaps beneath their windows, their clothes coarse, inadequate and rarely washed, parasites spread everywhere – on their skin, in their hair, and in their beds – their crockery scarce or nonexistent, often attacked by boils, herpes, eczema, scabies, pustules, food poisoning from the flesh of diseased animals, malignant fevers, pneumonia, epidemic flues, malarial fevers ... lethal diarrhea (not to mention the great epidemics, the diseases of vitamin deficiency like scurvy and pellagra, the convulsive fits, so frequent in the past, epilepsy, suicidal manias and endemic cretinism).[14]

Hunger real, hunger remembered and hunger feared drove peasants from youth to the grave. Hunger kept them working and living in dirt and dust well into the eighteenth century, making life for the majority, Camporesi comments, 'the antechamber of death'.[15]

Peasants did not doubt that they were members of the biological kingdom. Mites, lice, ticks, fleas and mosquitoes – each had their sting and bite, and all made human beings their food and spawning grounds. A southern Italian peasant of the twentieth century declared the peasant's community with small and hurting things when he said, 'We peasants are poor earthworms; we live with the animals, eat with them, talk to them, and smell like them. Therefore, we are a great deal like them.'[16]

The French historian and third-generation Annaliste Emmanuel Le Roy Ladurie sets historians of daily life looking at sixteenth-century skin and its diseases. They included 'the itch, ringworm, scabies, leprosy, St Anthony's Fire and St Martial's Fire'. Even peasant insults and curses made reference to 'scrofula, fistulas of the thigh, ulcers and abscesses'. 'Villagers,' he offers, 'as a new order of intimacy, much like that of chimpanzees and other monkeys, carried around with them a whole fauna of fleas and lice. Not only did they scratch themselves, but friends and relations from all levels in the social scale deloused one another. (The mistress deloused her lover, the servant her master, the daughter her mother.)'[17] The thumb was called the louse-killer (*tue-poux*).

Indeed, put most simply and most in opposition to what we ourselves idealize, peasants were dusty and dirty, shitty and smelly. They were fodder for bugs and vermin. They belonged to a world of small, nasty and invisible things.[18] They lived in a world without intimacy of space, place, skin, a world that did not have the means to cherish feelings, affections and companionship or to celebrate nudity and sexuality, fondling them with words and images.

Peasants observed that the smallest living creatures – bugs, spiders and worms – were creatures of dust. Worms appeared in compost piles, maggots generated in rotting meat, cockroaches were born from scraps of food that fell to the floor and mice sprang out of dirty boxes left in undisturbed darkness. And they knew throughout their days that they belonged to the kingdom of dust. It accompanied them on their skin, in their clothing, throughout their fields and within their houses; it was the smallest and finest thing they saw.

Peasants grasped intuitively what contemporary people strain to imagine: the eternal cycle of all living things. It made sense to them that God used spit and earth to make humans – after all, what else was available? – and they had no doubt that they, along with the mightiest monarchs, made good food for worms.

Men and women strove to rid themselves of dust and dirt, to rise above the muck and slime, the worms and vermin, the gnats and ants that surrounded them. With brooms and shovels and taboos and rituals they struggled against the contamination and pollution. With elevating conceptions, they made themselves another superior order of angels and spirits to transcend the body and biology that dragged them down into darkness. If culture were to do anything, it would be to insist that humans were not just the dust grovellers, dirt eaters, excrement makers and shit kickers they knew themselves to be. It would allow men and women to think – hope, believe – that they were somehow more than the Church's stern Lenten warning: *Memento, homo, quia pulvis es, et in pulverem reverteris* (Remember, man, you are of dust, and to dust you will return).[19]

MIRED IN MUCK TOO, ROYALTY AND ARISTOCRACY TAKE TO MANNERS

Since the beginning of agriculture, whose origins lay in the Near East approximately 8,000 years before Christ, court and city dwellers, we can surmise, labelled peasants as dark, dirty, stinky – and worse. If the Wicked Witch's magic mirror were to respond to the question, 'Mirror, Mirror on the Wall, who is the *dirtiest* of them all?', it would surely reply, 'No doubt! No doubt! The peasant! The peasant is the dirtiest, darkest stinker of them all.' Peasants were universally identified with the colour of the earth they worked and the skin that came with labouring in the sun all day long.

Peasants, however, were not the only medieval folk who itched and scratched, stank and were dirty. An everyday life of medieval and early modern courts, all the way up to Louis xiv's royal court of Versailles, would talk of cramped quarters, problems of disposing waste and infestations. Even kings and queens, not in command of running water and lazy about bathing habits, were also on intimate terms with vermin. Eugen Weber offers telling anecdotes from court life in early modern Europe in his text on European history. He describes a young French princess in 1700 who had to be instructed 'not to take lice, fleas, and other vermin by the neck to kill them in front of other people'. The ladies of the French and Spanish courts were so familiar with vermin and perhaps just so bored with them that they 'affected to train and feed pet fleas'. In an age when running water was scarce and baths rare, kings and queens stank. Some were notorious: 'The smell of Henry iv was so ferocious that his wife had to brew special perfumes to stand him, and Louis xiii [Henry's son] prided himself on taking after his father.'[20]

Royalty commonly sucked aniseed lozenges to sweeten their breath, made foul by rotting teeth and bad digestion. With noses guarded by perfumed handkerchiefs, aristocracy threaded their way through manure-filled streets in high-heeled shoes, in *zoccoli* of a foot or two's elevation. But neither high heels nor riding in a carriage could protect high society from sticky muck, rising vapours, swarming gnats and the purposeful splashing of the people of the street (known as *la rue*). Diane Ackerman points out that Louis xiv kept a stable of servants to perfume his rooms with rosewater and marjoram and to wash his clothes in spices. 'He insisted', she writes, 'that a new perfume be invented every day.' At his 'perfumed court, servants used to drench doves in different scents and release them at dinner parties to weave a tapestry of aromas as they flew around the guests.'[21] Nevertheless, these birds could not mask the palace's stench for long, as the building's many small apartments were without running water.

While some royal personages were celebrated stinkers, royalty and nobility alike increasingly attempted to separate themselves from the rest of pungent humanity. Their first baths and cleaning came from adopting manners and wearing scents. Manners gave a new outer face to upper-class daily life, according to Norbert Elias's classic *The Civilizing Process* (1939), composed of two volumes, *The History of Manners* and *Power and Civility*, and his latter *The Court and Society* (1969). Refining gestures and appearances, manners distinguished high society from the common riffraff and the dust and dirt, which went with life before.

In an early manual on manners, *Civility for Children*, Erasmus taught the youth of the upper classes how to elevate themselves above their own biology.'To wipe the nose on the cap or sleeve belongs to rustics; to wipe the nose on the arm or elbow to pastry cooks; and to wipe the nose with the hand, if by chance at the same instant you hold it to your gown, is not much more civil. But to receive the excreta of the nose with a handkerchief turning slightly away from noble people is an honest thing.'[22]

The high and mighty had to be taught how to go beyond the lowly stuff that came out of and degraded them. They had to learn not to disdain the picayune but to bring it – with the help of wig, comb, make-up, razor and toothbrush – under the control of civilized manners. After all, civilization, when deep thoughts, refined reflections and discriminating sensibilities were put aside, was largely about appearance, and appearance first required constant surveillance of the small accidents of the body. Everyday history must take account of defining manners and gestures, however slick or clumsy they may be.[23]

BECOMING A SOMEBODY ON
THE STAGE OF SMOOTH SURFACES

We see that as time went on, the privileged used many more goods and instruments, rites, occasions and decorations to elevate themselves beyond the blatant surface mortality of the many. Their first efforts were on the surface for the sake of outward show. In this way, early modern history is a period of individual manifestation and self-cultivation. As the upper classes cast themselves with care for the eye of the other – on lawn, at ball, at banquet – so they cultivated their inner selves with music, books and self-reflection, looking into the mirror of self-cultivation. This dialectic so at work in the upper and literate classes of Europe had its father in the French essayist

Michel de Montaigne. Montaigne left no stone unturned in his inner world or self in search of the meaning of life and the world. Nearly a century later, religious apologist Blaise Pascal (1623–1662) analysed man, regardless of his class and condition, to be forever in search of *divertissement* – distraction – in order to escape the terror of his mortal condition. For Pascal, religion alone sufficed man's sinuous and labyrinthine heart. And yet a century later, Jean-Jacques Rousseau (1712–1778) focused meaning in the search of his restless mind. Never at home in Paris or the court, and forever suffering inwardly the rejection of the other, Rousseau sought his repair and oneness wandering in the countryside and validation in what he judged his natural and spontaneous feelings. He would have the bedrock of his being be the sincerity of his heart.[24]

In early modern history, outer appearance as style, craft and fashion announced the world and to the world. Face, skin, cloth, shoe and comportment declared a person blessed. Grace and balance, accented by clothing, a wig and shoes, offered an initial profile, while etiquette, manners and comportment, like the walls of one's home, made individual bids to win appraisal.

Discretion in step, articulateness in word, and speed of wit bolstered the individual. Reticence retained rank and differentiated oneself from ignorant, brash and obsequious upstarts. As the peasant stomped, stammered and spat his way through his days, high-class and mannered feet glided quietly along the smooth surfaces of court, dance hall and garden. The body of an aristocrat was an elegant platform; his or her movements transfigured the body into 'a handsome decorated corporal carriage' that rolled through society with royal and elite appearance. Walking was put on display in solemn parade, causal promenade or organized dance (especially the minuet, sponsored at Versailles by dance master Louis XIV).[25]

For the classes that counted, everyday life was stylized down to nearly its every movement. Heir of Italian and Spanish manners, French *civilité, politesse* and France's honourable and courteous *honnête homme* offered an increasingly comprehensive guide to bodily appearance.[26] The English further adjudicated the proper display of emotion, gesture, posture and manner.[27] Etiquette instructed the kingdom on the proper way of bowing, doffing a hat, kissing a hand, waving a fan and kneeling – on one or two knees. Its prescriptions furnished a catalogue of proper surfaces and movements.

Clothes made the person and complemented the 'culture of appearance'.[28] Style and fashion – the forerunners of nineteenth-century glitz and glamour – wove a Shirt of Nessus for the courtly actors of the age. They could not separate self from dress. Giving heart and purse to the cliché that clothes make the man, as well as the lady, the court dressed to the hilt. On a more philosophical tack, clothing stimulated the human imagination. Clothes invited the fluid mind to imagine truth as dressed or nude.

The feminine body has always been the pearl of human shells. Gracefully dressed, a woman elevated everyday life – she was a pleasure to behold, a miracle to contemplate. Clothes advertised her as one being in public halls and altogether another (as modern art displayed) in her boudoir, her private bathing and dressing suite. Corsets, stomachers, crinolines, hoops, trailing skirts, rising embroidered collars, garters, gloves, fans, parasols, elaborate wigs, bonnets and preposterous hats supporting exotic plumage – even modelling ships – all played their part in generously engendering and then tethering the baroque Venus to her shell. From 1500 to the French Revolution, fashion held the upper-class woman in stern bondage.[29] She was expected to move freely despite yards of encumbering cloth. She was to move through the world without blemish. Somehow, her image was supposed to make her invulnerable to the splashing mud of passing carriages, and she was never to lose her boot in flight to sucking muck.

Appearance committed all, even the residents of Versailles, to a continuous battle against the daily rude intrusions of the body. Louis de Rouvroy, duc de Saint-Simon, contemporary commentator on Louis xiv's Versailles, introduces us to the inner spaces and thoughts of everyday court life. We learn among so many other things that the palace's quarters were small, cramped, confining and without plumbing of any sort. Residents fought daily skirmishes on behalf of fragrance and beauty. Baths, combs, powders and rouges were drafted for a lifetime of combat against uneven patches of skin, fickle and disobedient hair, lumpy and bony bodies, and outrageous pimples, boils and other protuberances. Beyond cosmetic wars against a resistant and repugnant body, residents also took up the cause of rumpled, soiled and sweaty clothes. Resisting all efforts and the cleverest techniques of beautification (the premier superficial science), and lurking just below the skin, was the everlasting antagonist: the body stinker, the body prankster, the body sneezing, belching, farting – alas ill, ageing and even dying, failing on so many counts to make the measure. Secondary layers of underclothes, inevitably soiled and bulky, were finally unconcealed liners, while nightclothes, shirts, chemises, petticoats and negligée (whose origin was an eighteenth-century French nightgown that mimicked the period's full-length women's day dress) forever tussled to secure warmth and protection while concealing unattractive lumps and gatherings.

Artifice had inherent limits in its contests against the beast body, as the many-eyed Argos public scrutinized and espied. Eighteenth-century bustles, for instance, may have succeeded in stealing seventeenth-century glances away from breasts to sumptuous derrières, only to have expanding hoops and alluring, lengthening trains trip her lady up or entangle her in tight places. The satirist Henry Fielding exposed the shams, frauds and masks of society, claiming that it was 'impossible to convey seven yards of hoop into a hackney-coach, or to slide with it behind a counter'.[30]

MIRROR, MIRROR ON THE WALL

The court that gazed outwards also looked inwards and disciplined itself. In the words of Annales historian Roger Chartier:

> When life at court located distinction in proximity, reality in appearance and superiority in dependence, it required of those who participated in it specific psychological gifts that are not common to all, such as the art of observing others and oneself, the censorship of sentiments and the mastery of passions and the internalization of the disciplines of *civilité*. A transformation of this sort modified not only ways of thinking but the entire structure of personality and

the psychic economy of the individual to which Elias gives
an old name, *Habitatus*.[31]

Eyes delivered the nascent modern individual to the face of the
mirror, the new commentator on self and milieu. In the course of
the seventeenth and eighteenth centuries the mirror, which grew
ever larger and more common, became the standard gazing pool for
those in search of their aristocratic and courtly appearance – and the
rendering of a judgement on who was 'fairest of them all'.[32]

The French historian Sabine Melchior-Bonnet writes of the
place and function of the mirror in the self-refining upper classes.

> By shedding its mystery, the mirror [by then perfectly
> flawless but ordinary] became an instrument of social con-
> formity and offered man the freedom of a solitary face-to-
> face encounter. The clarity and distance of the reflection
> offered a space of performance, a theater lending itself to
> disguise and show.[33]

Portraits and mirrors hung in the same room in close proximity, and
acknowledging this an undetermined number of artists with colourful portraits depicted their subjects looking at themselves in the mirror.
From different angles, they endorsed the same illusion, that this era's
bright and passing surface, especially its nobles and women, deserved
lasting adulation and glorious admiration. Such cunning writers of
the self as Montaigne and Pascal explored the splits of self occasioned
and amplified by the dissemination of the mirror. The modern individual played peekaboo with the self in the mirror, as he caught and
fashioned images of self at masquerades and dances, courtly entertainments and official ceremonies. Even though many of Europe's
kings sponsored masquerades, no place rivalled eighteenth-century
Venice, which led a French tourist to remark, 'the entire town is in
disguise.'[34]

The garden was another mirror and theatre of the strolling and
promenading self. The masses would wait until the late nineteenth
and twentieth centuries for public parks where they could play and

pose. Since Babylon, kingdoms had built great walls and crowned them with great palaces and great gardens that displayed a king's power, wealth, abundance, control of the landscape and an eye for the beautiful. More philosophically, the king's gardens reflected his willingness to spare no artifice in his nostalgic bid to regain Eden and restore the lost harmonious relationship with nature.[35]

Gardens multiplied in the Renaissance, and the passion for them (originally established around Roman villas and beautifully articulated on the Tuscan landscape) became infectious.[36] They became a matter of stylish necessity and competitive experimentation. Stating one's place, taste and power on the landscape, gardens figured prominently in an estate's presentation and supplied ample reason, as they did at Versailles, to tax budgets beyond their limits. An extension of church, court, estate and country home, the garden framed open-air stages for festivals, pageants, balls, concerts, fireworks and other spectacles, and projected idealized perspectives, grids, curves, contours and images of orderly and luxurious life. They were a distinct, different and imagined life in the everyday world.

The garden offered a stepping stone into the surrounding countryside, itself a landscape tamed, stylized and made pleasant, as the body itself and indoors were increasingly made. Promenades in carriages and on foot that began in and around estates led a greater distance to smooth riding and walking lanes in suburbs, and then on city ramparts and select city avenues. The garden had given rise to the ethereal proposition that the world was to be gone out into and enjoyed.[37] By the end of the eighteenth century, gardens (which could be reclusive hideaways) also cradled subjectivity and the love of nature that accounted for generations of country walkers, botanizers and romantic explorers and hikers.[38] They incubated prelapsarian dreams of Edenic happiness.[39]

GOODS ACCUMULATE AND DREAMS OF HAPPINESS MULTIPLY

Music and books offered other stepping stones into cultivating the happy imagined life. Indeed, as if to deny the hard, dusty, dirty, animal truth of life of the many and the age, more and more of those with means took that world to be what society made it and they dreamed it.

Beyond the manners and exclusive fashions of court, society at large began to take itself in hand in the eighteenth century. Works and dreams and happiness converged in self and were projected into the present and future. Monarchs began to map and control their lands, as their administrative powers extended. They equipped themselves not just with palaces and gardens but also with armies and corps of officials, which were noted more and more in the city and even parts of the countryside. As European ships regularly probed and fought for control of the Americas and the seaports of the world, European markets, commerce and goods expanded. Goods increasingly defined the terms and conditions of our everyday life. Buildings and homes offered space and comfort to the well off.

Life increasingly for the well off was lived among and by things. The subtitle of Daniel Roche's *A History of Everyday Things: The Birth of Consumption in France, 1600–1800* tells a great deal of how things came to fill and even rule lives and ideas of comfort and happiness.[40] The first three chapters of Roche's book tell the story of increased production and the expansion of ordinary and luxury consumption and explore the agency of towns, trades and inventions. Under the rubric of 'ordinary life', he studies the rural house between tradition and innovation and in relation to improved heating and lighting and the increase of wood and coal supplies. The work concludes with 'Furniture and Objects', 'Clothing and Appearances' and 'Bread, Wine, Taste'.

Editors Tara Hamling and Catherine Richardson's *Everyday Objects: Medieval and Early Modern Material Culture and Its Meaning* supplements Roche's material history.[41] One essay starts with the question: what sense can we make of a hat, offered as a betrothal gift and then sought in return in court when marriage plans have ended? No doubt for the active and interested mind, with a bent towards material anthropology and archaeology, such hats are everywhere in human life. Or, as I extrapolate from Richardson's telling essay 'A Very Fit Hat', our lives, narratives, times, crafts and classes belong in some measure to things possessed and used.[42] This work has rein-terpreted twentieth-century philosopher Gabriel Marcel's *Being and Having* to read 'Having Is Being'. And these goods not only deter-mine how we work to have and use them but also define us and even determine our status and how we see, touch, hear and taste the world; they supply the means by which we eat and entertain others and make ourselves at home in the world.

Objects in Hamling and Richardson's book escape sweeping generalizations of materialism, technology, production or even recently popular histories of consumption. Following six principal parts – Evidence and Interpretation, Skills and Manufacture, Objects and Space, Sound and Sensory Experience, Material Religion and Emotion, Attitudes towards Objects – a second table of contents, of objects and types of objects, divides the book into Clothing, Shoes, Tableware, Musical Instruments, Books, Portraits, Domestic Goods, Ritual Objects and Buildings and Fixtures.

Some objects are precious and singular; others are common and ordinary. They are found in different conditions – venerated and discarded, and used and repaired, as is so nicely pointed out by Sara Pennel's essay 'For a crack or flaw despis'd'. Their place and impor-tance in social life belongs in some cases, such as the drinking mug, to the efficient plane of the moving hand and arm and the tilted head and poised body. In the case of other objects, such as shoes, clothing or a teetering wheelbarrow, the object is truly grasped only in rela-tion to the act of walking and its appearance to the person on foot and in motion. Objects, like pins, can define the clothes we sport and the interior pricking of the folded fabric we wear, as Jenny Tiramani points out in 'Pins and Aglets'.

Also affording entrance to everyday senses and tastes, there was the use of tea and coffee, and beer and other alcoholic drinks, which socially opened the door to salons and more popular houses and taverns. The use of tobacco likewise spread. The subtle waves of alluring and fly-chasing fans caught eyes, while the clanging of bells on steeples and the ting-a-ling of Communion bells still called people to church and altar. As hosts of brass and string instruments, then harpsichord and piano, swept souls and expressed the sentiments of well-dressed and well-mannered folk, so were rustic pipes, medieval pipes and bagpipes played, especially in Ireland and Scotland, to accompany both riotously joyous and solemn occasions.

Things measured the richness of a civilization. Collecting and mixing and making things created museums, documented explorations and inventoried the bounty of nature and crafts. They additionally offered points of curiosity and presented objects for touch and examination, analogy, hypothesis and speculation.[43]

Technology offered improved mechanics. The steam engine provided a new source of power for pumping and milling. And commerce and state joined in the building of better ocean-going ships and inland canal systems. This, in addition to advancing agronomics, engendered commercial agriculture, which helped underwrite the beginnings of the steady growth of population in eighteenth-century Europe. Across Europe and Russia, the state itself directed and stimulated production, while business entrepreneurs' banking grew and flourished in England and Western Europe. Improved land and water transportation assured a greater distribution of goods. In a world knitted together by prospering and seafaring nations, more colonies and commercial and civic centres sprang up and were in cooperation and competition as they sought the applied benefits of secular and practical learning.

To use a contemporary phrase, a climate of innovation encapsulated Europe and colonies across the globe. The market was increasingly understood to be advantageous to society as a whole. The civilization's very advance, equated by some of the literate elite to the advance of humanity, depended on a growing and mutual sharing of knowledge of crafts, trades and invention. This defined a central goal of Diderot's great *L'Encyclopédie*, published between 1751 and 1772. Additionally, gathering humanity into a single active entity in time, exploration and trade resulted in more and enhanced private collections of the entire world's materials (plants, animals, shells, rocks and minerals) and artefacts of all stages of indigenous and historical material cultures. The most prominent national museum of the era was the British Museum, opened to the public in 1759. Correspondingly, the eighteenth-century spread of subscription libraries in England and the West offered, as the books themselves did, a composite of human knowledge, learning and skill.

In sum, the middle class stood in ever greater control over the improvement of life. The eighteenth-century urban person had more goods and objects – and as an ever rich composition of people, the middle class lived and thought of themselves as belonging to and making a superior world. Public life offered multiplying distractions and displays, while domestic life afforded increased comfort and ease, and grounds for temporary retreat from personal rivalries and civic affairs. Utopian intellectuals – spearheaded by the *philosophes* in France – took the boldest leap of confident optimism, daring to foresee humanity as the end and source of its own eventual happiness.

Objects, thus, opened the door to life. Rooted in expanding materials, tools, energy, technology and production, distribution and consumption swelled and work and commercial activity grew. Objects did more. Things defined space and movement and accounted for new dimensions of common sensory experience. Objects defined houses and estates and staged exclusive lives. They furnished new metaphors for human actions and being.

Truly, things talked to and about everything and everyone. Sugar and the spices, such as pepper, cinnamon, ginger and turmeric, tell a great deal about the fortunes of global trade and changing senses of taste, while the tomato and the potato tell how New World crops changed European diets, tables and fields. Clothing, shoes and tableware all encompass long histories – the origin of the three-pronged fork has proven of special interest – sweeping in their trains stories of gestures and manners. Then, too, to change tunes, there is the growing hoot and toot of musical instruments and the production, use and effects of books in the service of diverse wants and audiences. Domestic goods, calendars, portraits and even ritual objects defined the inner space of the home, which filled the thoughts of early minds.

The most prestigious objects, valuable and unique, elevated their owner – and even, as in the case of precious metals and porcelain, shored up royalty's sovereignty. Conversely, the most rude and ordinary degraded the status of their owners.

Books, for instance, illustrated and accumulated the glorious past and associated their owners and readers with it. If enhanced with decoration and finely printed, books constituted a prima facie claim to status and prestige. Their display wrote in a single sentence what the individual and family read, thought and possessed.

Books, however, significantly did something else. They provided the literate with an inner space of privacy – a corner into which they could escape from the hubbub of the quotidian. The book, or better yet a private library of one's own, formed a cubicle of privilege for those who wished to escape the world. Books organized minds while transporting readers across times and places, on journeys to exotic places or back to the antiquity of Rome and Greece.

The book became the vade mecum, the companion, of all those who cultivated their sensitivity and followed an inner path. One reader chose a book as his or her path of lay mysticism. Another sharpened ironic reflections on the honing wheel of the classics. Others, anticipating Romantic literature, explored their own heart's inner feelings and generous sympathies for a sorrowful protagonist like the one in Goethe's *The Sorrows of the Young Werther* (1774), who boasted of his inner self: 'I am proud of my heart alone, it is the sole source of everything, all our strength, happiness & misery. All the knowledge I possess everyone else can acquire, but my heart is all my own.'

At the same time, books played different and more common roles in the home. They took the form of practical manuals. They were put into service as almanacs and calendars, and they held wondrous pictures and curious illustrations. Expressing sentiment and sensibility, images played an increasingly important role for all in early modern history, even for iconoclastic Protestants. The faces of cards (not identical across time or place) in Elizabethan Catholic England offered 'talismanic protection' and lent themselves to meditation and prayer. Texts, ornate and image-filled, cradled devotion in luxury and prestige.

Books led minds afar. They reached as deep in space and mind as interested readers could travel.[44] Unrivalled in reach and their hold on minds, books – material objects and commodities – wove distant correspondences and invisible associations. They heralded glorious cultures and made the private selves of personal letters public – made revealing hearts a commodity on the market of expanding sympathy. Bold displays of individuality, cultivated privacy and expressive sentiments were all on display in eighteenth-century literature.

Books enhanced eighteenth-century individualism, be it that of royalty, aristocracy, *haute bourgeoisie* or even the merchant class of prospering cities in Europe and many of the colonies. In the mirrors of books, select readers could join the ranks of Plutarch's famous Greeks and Romans, and they could adorn their swelling personal and household goods with decorative and aesthetic monograms as if their initials had the same claim to recognitions as was given to coins, the currency of fame – kingdoms and republics.

Books, monograms, vases, pots, all the other everyday things give the social historian material and cultural testimony to past lives. Things echo as well the domains that existed between decoration and representation, utility and fashion, value and sentiment, ordinary and festive, individual and collective meanings. Far more concretely, which may be to the preference of the everyday historian, objects indicate sources of production, invention, distribution and dissemination. In accord with the Latin legal phrase *res ipsa loquitur*, things truly do speak for themselves, by origin and spread, quantity and quality. In early modern Europe they put on display the manufacture of porcelain, clothes, paper and metals. Things estimate the capacity of society literally to shape and form objects in the light of such desirable characteristics as strength, durability, malleability, translucency, transparency and colour.

FREE OF PLACE AND OUT OF ORDINARY SELF

Travel led one out of home and self to other worlds and to a higher status at home. The eighteenth century is rich in self-conscious travellers, who flocked abroad for curiosity, education and reasons of class.

In distant places, literate travellers could find new worlds around them and new selves within. Travel abroad, especially for the upperclass English, became a rite of passage, which became a prerequisite for Victorian England: to travel abroad, usually France, was a way to complete an education and take up one's status as a worldly and sophisticated person. Like the book one read and the art and music one preferred, a trip taken and commented on was a way to display the complexity, the acuity and perspicacity of one's mind.

As land travel, though still rough and rustic, increased its speed and regularity along travel circuits in northern Europe in the eighteenth century, the aristocratic and upper middle classes turned their travels around estate and town into a circuit of decorated carriage promenades.[45] In *Le Promeneur à Paris au xviiie siècle* (2007), Laurent Turcot traces the path of promenading in France.[46] He illustrates how it led from court and garden to Paris's boulevards and ramparts in eighteenth-century France and set the stage for the nineteenth-century urban *flâneur*. Turcot's aim, in effect, was to provide a historical background for Marxist philosopher and literary critic Walter Benjamin's influential but unfinished work on everyday Paris life and thought in the 1820s and '30s among the arcades (those icons of iron, glass and cloth manufacture) and those 'historical scouts', those intellectual *flâneurs* quintessentially represented by Baudelaire – himself 'an allegorical genius' who metamorphosed Paris, the literary centre of the world, into poetry. Benjamin's exploration also follows the outer and inner trails that led from eighteenth-century aristocracy to nineteenth-century street democracy.[47]

Just a few steps forwards in time there emerge whole breeds of distinct urban walkers – boulevard window shoppers, the long-commuting city worker, gawking visiting country folks, parades of foreign tourists and other sorts of pedestrians and commuters, who make everyday urban life inseparable from urban travel. Ahead was the monumental work of the great nineteenth-century maker of modern Paris, Baron Georges-Eugène Haussmann, who in the aftermath of the bloody barricades days of 1848 and in the service of Napoleon iii recreated Paris to assure the movement of police and armies and the circulation of foot and wheeled traffic. To achieve his goal he undid the long-standing accretion of streets and enlivened the city by widening streets, tearing down neighbourhoods, erecting new housing and connecting shoppers' boulevards and avenues to the city's new railway stations. His greater goal was a safer, healthier and more efficient city, a city worthy of being a modern nation's capital, a true city of light and the guiding beacon of an orderly and prosperous nation. Insofar as he succeeded, everyday street life, as it was known from 1150 to 1850, was unravelled and all were put on the clock set and syncopated by the arrival and departure of the train, which great machine and thing whistled Paris and the world into a new order. But this is to get a chapter ahead of ourselves.

Already in the eighteenth century, Europeans and colonial leaders put themselves on a freshly made and expanding map. Trade and travel offered a great stage for aggrandizement and imagination, as commerce spread and centralizing states – exemplarily France – knocked down the walls of castles and cities at home and pried open ports around the world. They inventoried nature at home and abroad and traded with all and taxed whomever and whatever they could. At the same time the rich bathed in goods and sunned themselves in courts and gardens, societies annexed the world, its resources, its goods and potential to their economies.

And, as we will see in the next chapter, all this was done all the more with the coming of the Industrial Revolution starting at the end of the eighteenth century. Wood, coal and steel accounted for powerful engines and machines, which despite human costs and social dislocation created a greater abundance than ever before. Money greased all gears and levels. New goods and products produced large dreams and schemes. Sons and daughters became consumers and citizens, while intellectuals conjured a world of man's own making.

This great revolution collectivized and standardized everyday life. It also differentiated the means and dreams of the many. Thanks to industry, market and goods, a portion of the middle class became a self-entitled aristocracy. At home their private and domestic life blossomed and in select quarters created intimacy.[48] In the public square, as the Third Estate they increasingly took themselves – as expressed by the Abbé Sièyes in *What is the Third Estate?* – to be the makers of the nation and the source of its value. On the eve of the French Revolution, this political manifesto argued that common people were the true heirs of the past and the living promise of the future.

5

The Mechanizing of Work and Thought, and the Acceleration of Life and Individuality

Perhaps the 'global turn', for all its insights and instructions, has hit a point of diminishing returns. The fact that contemporary technology, economics, and politics have made us so acutely aware of global connections in our own day does not mean that past events are always best dealt with by setting them within a similarly vast context. 'I could be bounded in a nutshell and count myself a king of infinite space', said Hamlet. Many of the most interesting historical phenomena – think only of the origins of most major world religions – have started with rapid, incredibly intense changes that took place in very small spaces indeed. Perhaps it is time to turn back to them.

David A. Bell, 'This is what Happens when Historians Overuse the Idea of the Network'

The nineteenth century in Europe was made by two great revolutions: the first, the French Revolution, which lasted until 1789, and the ascent of Napoleon in his coup of 1799, declared the end of the feudal, royal and clerical order and a new eon of rights for all men; and the second, the Industrial Revolution, bequeathed work, wages, power and goods to the many. They both transformed everyday life by ultimately assigning political rights and expanded consumer choices to the individual.[1]

Understood as the explosive decade from the taking of the Bastille and the fall of the monarchy to the ascent of Napoleon, the French Revolution – in the spirit of the age and the American Revolution – set forth a universal declaration on behalf of humanity and the individual citizen.[2]

In August 1789, the National Assembly started an ongoing festival of declarations. With dizzying sets of ideal and utopian proclamations, citizens, once disdained as the rude mob of town streets and the savage peasants of the countryside, were elevated to a new status. Equal, free and fraternal citizens composed the public order of law and rights, which both encompassed and enshrined everyday life. Revolutionary Paris became the stage of the world auguring with changing governments and mobilized crowds.[3]

The Revolution, with its boldest language and legislation, struck down the hierarchy and privileges of the old order of aristocracy, Church and guilds in the name of equality for all under the law and the oneness of humanity. On the one hand, it banished feudal obligations, which still structured much of rural life. On the other, it ended the state system of censorship: citizens could speak, write and print freely. Declaring space public, the Revolution opened streets and roads to signboards, petitions and assembly. It spread democracy by renaming streets, squares and buildings and, in addition to the new framework of rights and the authority of democratic government, which soon included emergency conscription when the nation was judged in danger, it established a brand new paper currency, the *assignat*, to govern public transactions. (The *assignat* was based on expropriation of Church lands.)

But the French Revolution seized minds and bodies with more than words and paper. It made its boldest strokes with terror and blood. Its engines were still erratic, its government nervous and its state power hungry. The drama of unfolding events associated with the Revolution turned the new nation into daily theatre for its new citizens. The pace of things was too quick to give it distinct form in the architectural and decorative arts; it settled for taking the crosses off graves, removing Christian symbols and even converting iconic Notre Dame to worship for the new national religion, the Cult of the Supreme

Being. The Revolution renamed the months and would have its own history – as if the new axis of time – mark a new era, as Christ had.

The Revolution enacted itself on the public square. At Place de la Révolution, the revolutionists put in service the newest and most efficient machine, the guillotine. Called by its advocates 'the people's avenger', during the Reign of Terror (September 1793–July 1794) the guillotine decapitated king and queen and eventually the radical Jacobin and head of the Terror, Robespierre himself, along with approximately 30,000 more people in Paris and elsewhere in France.

The Revolution also declared itself in dress. Its citizens wore far less ornate and expensive clothing.[4] They shed the knickers with silk stockings of the aristocracy and elite and put on long cuffless pants, so they became the *sans culottes*, who trudged off to war on foot across Europe as the first citizen army, waving the revolutionary tricolour flag of blue, white and red.

Beyond the stormy course of the Revolution and creation of constitution, democracy and a new form of government in nineteenth-century France and Europe, a new soul had been bred into the majority. The Revolution inwardly designated all potentially as equal members of humanity and as individuals of worth and rights in the market and streets, in speech, assembly and contracts. As if incorporated in a new communion of humanity, the individual hereafter was citizen, member of the nation and fresh participant in all facets of everyday life.

THE GRIND AND WEAVE OF DAILY LIFE

The Industrial Revolution mechanized, standardized and accelerated the movement of everyday life. On an unprecedented scale it utilized natural resources, used new materials and engines, consolidated and regimented society and made bountiful goods for life across the world.

With mines and factories, with concrete, iron and steel, and with canals, railways, roads and steamships, the Industrial Revolution redefined manufacture, invention and production; it ordered and structured the activities of society, aggrandized the military and centralizing powers of nations and accounted for the extending reach and new goals of a truly global trade.

Vastly expanded and accelerated transportation and near instantaneous communication entered humanity into a new order of speed. Urban centres gained unprecedented control of water and liquids and of energy, while public and private lighting turned night into day, enhancing safety, health, theatre, surgery and pleasure. Industry's creations and products metamorphosed town and country, increased their proximity and interaction. New orders of having and powers of spending multiplied wish and possibility.

As I hope to suggest in this and following chapters, the Industrial Revolution was an ongoing transformation of nature, society and everyday life. It exceeded all calculations of short- and long-term material and psychological effects.

THE INDUSTRIAL REVOLUTIONS

Beginning in the second half of the eighteenth century, the Industrial Revolution joined capital, machines and factories to unprecedented levels of production. It increased Europe's and the world's exploitation of natural resources and use of energy, and expanded transportation by land and water. It devoted human activity and intelligence to the making and distribution of goods. All this fuelled dreams and power that made perennial ordinary life extraordinary in its mutating forms.

The Industrial Revolution extended human powers over nature and society.[5] It assured the power of the concentrated many over the scattered multitudes: the city's dominance over town, village and countryside. Though not to be understood independent of the rise of the central state in the eighteenth century and the birth of the democratic nation state in the second half of the nineteenth century, the Industrial Revolution transformed the human landscape, ultimately superseding the millennia-long prevalence of peasant and village life.

NEW GEOGRAPHIES

The historian of everyday life must recognize that the Industrial Revolution proved equal in the transformation of humanity to the

Neolithic Revolution, with its agricultural fields, gathering villages, specializations and rising cities and great civilizations. Nowhere is the speed and transformative power of the Industrial Revolution on the landscape seen as clearly as in North America.

On the cutting edge of the Industrial Revolution, forests were hewed down in New England, the Midwest and even the West. Mines were drilled and dug wherever minerals were found or suspected. Across the whole short-grass prairie, fields were opened, wetlands drained and tiled, rivers channelled and transcontinental tracks laid. New and paved roads followed. Towns were designed on company drafting boards down to the layout and names of streets; they propagated across the entire trans-Mississippi countryside from the Great Lakes and Dakotas to Texas. People arrived by horse-pulled wagons, while supplies for stores, prefabricated houses, buildings and even churches came by train. Of course, the first economic function of the train was to supply farmers' needs and to collect their harvests and products to sell in distant cities and ports. So, as if to jump space and time in a single Superman bound, tracks colonized and imperialized the entire trans-Mississippi American countryside in the three and a half decades from the Civil War to the start of the new century. Peasants from the Old World set to work fabricating and inheriting ready-made lives in the New World. Everyday life cannot be written there or then without reference to this unprecedented and compressed revolution.

Capital threw its power behind the metamorphic powers of machine and industry. Construction cast up dust everywhere as new landscapes were formed and edifices raised. Work and activity afforded a world of fresh sights, sounds and smells and perceptions, of emotions and experiences. The earth was flattened and levelled, made ready for democracy, in which everyman was king. Public and private worlds were made ready, smoothed and easy for walking feet, bodies and taking and grasping hands.

Invention, a new road to wealth and power, boldly designed and drafted everyday life and its instruments and goods. Though not with immediacy and universality, the world nevertheless became ever more malleable to collective and individual will, wish, hope and dream. It gave credence to the proposition that having is being. Life bubbled over with the surging streams of new and novel things.

Increased food, adequate and even comfortable housing and improved health incubated minds with replenished imaginations, fresh wishes and reaching fantasies. Goods and well-being, which gave physical vibrancy to democracy, engendered things and thoughts, which were generous and sublime, vulgar and capaciously greedy. Everyday life exploded. In this way the material grew active minds, which were sources of rivers of possibility. New selves and new worlds became companions and coordinates of everyday life in the era of industrial democracy.

With profound implications for everyday life, industrial centres, in tandem with financial and political centres, became national and global hubs. Utilizing world resources and labour markets, Europe and North America altered their own and the world's material and social environments. With dynamic energies and acute eyes and trained hands, the Industrial Revolution changed the equations of necessity and possibility and made a world turbulent with disorder, ambition and wish.

Such immense change meant industrial society had a dark and bright side. The dark side was a grinding work regime for all, including women and children. Especially in its first generations on to the closing decades of the nineteenth century, everyday life meant crowded, filthy and unsanitary living conditions. There were long daily trudges to and from work. They passed through crowded and unpaved streets, with no public toilet en route. Low wages and irregular work cycles meant times of scarcity. Emerging protests and early stages of unionization formed a common story of a community's 'heroic days', while those at the bottom were without home or family or garden in the countryside to which to retreat. Everyday historians tell mortal and loathsome tales of desperation and abandonment, and they know that only in the last decades of the nineteenth century did births exceed deaths in London, that great mill of national mortality.

The bright side, conversely, as family historians of the nineteenth century frequently record, was that wages were collectively made and accumulated and homes were bought and improved – and surplus money meant leisure, education and choices. As can be counted in wills, tables, chairs and beds had become more abundant in common dwellings. City newspapers reveal in their advertisements a growing plethora of objects and goods for all, as well as the coming of fresh water and sewerage lines, lighting and electrification, and the introduction of education, police and sanitation. In effect, the darkest corners of life were cleaned and lit, and hope beamed that there would be a long and full life for the majority.

In effect, the Industrial Revolution changed how people lived in space and time. It redefined how they experienced their own body, work and daily life with others. Redefining necessity and discipline, it made wages and money conditions of survival, leisure and prosperity. It also joined individuals and families to communities and public places for leisure, while it offered willy-nilly enlarged domestic and private space in which youths could hatch ambitions and dreams.

Women seized the chance. Across continents and classes, Western women, with the support of men, set claim to political and civil rights. Winning limited voting rights in Sweden, Finland and some western U.S. states, poster-carrying and parading suffragists appeared on the urban American and European landscape. Preceding and in conjunction with this movement, women took up new roles in public and private life, redefining individuality, sexuality and career and proposing new concepts of man and woman, home, child and intimacy.

STEAM HISSES AND DUST FLIES

The Industrial Revolution, which began in England and first spread to northern Europe and North America, transformed landscapes and industries, remade national economies and shaped everyday lives.[6] Steam-powered mine pumps increased production of iron and coal, ran the new factories and drove trains through life as made and known up to that point.

The train came after the canals. A barge trip through Belgium and Holland illustrates how this land won from water was drawn anew by iron and concrete structures. Every lock and bridge displays the engineering of rivers and building of canal systems, which turned waterways into highways for the transport of natural resources, manufactured goods and immigrant peoples. Overseas the two great feats of engineering were the Suez Canal, completed by the French in 1859, and the Panama Canal, started in the 1870s by the French and completed by the Americans in 1914. They formed new routes between the Atlantic and Pacific.[7]

The all-purpose steam engine powered the repeating looms of small workshops that furnished cloth to society and empire. The steam engine, with its vast power but insatiable need of fuel, drove the pumps that gathered, dispersed and channelled the waters, which dried mines, replenished canals, filled wells and scoured and shaped surfaces.

The steam engine took over much of the work once allocated to wind and water mills. It drove the second, heavy phase of the Industrial Revolution, which began in England at the start of the nineteenth century with the manufacture of iron and the use of coal. The heavy phase of revolution produced the tools that made things and other tools, and constructed visible and subterranean structures, which characterized the industrial environment with awesome sights and sounds, covering surfaces with oily lubricants and covering the atmosphere in dusty haze.

Steam powered trains and ships.[8] It geographically demarcated the older commercial zones of Europe from the newer industrial zones. It distinguished those parts of the Lowlands abiding in the shadow of the more leisurely grinding windmill from those belonging to the more recent and regimented discipline of steam, coal and iron.[9] It accounted for the vast difference between rural life, measured by seasons and millennia, and urban life, which clanked and clattered by hour, factory whistle and pressing orders.

By the 1840s, the revolution that began in Britain and Flanders had already spread to regions in Germany and realized the emergence of industrial zones in France. By 1850, 5,000 steam engines were already at work; 3,200 kilometres of railway track had been laid down; and displaced craftsmen were experiencing the competition of the cheaper and the machine made. Steam engines increasingly partitioned old and new everyday life.

With steam machines and metal shovels and drills, engineers incised the surfaces of the earth. The engineer was no longer the isolated architect. Instead, now called a civil engineer, he was the aggressive agent of earth-changing. No longer bound by past social order and now on behalf of commerce and production, speed and volume, the civil engineer, encapsulating everyday life, created a landscape of design dictated by the requirements of the tracks, factories and new industrial sites and cities.[10]

New materials joined the steam engine, train and machines in making the great material revolution that reconstituted daily life. Iron and concrete framed modern urban life, which admittedly was raised as well by brick and wood frames and planking. Their combined strength and malleability produced the beams, plates, arches, trestles, shells and force-deflecting catenaries to furnish skeletons of such dominant structures as bridges, tunnels and large buildings. Iron, or more correctly wrought iron and cast iron, and increasingly steel (an alloy of iron and carbon) formed both spine and decorative visage of modern structures and landscapes.[11]

Iron and then steel etched themselves on the skyline. Steel, used previously in the manufacture of sharp and strong-edged swords, daggers and tools, took its place in macro-construction in the 1850s, when it became available in sufficient quantities thanks to the Bessemer process, which was the first inexpensive industrial process for the mass production of steel from molten pig iron. The iron and steel that shaped the macro-world also flooded our great-grandfathers' basements and work sheds with hand tools: axes, hammers, wedges, vices, saws, pincers, drills, chisels, files, rasps, planes, scissors, wrenches, screwdrivers and measuring devices. Daily life increasingly turned on these tools for sawing, chopping, hammering and smoothing; and tool cases filled with screws, nails, bolts, nails, pins and locks to secure our goods. Metal tools and machines morphed themselves into the era's body and gestures; the instruments of work and action became the words and concepts of acting and achieving.

Concrete complemented and enhanced iron and steel in modern building. A far older and perennial building material, versatile concrete, a near all-purpose material (which the Romans used to supplement their stone, brick and even wood structures), filled in riverbeds, lined water and sewerage tunnels and supplied pilings and foundations, basements, walls, flooring and even roofs. Utilizing improved British formulas for cement, concrete, by virtue of its strength, durability, malleability and fire- and waterproof characteristics, became an indispensable material for building and engineering the modern world.[12] Its pervasive use, especially in foundations, beams and flooring, outstripped that of rock, brick and even wood. Its grey, dull, flat face defined a dominant countenance of modernity. Reinforced by iron rods, concrete joined with steel I-beams to erect the great majority of bridges, viaducts, tunnels, wharves and docks, multi-storey buildings, roads, stairways and pavements. Concrete also served the expanding revolution in transportation, superseding stone for foundations and gravel, macadam and asphalt for surfacing roads, highways, pavements, driveways and, more recently, car parks.[13]

TRAINS AND STATIONS

As suggested above, the train was the single machine that materially and sensorially created modern life. A steam engine turned on its side and mounted on wheels, the train, first fed by wood, then coal, marked the excitement and power of new beginnings. It started with hissing, chugging and churning. It rolled forward, accelerating, with the clatter of pulling and swaying cars as it took on the irresistible momentum of the new order. Its belching soot and trailing smoke and its piercing whistle cut landscapes in two and punctuated the day's schedule into the hours and minutes of its arrival and departure. Its screeching halt came at the station. The station, the point of discharging and loading, became the command centre of modern life, supplanting the historic centre of town. It not only marked speed, efficiency and volume but it embodied an aesthetic of importance. I think, for instance, of any main railway station or especially the interior of Antwerp's central station, which is modelled on a decorative Baroque altar and welcomes its arriving passengers into communion with the modern city.

The train was the umbilical cord of industrial life. It integrated space and people in the kingdom of speed and progress. It intensified the mixing of peoples and classes and the exchange of materials and goods. It fed the reality of democratic society and the spread of capitalism. Underwriting migration and popularizing travel and holidaying, it knitted farm, village, town and city (and soon world) into one. Additionally, the train synchronized all facets of social and commercial life. Railway time set national daily time. The face of the station's clock and the factory's whistle syncopated workaday life.

The train wove everyday lives together. People met at stations and in class-segregated train compartments. While integrating commerce and society, the train cast a spell over nineteenth-century dreams. It was in all senses phenomenal.[14] Like the sparks, smoke and sounds it spewed, it flooded the world with sights, sounds, images and ideas of modern times. It hurtled passengers along at what were initially such bewildering speeds as 30 and almost 50 kilometres an hour. It changed perceptions and conceptions of space, both fragmenting and joining surfaces as it moved across swathes of land, accelerating and decelerating as it went.[15] Out of a compartment's glass window, scenes were sequenced, juxtaposed and blurred together.

The train remapped Europe, North America and the world. In the 1840s railways overtook canals as the spine of national transportation. In Britain railways grew a hundred-fold from 1830 to 1860. Total track length had multiplied in those three decades from 158 to 16,790 kilometres. In 1853 in the United States, the first 'union station' was established as far west as Indianapolis. In 1869, a gold spike joining the Union Pacific and Central Pacific completed the transcontinental railroad at Promontory Summit, Utah.

In all senses the railways became the medium for national integration. Bismarck so adroitly showed in his Blitzkrieg war against Austria in 1866 that railways could be used to win wars by the speedy delivery of armies to the front. Also, railway stations and converging tracks formed hubs for developing interurban lines. Located around the points of the compass, terminal train stations served as ports to the city.[16] Also, by the end of the century railways arrived at nearby sea ports, which were served by iron steamships, which carried immense volumes of cargo, tourists and poor immigrants (like my grandparents from Sicily), across the globe's latitudes and longitudes.

With the expanding railway system and its growing stations came another invention, one that jumped space with the speed of a finger tap of a dot or dash. The telegraph, which grew out of early nineteenth-century experimental work with electricity and magnets and was first established in the 1850s in the United States, sent messages wherever its continental and oceanic cables reached.[17]

Trains were central to industrializing and forming modern life. The tracks assigned vitality to places. Their stations were the embryonic life of villages and the full-blown hub of accelerating life in urban centres. The daily metronomes of society's activities, trains muscled society with the exchange of people and goods, troops and weapons.

ACCELERATING OUTWARD, SPEEDING INWARD

For many intellectuals the train was the unwanted 'machine in the garden', to borrow the title of Leo Marx's 1964 book. American philosopher and naturalist Henry David Thoreau, for example, saw the train as slicing through the honest countryside of natives and frontiersmen. Loud and disruptive, it annexed the pastoral countryside to expanding urban and moneyed interests. Abundant praise for industry's achievements was met by countering complaints and laments for forsaken villages, lost traditional communities and dreary, smut-filled landscapes. Indeed, opposing visions of emerging industry in the first decades of the century turned on a conflict between eulogies for rational engineering and counter-attacks from an energized Romantic sensibility on behalf of the virtues of the old order and the victims of the new world of factories, mines, trains and the huddling masses of train compartments, ship hulls and close city quarters.

Differing sensibilities framed life in the century of revolution. With sensibilities antagonistic to Enlightenment rationalism and systematization, Romantics led by Sir Walter Scott turned their admiration to the Middle Ages and its rising spires and maligned Gothic intricacies. Both Neoclassical and Romantic public and domestic architecture filled the post-Napoleonic world, as many cherished the idealized village and symbolic communities of the Middle Ages. In France, some cheered for Napoleon III's urban planner Baron Haussmann, who sought to open Paris by building boulevards that would facilitate modern transport and permit the speedy and efficient deployment of cannons and troops against the rebellious masses and their proclivity for blocking streets with barricades and paving stones. Others lent their sympathies to the lower and hidden classes, such as those depicted by French caricaturist Honoré Daumier in his drawing of humble people huddled in a third-class train compartment.

Nostalgia and progress battled their way throughout the nineteenth century. Neo-Gothic architecture inspired the British Parliament building, whose foundations were laid in 1840, but was also manifest across the extravagant facade of St Pancras railway station, known as the 'Cathedral of the Railways'. The celebrated Crystal Palace of cast iron and unprecedented sheets of glass, built in Hyde Park to house the Great Exhibition of 1851, with its 14,000 world exhibitors, did not win the heart of anti-Western Fyodor Dostoevsky, who judged it and the modern city 'an anthill'.[18]

By the end of the nineteenth century, the vast majority of Europeans and North Americans found the compass to their lives in terms of their proximity to railway lines and the means by which they migrated from village to town to city. Everyday biographies, forming the substance of family histories, turned on stories of going barefoot, a first pair of shoes, walking to and from work, and the days – which don't come for most until the end of the nineteenth century and first decades of the twentieth – when one could afford, thanks to public transport, to ride to work. Normal days for the majority meant immense amounts of walking, when public transport remained relatively expensive in proportion to wages, and going on foot was a way to save pence.

WALKING AND RIDING INTO MODERNITY

Paris was, along with London, a premier example of the making of the modern city. Carved into twenty *arrondissements* (districts), Paris stood ready for a new era in administrative and police control of traffic and crowds. While there were relatively small but increasing numbers of Paris residents in the closing decades of the nineteenth century who made use of the omnibus, the great majority still resorted to shank's mare for speed and economy.[19] Walking still remained the most efficient way to traverse a distance up to 5 or 6 kilometres separating work and home. It remained the cheapest way for the vast majority of workers and middle class to get about. The Métro was installed only in time for the Exposition Universelle of 1900.

As the working class relocated itself in the closing decades of the century from the expensive city centre to the north and northwest centre, so central Paris was sensually reconfigured for its middle-class daily walkers. The older auditory and olfactory environments, once familiar to the Paris walker, were removed as well as broom and shovel could. Familiar echoes no longer reverberated in pedestrian ears. Gone were songs and shouts urging the lower classes to buy used clothes, old hats, eggs, hazelnuts, cabbage, chicory, baked potatoes, almanacs, frogs' legs, rabbit skins, rats, guns, bullets, handkerchiefs, firewood and water.[20]

The salaried middle class and working class grew in numbers on the everyday walk from home to work and back. Many zones saw an increased number of leisure walkers and strollers. There were more and more shoppers who, singularly and arm-in-arm, sought the amply displayed goods of the *grands magasins* concentrated on the *grands boulevards*. Paris, filled with commodities and radiant with them, became one immense illuminated shop window as well as site of world's fairs in 1878, 1889, and 1900. Swelling numbers of tourists and provincials came to Paris to gape and gaze and be awed. The city street should no longer belong to the crowds that the French once called *la rue*.

Urban traffic delivered Paris and the world to new senses of time and distance.[21] Foot speed was no longer the universal measure of speed. The railway and the telegraph standardized the twenty-four-hour clock. The railway and urban transport systems saw a seven-fold increase in use in France, England, Germany and Austria-Hungary between 1860 and 1900.[22] They delivered millions into the city for work and business and dispersed millions to the surrounding countryside for recreation at racetracks, fairs, golf courses, amusement parks and beaches. In effect, an entirely new grid framed everyday life and movement.

LONDON AND PARIS BAPTIZED IN WATER AND LIGHT

Water was distributed thanks to great productions of cement and metal pipes and pumps regimented for cleaning up the city. Fresh and pure drinking water and effective sewerage lines were true and first agents of public health in overcrowded environments. Along with a shower of administered light, water washed away the foul and dark side of life. People dressed and looked better, and smelled less. With new spaces and fresh bodies, privacy and intimacy were universalized skin to skin and breath to breath.[23]

In the very hot summer of 1858, the Great Stink engulfed London, disbanded Parliament and drove the government to undertake the cleansing of the metropolis.[24] Heat, rain, overflowing cesspits (some 200,000 in total), primed directly by run-off from newly installed flush toilets, turned sodden soils into waste-saturated air. All surfaces were slippery and putrid. Driven by health, taste and commerce, London took up the Herculean task of cleaning its Augean stables.

The clean-up first relied on hand tools – brooms, shovels, rakes, pitchforks and scrapers. It called into service rags, whiskbrooms, brushes, big street brooms, bins and carts. Street cleaning was principally devoted to gathering and carting off waste and manure. Proving ultimately more important than street cleaning and its legions of 'nightshade men' – haulers of manure – were the installation of new water mains and sewers, which prevented citizens' water supply contaminating run-off.

Coincidental with the urban clean-up in the closing decade of the century, there was fostered in the middle class a growing duty and discipline of personal and domestic cleanliness. The world was increasingly seen through shiny glass windows and lived on clean and polished floors. Foot scrapers, overcoats and vestibules stood vigilant guard at the front of better dwellings. People of means and pretence wore gloves and hats and scented themselves with perfumes to shield themselves from the mud, dust and foul smells that went with the roads they travelled. Of course, hands still smudged, fingernails contaminated, and waste from skin, scalp, nose and ears was everywhere.

Personal hygiene and city planning, however, played a far less decisive role in cleaning up metropolises than in letting abundant water and light flow in. These two elements transfigured the darkest and dirtiest faces of the city.

Each extension of the water system enhanced people's life, health and beauty. Driven by steam engines and with pressure valves and interconnected piping, city water systems supplied an inexhaustible spring. Water, the earth's first and oldest cleanser of surfaces, defined modernity as clean and healthy. Moved by cast iron, steel and cement pipe and technologies of plumbing, public water became the most docile, ubiquitous baptizer of modern times. It made fields fertile, turned grasses green, filled gardens and parks with flowers, and yet also cleaned towns, homes and their residents. The historian Asa Briggs judges the hidden networks of pipes, drains and sewers one of the greatest achievements of the age.[25]

However, before the public could present itself as clean and wholesome, it needed to be seen in a new light. Electric lighting did the trick; it changed every surface on which it lit. Light was industrialized, to reference the subtitle of historian Wolfgang Schivelbusch's *Disenchanted Night*.[26] Humanity for the first time stepped into the 'age of administered light', to use the words of Gaston Bachelard.[27]

With a broader and brighter beam, electric light over half a century lit up city and then countryside streets, kitchens, front rooms, bedrooms, porches, and dance halls and theatres. It guided ships around shores and provided signals and beacons to direct and synchronize a moving society. It took the form of headlights added to cars, trains and all moving vehicles. It changed the meaning of stage lights and allowed night-time surgeries. It cast penetrating light even into pitch-black mines, basements and farmyards. Lighting put a luminous glow on things; goods and surfaces became effulgent; colours stood forth. The world shone and was translucent as never before.

A GREAT FACELIFT

With water and electricity as its servants, society could extend the imperative to make clean, beautiful and healthy all phases of everyday life. Industry supplied implements, containers and fabrics for sanitation, hygiene and beauty. Whole markets opened up, aimed at woman as domestic cleaner and woman as princess beautiful. Education taught body hygiene; dance halls and city walks flaunted looks, while athletics paraded the body, strong and fast, in public competitions. Commerce profited from the democratizing notion that all should be clean, healthy and good-looking; and there should be a medicine for every malady.

As if locked in a great war of light and darkness, as one branch of heavy industry made and kicked up dust, so other branches, led by the emerging chemical industry, sold cleansers, cleaners and industrial solvents of all sorts. The use of soap increased manyfold in the nineteenth century, as did bleaches to turn clothing white and waxes and polish to put a fresh buff on all things. Small companies cast their fortunes with innovative abrasives, paints, files, sandpapers, brooms, brushes, combs, razors, toothbrushes, carpet sweepers and vacuum cleaners.

Brooms, brushes, rags and a pipeline of chemicals diversified women's cleaning regimes, enhancing their daily and seasonal obligations at home, which were all about washing, cleaning, polishing and shining surfaces. Other new products equipped the woman to scent, shape and disguise herself for a day job and an intimate life at night. Soaps, shampoos, dyes, toothbrushes, pastes, combs and razors joined the battle for clean body, hair and teeth, while cosmetics, colognes, fragrances, eaux de toilette and mouthwashes prepared people for their day's bid for public decency and respectability. Glamour, yet another facet of the model nineteenth-century Victorian life, beaconed new and fresh times. It solicited not just a glance but riveted public attention and prolonged discussion.[28] Of course women, their faces and bodies, became the beacon star of this fresh, alluring sky.

Between 1870 and 1930 surfaces and inter-surfaces of people and things, indoors and out, were smoothed. Taking the rub out of things made for easier rolling for gears and machines and for placing skin against skin. In the essay 'Commonplaces: History, Literature, and the Invisible', Eugen Weber anatomizes this 'superficial transformation' of the skin of things.[29] There were progressively fewer swallows in Paris because 200,000 horses, which annually produced 50 tons of manure, were steadily replaced by Métro, car and truck, leaving less waste for birds to glean and peck. The official cleansing of water and the first sewerage lines, the former a decade or two in advance of the latter, multiplied and steadily reached more and more public buildings and private dwellings. Households and their dwellers cast their ballot for cleanliness and decency by the simple act of flushing: all went *tout-à-l'égout*, down the drain. Rubbish, another sort of waste, was disposed of by means of the uniform and universal metal dustbin (*poubelle*) and regular urban collection as organized by Monsieur Poubelle, a Paris administrator who introduced hygiene measures near the nineteenth century's conclusion.

Speaking of Paris and appearance, the coming of the *pissoir* in the 1880s diminished but did not eliminate public urination. Defecation, spitting, nose picking, hand wiping, and body and genital scratching and other uncouth gestures, along with scatological language, steadily disappeared from common sight and thus became increasingly remarkable and censorable. The scatological took a step backwards in popular culture, on crowded Métros and around the Sunday table.

Wooden clogs fell increasingly silent as country folks were put in shoes and set to walking on cement pavements. Only the poorest of the poor padded about barefoot. Shoes increasingly fitted the feet of their owner, were kept in good repair and were even polished at home in preparation for Monday's work. Young country girls, a great addition of farm-freshness to grey city life and work, bloomed brighter in colours and manners, with disciplined and socializing employment in shops and especially the new institution, the department store. Women were less prone to expose their derrières to do their business on the way to work and increasingly smelled like a bed of flowers rather than the bed in which they slept. Scented and dressed colourfully, they gestured more discreetly. Bawdy women increasingly found their orbit circling saloons, bars and dark streets.

The blind, deaf, disabled, lame and maimed that once filled the streets were proportionately displaced by workers and shoppers and young and fresh recruits to labour, money and leisure, thanks to multiplying jobs, better wages and improved health. Youth even filled neighbourhood streets with playful antics and, with girls around, young men paraded like proud peacocks on their days off. Picturesque scenes and pleasant senses multiplied. Daily life increasingly had sweet and soft seams as baths, showers and dances grew common.

By 1900 Paris boasted the creation of nearly 350,000 electric lamps, which banished a lot of real and imagined stalkers from the Paris night. Spitting, a common habit until then, became less acceptable; those with handkerchiefs were expected to use them. At the same time, with more and more available public urinals and bathrooms, both sexes were less likely to use a tree, the side of a building or the mere turn of a back as the shut door to their toilet.

The writer Stefan Zweig observed a similar development in the Vienna of his youth. In his *World of Yesterday* (1942) he wrote that dim streetlights had been replaced by electric lights; people moved about in horseless carriages with a new rapidity; it was no longer necessary to fetch water from the pump. The masses became handsomer, stronger and healthier. Sports steeled their bodies. Fewer disabled, injured or diseased people were seen on the street. Science, he held, was 'the archangel of progress'.[30]

Cleanliness, self-control and discipline went hand in hand in Vienna and, I conjecture, across Europe with the emerging pedestrian, commuter, shopper and factory worker.[31] Near mid-nineteenth century, etiquette took control as the middle class started to dominate city life and streets.[32] The middle classes, who began as best they could to clean themselves up and made house cleaning a daily affair, began to regulate their bodily behaviour and appearance in public.[33] The bourgeoisie and, imitatively, that new amalgam of working and middle class, quit frenzied dancing and transformed disgust into an internal monitor of external behaviour. Perhaps Freud's superego was discovered in the eye of passers-by on the streets of his hometown, Vienna.

Across a wide spectrum of wealth, traditions and place, middle-class individuals took up the Victorian life.[34] They took up the duty to be a model of private and individual life. Enhanced by a century of constitutional rights, secular education and Romantic aesthetic subjectivity, with greater goods, space, means and choices, the middle-class individual capitalized on the self-definition afforded by increased privacy, intimacy and uniqueness. In his five-volume history of *Bourgeois Experience from Victoria to Freud*, Peter Gay takes up the development of the bourgeois individual under the following rubrics: the *Education of the Senses*, *The Tender Passion*, *The Cultivation of Hatred*, *The Naked Heart* and the *Pleasure Wars*.[35] The writer Theodore Zeldin offers a multifaceted exploration of the heterogeneous factors of the inner side of person, family and everyday life in his *Intellect, Taste, and Anxiety* (volume II of his *France, 1848–1945*) and his *An Intimate History of Humanity*.[36] At the same time, middle-class individuality located some of its dynamics in differentiating self from common people and emergent mass society. Indeed, as it falls to the everyday historian to discern, lives were played out in a process of distinguishing the self, both as an individual and as a class, from those above and below.

A QUICKENING PACE

However, we must not get too far ahead of ourselves at the turn of the century attributing the full evolution of modern society as regulated, healthy and youthful. Like urbanites everywhere, Parisians did not relinquish using the streets to assemble and voice their demands. However, when they did, they were more and more likely to do so not as a spontaneous action but under the plans and auspices of organizing groups, which used demonstrations as a means to express their complaints and exert their power.[37]

The newborn Third Republic mingled everyday life and politics during the years following the Franco-Prussian War (1870–71). The residents of Paris followed their passions and interests to the streets, whose very names were intermittently changed to match mutating causes and changing regimes.[38] Parisians took to the streets in 1873 to voice their support for the presidency of General Marshall McMahon. In 1888 an immense crowd gathered along the route of Victor Hugo's funeral procession. In 1889, en masse, they filled the streets to join in the hundred-year celebration of Bastille Day.[39] With sticks and stones, students and intellectuals engaged in street fights starting in 1898 to contest the innocence of Captain Dreyfus, who was falsely accused of treason by government, army, conservatives and French nationalists.[40] Finally, multitudes enthusiastically turned out to welcome another war against Germany in 1914, which as never imagined would truncate progress and return life to survival among warring machines.

But despite the large passions involved in these events, the power and spontaneity of the crowd had been diminished. As the streets in measure had been swept clean of disease and crime, so had much of their mob-and-crowd aspect been mopped up. Protesters were better policed and under greater surveillance.[41]

Perhaps of even greater note for the social conditions of everyday life up to 1900 and possibly the First World War, Weber, speaking of the streets of Paris, claimed that the majority of pedestrians appeared and smelled as they always had. They didn't bathe or change their clothes regularly. Nor did they brush their teeth or visit a dentist.[42] Even though fashionable people had taken to wearing white shoes, the majority wore the single worn brown or black pair they owned. Barefoot children still enviously peered through shiny glass shop windows; workers and newly arrived immigrants from the countryside still trudged their way through without knowing how or having a sou to take a ride on the Métro.

In city, town and across the French countryside, the majority were still deprived of space and things. They inhabited small, damp quarters, which were without access to running water and indoor toilets. (Even hospitals still did not have an abundant supply of running water, and Paris' richest people, who had indoor toilets, did not have bathrooms and had only a single tap of running water on each floor.)[43] Many streets still remained without sewers. 'By 1903 only one Parisian house in ten was connected to the [sewer] system.'[44] The turn of the century across Europe and North America still belonged to the horse and dray (a low, heavy cart without sides), one of whose principal uses was found in hauling the city's abundant manure for nearby suburban farms and market gardens.

In the countryside, the walking speed of man and beast still measured primary distances between home and field, village and neighbouring villages and market. For much of rural France, where in 1891 two-thirds of the population still lived in small rural parishes of fewer than 5,000 inhabitants, adjacent provinces were as remote and mysterious as other continents.[45] In contrast to their quick-footed, scurrying and unencumbered city pedestrian cousins, peasants still trudged the land as their ancestors had. They continued to discipline their bodies to walking and working the land.[46]

Dust, dirt, muck and darkness still enveloped life in rural France and Europe. Paved roads didn't reach deeply into the countryside. Water and waste systems had not yet been installed. Women, with the exception of those who could afford to buy the circulating water hauler, spent their mornings carrying water home from the town's single fountain or well. Electricity had not reached villages.

Everyday life in the countryside remained precisely what it had been for centuries. Streets there were often unpaved, barely lit and narrow and winding. There was only, if that, a small walk to promenade and a small square where a newly formed local band – a military band commonly – might play on Sundays. There were few stores, little shopping and minimal social interaction between classes. Only market day interjected a sign of life into what the youth felt to be dead towns.[47]

Yet an essential difference existed between the old and new way in city and countryside alike. Both were irreversibly being woven into the same embracing and regimenting nation. Communication and transportation had fashioned a great tapestry of space, speed and mind. Abundant goods and improved housing, even when only seen over the fence and imagined as some place down the tracks, created realms of wish in everyday minds. Distant places sparked local minds with new possibilities and conjectures about migration bringing another and a modern life. Education likewise made elsewhere a hope and possibility.

Even in the countryside some rough majority imagined themselves as one day being free of their own dingy quarters, stick-in-the-mud family and smelly, stubborn animals. Biographies grew out of dreams – of travelling smooth and wide avenues and being colourfully dressed among bright objects and gay people. Simply being someone else, somewhere else! They hungered for bigger towns and cities – Paris, London, Vienna, Berlin, Rome and other amazing places. There they would be paid real money, money all their own – perhaps to be a clerk, railway employee or teacher – to sit in an office chair all day long and manipulate words and numbers. They would disencumber themselves of that world that forever had harnessed their parents and grandparents.

Upper-class urbanites looked across the fence in the opposite direction. Taught Romantic sentiment for a century, city people idealized farm, village, nature and countryside. They imagined farms and woods as places free of congestion, machines and noise. This was for middle-class country walkers a spiritual resource – a place where they could return to their true and natural selves. As Jonas Frykman and Orvar Löfgren wrote, expeditions into the countryside were 'based on collecting beautiful landscapes' and actually occurred around planned footpaths and guidebook listings, while newly erected sightseeing platforms structured the enjoyment of the scenery.[48]

By the beginning of the twentieth century, city and countryside had become, at least for the reflective middle class, each other's mirrors.[49] However, more than mutual projections joined them in national life. Institutions also integrated town and country by providing citizens with similar experiences, laws and rights. At the same time, mass transportation and communication increasingly synchronized entire nations' experiences with surging rivers of goods, increased opportunities for work and money, and individual choice and identities. To the profound disappointment of international socialists and other pacifists, peasants and workers alike from different nations enthusiastically marched off as citizens in nationally regimented steps towards the same unknown war. Improving everyday life experienced a terrible blow with the scarcity, separation, destruction and killing of the first fully industrial and democratic world war.

How do we calculate the millions of individual deaths that occur in wars of a national, mass, mechanical age? After Verdun the Somme was the second great battlefield on the Western Front; there between July and November in 1916 Great Britain lost 400,000 soldiers; France, 200,000; and Germany 400,000–500,000. Each death registered in countless ways in lives and hearts at home, yet how to forget, remember or calculate each or all. In the interwar years the memories and meaning of veterans and paramilitary groups publicly enacted remembrance. In my poem 'The Sum of the Somme, Another Century's Gethsemane', I ponder the possibility of counting those war dead of a century ago.

A battlefield in the great bend of time,
A mere season's pull of oars
Along a river
Through a hilly landscape
Populated with towns like
Ginchy, Guillemont, and Vimy,
Where the Canadians burrowed, tunneled, and battled
Below torn, shredded, but sheltering earth.

And then there was Delville Woods,
Where on July 14 South African troops went out
3,000 strong
And returned on July 20
At 140.

Invite the living to conjure the past,
Tell them about messages sent by
Pigeons, drums, telephones, signal flags, and telegraph.
Help them imagine No Man's Land.
Chew every metaphor into mind's cud.

But see now in the fields
That cows graze around stone crosses,
The mounds of sugar beets heap up at the end of once
    blood-bitter fields.
Listen to the whine of power mowers cutting memory lanes
Among grass-covered knobs and knolls,
And do not be too harsh with yourself
For your flitting, speeding empathy.

Remember that, like a great nervous shutter,
The mind's eye opens and closes with a blink.
It is hard to stay awake counting the fallen sheep
Of another century's Gethsemane.[50]

6

Inventing Our Ways and Designing Our Days

Social life, which once offered an example of relative
permanence, is now the guarantor of impermanence ... No
social value any longer underwrites the time of consciousness.

John Berger, *And Our Faces, My Heart, Brief as Photos*

As much as historians, by disposition, are against homogenizing
lives and narratives, they must structure their enquiries and
frame their narratives with generalizations if they are to be true
to modern times in which at ever greater rates across ever vaster
distances nations, economies and peoples expand and interact.
Every step towards writing global, national, regional and even local
histories involves referring to whole societies and changing spans of
periodized time. Everyday history is not an exception. As much as
it purports to deal with the immediate, common and concrete, the
writing of everyday life must refer to the influences of popular and
mass society at large.

Everyday life becomes increasingly a matter of changing landscapes and environments. Its description must be made in terms of
growing economies and societies. The everyday historian's description and analysis, ever dependent on economic theory and sociology,
must be made with reference to dominant and emergent technologies
and the diversification and homogenization of class, income, wealth
and prestige. The everyday historian classifies individual regions
and particular groups by their inclusion under or opposition to

national politics and law. Even matters essential for the definition of local places and peoples – I think of the illegal, rebellious and multi-layered clandestine culture as a set of ideals and behaviour – merit the larger optics of the spread and control of national authority and developing social sciences, especially sociology and economics.

Historians of modern and contemporary everyday life find their minds actively switching back and forth between individual and general, place and society, regions and nations. No sooner do they focus on one than they point out and move towards a multiplying many. Distinctions are generated with comparisons made by the contrasts, juxtapositions and even contradictions.[1] In any one community, there are elemental differences of sex, age, marital status and health. There are equally primary differences between individuals and groups, generational variations; those who occupy the centre of things and those who reside on the periphery; and even those who live in accord with traditional and conventional ways and those who turn the local upside down with overt changes in nudity, sexuality, homosexuality and lifestyles. Cross-hatching all these distinctions are differences inevitably drawn between worlds of village, town and city – what is traditional and communal and what becomes public, innovative and flagrantly progressive. In conjunction with this, the everyday, ever existing in and straddling consciousness and unconsciousness, undergoes fresh bifurcations of the private and public as the real and imagined redraw the ambiguous boundaries of the hidden and clandestine.

Outsiders populate the rich real and imagined underside of everyday life. Born out of counter-definitions, they are judged parasitical, illegal or of an asocial or devious impulse. Their genesis, revealing the spirit of the historian, is considered to be misfortune, perversity, bad times or a counter-culture. They survive, especially in the Spanish picaresque tradition, by guile and wits or what they can beg, borrow or steal. The reader of nineteenth-century novels can draw long lists of those who live on the edges of society – collectively characterized in France in the aftermath of 1789 as dark, dirty and ominously dangerous classes. Emerging in the same period, eccentrics, *flâneurs*, artists and students filled Bohemia, while tramps and beggars, pimps and prostitutes, gamblers, drinkers and other 'children of the night' filled out the alleys and waterfronts. Karl Marx imprecisely described the latter as the *Lumpenproletariat*, while Charles Baudelaire authenticated the agony, passion, flesh and dreams of drug-takers and others in his *Les Fleurs du mal* (1857).

Characterizing the poor, who were often taken to be the true heart of daily life, generated a whole analytic literature in addition to fiction (most notably the novels of Charles Dickens). The conditions and potential of the poor first derived from late eighteenth- and early nineteenth-century theory, to borrow an outline from Gertrude Himmelfarb's *The Idea of Poverty: England in the Early Industrial Age*.[2] Natural and economic explanations of the plight of the poor as well as advocacy on their behalf could be derived from the writings of Edmund Burke's non-interventionism, Jeremy Bentham's legislative principle of the majority, William Pitt's positive interventionism, Thomas Paine's revolution against the old order on behalf of a new humanity, and Thomas Robert Malthus's analysis of their condition as a cyclic result of their geometrically increasing reproduction against a mathematically increasing food supply. More systematic considerations came with the period of reform, defined by three Reform Acts, of 1832, 1867 and 1884. Then a paradox arose, which surely haunts the student of everyday life in the modern and contemporary worlds: an overall advance in conditions comes with an increasing number of poor consolidated and placed on government rolls and, once so placed, the debate increasingly focuses on the matter of who are these poor, what are they entitled to do, and what should the government do to maintain them or help them escape the everyday life of poverty? The issue of the poor, which tested and continues to test conservative and liberal like, provoked more radical solutions by early nineteenth-century reformists and revolutionists. They suggested that the poor should take their fate into their own hands. In his *The Condition of the Working Class in England* (1845), Friedrich Engels, who worked so closely with Marx, argued that capitalism proletarianizes the poor, making them a distinct class with a fate and rights of vindication of their own.

Simultaneous with such broad inquiries into questions about the economic description of the underclass, accounts of crafts lost to industrialism arose and – again to rely on Himmelfarb – particular approaches to 'the undiscovered country of the poor', which were developed around London as a special case, the investigation of public health (especially typhoid), the moral physiognomy of street cultures, and also inquiries into the 'ragged classes or dangerous classes'.[3]

KNOWING THE PARTS BY THE WHOLE

In the Marxist tradition, two twentieth-century British historians in particular opened the gate to exploring the everyday life of the working class. Eric Hobsbawm, co-founder of the influential social-cultural journal *Past and Present*, used Marxian historiography to write a developing social history of the working class woven out of the Industrial and French revolutions. A primary emphasis was on how consciousness, policies and organizations were rooted in everyday life.[4] In *The Making of the English Working Class*, E. P. Thompson argued that class is a historical phenomenon, 'unifying a number of disparate and seemingly unconnected events, both in the raw material of experience and in consciousness'. And with apologies to the Scottish and Welsh traditions of labour, Thompson made it his goal

> to rescue the poor stockinger, the Luddite cropper, and the 'obsolete' hand weaver, the 'utopian artisan', and even the deluded follower of Joanna Southcroft, from the enormous condescension of posterity. Their traditions may have been dying. Their hostility to the new industrialism may have been backward-looking. Their communitarian ideals may have been fantasies. Their insurrectionary conspiracies foolhardy. But they lived through these times of acute social disturbance, and we did not. Their aspirations were valid in terms of their own experience; and, if they were casualties of history, they remain condemned in their own lives, as casualties.[5]

If not in conformity with a Marxian interpretation, the history of everyday life must nevertheless depict daily life at any one place in the context of an age of 'industrial culture and bourgeois society', to use the title of German historian Jürgen Kocka's work devoted to analysing the dynamics of business, labour and bureaucracy in the flawed formation of modern German society.[6] Any particular study of the nineteenth century must include the dynamic and transformative effects of the century on society as a whole and on its parts. It could not be otherwise in writing of a time characterized by such industrial productivity, increasing population, immense social mobility, the spread of domestic and foreign markets and the formation of an inclusive democracy. The nineteenth century was idealistic, optimistic and truly utopian, beyond all other centuries. It gave rise to the modern political spectrum and its ideologies. Constitutional liberalism, egalitarianism, democracy, socialism, communism and also nationalism fed energies across Europe and the West that were pushing for life to go beyond the dictates of necessity to include the swelling hopes of possibility.

As historians previously tended to focus on unique European, particularly Western European, paths and tragedies en route to freedom, democracy and the realization of nation states, so in recent decades historians for a variety of reasons and disciplines have sought to treat nineteenth-century Europe within a global perspective. Singular in his efforts is the German historian Jürgen Osterhammel, whom some have praised as 'the Braudel of the nineteenth century', in his narrative of the nineteenth century from a global perspective, *The Transformation of the World.*[7]

Surveying the forces that shaped everyday life, Osterhammel assesses the growing integrative powers of state, which with diverse institutions and agencies strengthened, mobilized, disciplined and commanded society itself. He offers such compelling themes relevant for the transformation of everyday life as the expansion of energy and industry; paths of economic development and spreading and improving wages; penetrating networks of communications, trade, money and finance as well as the growth of knowledge afforded by literacy, schooling and the exporting of the European university abroad. Also penetrating nineteenth-century life was the dissemination of civilization and its ideologies and prejudices, and 'concepts of religion and the religious'. In the broadest and most democratic sense he bundles diverse quests for freedom under the concept of emancipation.

Osterhammel concludes his work on the nineteenth century as an epoch constantly preoccupied with appraising its place in space and time. It completed modernity begun centuries earlier by affording a long-term rise in income, a transition from a status to class society, the growth of political participation and a shift in the arts away from imitation of tradition to creation.[8] Although the First World War, Osterhammel argues, marked the end of the century itself, introducing the frightful consequences and imbalances that were played out in the first half of the twentieth century, nineteenth-century dynamic transformations dominate today.

Osterhammel identifies five driving forces of the transformative century. First, the asymmetry of growth defined by increased productivity of human labour profoundly enhanced industrial production and far-reaching commerce. The opening of new frontiers and the expansion of colonies increased economic imbalances, while the destructiveness of weapons and the greater control yielded by the state apparatus exceeded society's ability to absorb and pacify them. Second, one force of disequilibrium was the accelerated mobility as witnessed by emigrations to North and South America and Manchuria, and the resulting relocations of peoples from 1870 to 1930. There was the expansion of world commerce abroad and the acceleration of movement and integration by train and tram, which eclipsed the dominance of going on foot. Third, ideas themselves forever tipped the balance. Transmission of ideas and cultures by new media and translations produced cross-cultural appreciation, on the one hand, and that profound global debate between modernizers and advocates of traditional cultures on the other. Fourth, the century spawned worldwide conflict between hierarchy and equality. And fifth, despite failures in democracy and colonialism, the nineteenth century saw the initiation of worldwide emancipation. These manyfold imbalances – be they called wars and revolutions or extremes of material means and ideals – hatched forces and possibilities, means and movements, making the world of 1900 the vital century so alive to the dynamics and transformations that have accelerated and been concentrated in the aftermath of the Second World War.[9] All this ended what might be defined as the relative autonomy and insularity of everyday life for Europe and America and foreshadowed its end across the world in the course of the twentieth century.

Joining Europe and the West to the world at large, Osterhammel, relying on Max Weber and social science abstractions, affords an array of insights in which the everyday historian can construct the formative dynamics and changing condition of daily life in the nineteenth century. He brings forth the totally shattering or corrosively penetrating forces that ended the autonomy and the homeostasis of numbers, rituals, materials, landscape, work and authority that had integrated everyday life into a functioning whole. Compelling local and regional historians of daily life to widen their scope, he focuses attention on the *asymmetrical* forces of energy, materials, labour, knowledge, speed and central state, which were first concentrated in cities and then exported, with all their potential for disequilibrium, to towns and the most distant fields and villages of the world. Making local history global and universal, all that it had never been, these forces dislocated peoples and places past and they turned individual minds (however remote in space) into theatres filled with strange fears, fresh possibilities and opinions and hopes about distant markets, nations and the very place of man amid things, society and family. In the nineteenth century, the outside world entered the village – *la république au village* – and accordingly the village, body and soul, not without anxiety, turbulence and fracture, joined the world.[10] The difference between the traditional country and the progressive city was often given a moral cast, playing out in modern literature as the struggle of wholeness and innocence versus worldliness, money and luxury.[11]

All this permits the everyday historian of this period to plot and narrate his story dramatically against the background of the great transformation of peoples, places and times. Even in his most local studies, be they focused on transformations within a place or migrations out, he can potentially lay claim to telling a part of a dramatic and moral, national and even global story.

SWEPT UP IN DRAMATIC CHANGE

In 1900 the world was in the thick of change. Daily life in European and Western cities and port cities everywhere provided new skylines. Senses and ideas, along with needs and aspirations, were altered. Things and people moved as never before. New materials and goods were the pistons of economic democracy. Environments in city and countryside were transformed. Buildings and structures grew in size and volume; subterranean structures took the form of networks of tunnels, water mains and sewers; and wires ran, while bridges, trains and steamships linked distant peoples and places.

Also, shadowing and even defining daily habits and conformities, governments multiplied and their organizations, bureaucracies and laws organized lives. Schools, libraries, armies and public health made a newer, smarter, healthier and more obedient citizenry. New emotions and sensibilities tried new fashions and styles and put on uniforms.

What inevitably remains a subjective construction prompts me to say: a sense of ownership grew as the public realm was expanded and people, on all levels, took their lives in their own hands. Counter-balancing senses of alienation, a majority of people took themselves to be participating in a giant project of betterment. Proof was that wheels turned, factories hummed and the promise of improved wages (often battled for) raised hope. The promise of more things and leisure tomorrow stamped the day, and a majority witnessed improvement emerging from their work, wishes and votes.

Despite preachments of the reality of class warfare and loss of tradition, which were heard from both sides, the majority, refreshed with energy and hope with each generation, persisted in believing in their new city that with just a 'little luck' and 'hard work' they – or their children – were heirs of today. Their expanding claim to future fulfilment was based on identity as a national citizen, role as a wage earner and consumer, and enhanced place in society as an individual with rights and choices, and membership in a family with mutual obligations and affections. Increased public space, domestic privacy, leisure and personal choices helped create the intimate person, whose body and private space were elevated under the emotional choice of love to the highest order of human experience. Of course, nudity and sexuality became realms for elaborated pleasure, escape and expressive individuality.[12] A common way to fame was having fashionable and even increasingly displayed photogenic sex appeal.

None of this precluded near omnipresent nostalgia for idealized simpler times past or the embrace of upper- and middle-class ways, which had been swelling for at least a century and a half, and the cult of the private life.[13] For, after all, homes and goods increasingly anchored the majority's hope and dreams of happiness, despite daily ripples of consciousness of nudity and sexuality, ample prostitution, flashes of clandestine lives and common and even corrosive alcoholism in the working classes. Though not universally or instantly, even workers' conditions improved as they were able to improve their dwellings – escape cellars and bid farewell to shacks, cottages and lofts in barns and got larger apartments and houses of their own, even if they still shared and paid for their dwelling by renting to immigrant cousins and fellow immigrant boarders.[14] Lined with soft and clean surfaces, decorated by calendars and commemorative trinkets, these dwellings were turned into homes, which ideally weren't transitory nests but lifetime dens – a lasting centre and anchor of self in place, the condition of privacy and the source of intimacy.[15]

More and more, workers mistook themselves – their pleasure and good – with their middle-class bosses. Even if water and sewer lines had not reached the majority, masses now had access to a private outhouse or stair. Although very few even got a bedroom of their own, they could enfold themselves in the day's paper, ensconce themselves with friends and cards and darts at the local pub or take a walk down a good street and, at least on Sundays, dress the part of well-being: put on a fresh shirt and their second pair of shoes, see their daughters clothed in bright dresses and as a family carry on their own promenade.[16]

First for city dwellers, then townspeople, and only later, with considerable variation of remoteness of place and region, for country folks, the industrial democratic order promised more than work and money. It proffered respect and dignity and stuffed daily dreams with a plethora of images of the things and situations that stand for the coveted life of security and plenty. Modernity as completed by nineteenth-century engines of change won the majority to its discipline not just by wages and relief of arm and leg but by pleasing and captivating hearts.[17]

Modernity transformed the interface of society and world. It presented eye and touch, which equals in measure soul, new, smoother, brighter, varied surfaces and, if I may, a plethora of surfaces. It redefined ordinary sights and common touch. With glass in every window and now increasingly bountiful light beginning to shine indoors and out – at least in advancing cities – it was hard not to celebrate the world with leisure, colours and arts. There was a plethora of objects to be had; abundance tantalized imaginations when window-shopping, passing the plates of glass, mirroring the things and lives that could be.[18]

Other stimuli stole everyday eyes, ears and hands for modernity. Machines and industry materialized new places and lives. Blinking lights and flashing signs invited the many to the dance hall, the amusement park and – in Paris – the Folies Bergère, which dated from 1869.

The printing industry gathered in the entire world – with representations real and imagined, long known and recently discovered, remembered and planned, sought after in the future and missed in the past. Newspapers netted society's interest with printed pages. They formed democracy's daily habits. They did this by covering daily and recent happenings. Aside from a place and a reason to stop off on the way to and from work or occupy a newly purchased easy chair, newspapers seed a fresh mind, with hot opinion, serious judgements and wonders of daily life; they were the scorecard of society's deeds and hopes; in many ways, they wove themselves into the day's conversation. Morning editions sought first attention to the day's happenings, while evening editions tallied the day's – or a week, month, even a year's – consequences. Audience and profits determined the cast and depths of a paper's nets. With headlines announcing a day in a place, region, nation or the world at large, articles gave content and depth, even enlightenment, to ongoing subjects; feature stories vied for the free time and taste of its audience. Advertisements, for all things purchasable, sought to win readers' interest and wallets. Reflecting and making everyday thought and prejudice, newspapers showed that there were wide latitudes between telling the truth, relaying information and winning interest.

Societies were increasingly dependent on literacy, and with reading and shuffling went sitting. There was a veritable explosion of chair manufacture starting in the eighteenth century and diversifying in form throughout the nineteenth century.[19] Desks and chairs furnished floods of offices and stories of high-rise buildings filled with armies of white-collar workers. Increasingly, especially for the middle class and a select number of the working class, everyday life, as lived, judged and, of course, imagined, was life as read – and projected in words and the images and sentiments words convey. Words were woven into images, and images into words, and, of course, numbers remained a vital part of the mix; and so the fabrication and fabric of the modern mind occurred.

Matching literacy in importance for the new working immigrants was learning how to get around a city, which meant how to find work, go shopping, the quickest and cheapest ways to get somewhere. My Aunt Milly argued that her and my dad's oldest cousin, Joe DeCarlo, born in Sicily, kept his ranking in the family not just because he had the loudest voice but because he also knew how to take the city bus and get a transfer to go from one bus line to another, and thus travel for the same price to what were thought inaccessible places for those without cars.

And perhaps counting counted most. It surely was the equal to reading or knowledge of how to get around, and whom to get around with. Numbers calculated wages – daily, weekly and annual income. They equipped you to enter the market as a kind of equal – someone who could weigh, compare, shop and bargain. Numbers were king when it came to big purchases, like that of a small business, a piece of property or a home (which might mark the single most important transaction in a lifetime for many). Numbers ruled one's understanding of cost, loans, interest, upkeep, duration of payment and potential return. Whole fortunes, so to speak, were made by knowing the times table. The quantitative sides of life dramatically increased in the nineteenth century.

MACHINES AND ENGINES, PLANES AND CARS

By 1900, the beneficial effects of the Industrial Revolution, supported by the expansion of commercial agriculture, social organization and public health, had occurred, as historians of everyday life must reference, across much of Europe and the West and had begun to penetrate the world's outposts. Europe's population alone had approximately tripled in a century from 180 to 500 million, without even accounting for the virtual settlement of Canada, Siberia and the trans-Mississippi west. People had been set in profound and irreversible movement.

Colonies and new settlements experienced dramatic growth. Metropolises, the greatest of the cities, had proven to be the greatest magnets for migrations, their populations multiplying five-, ten- and twenty-fold over the course of the nineteenth century. London, foremost in growth among the world's cities, had proved a great death mill up to 1850, with a death rate far in excess of its birth rate, until a great reversal of these trends thanks to improved sanitation, public health, housing and urban order.

Urban skylines proclaimed the surging metropolitan order. Buildings, bridges, roads and skyscrapers announced it, as had the spires and towers of the twelfth- and thirteenth-century cathedrals. The four Expositions Universelles, held in Paris in 1855, 1867, 1878 and 1889, commemorated themselves with the erection of new structures of steel and glass. The Eiffel Tower, built for the 1889 exhibition, revealed the bare bones of steel-frame modular assemblage.

France celebrated the American centennial celebration of 1876 with the gift of the Statue of Liberty. Standing in New York's harbour, it was a visual portal to the New World and prospects for a new life in a new place. A massive work of freestanding copper, the Statue of Liberty signalled to millions of immigrants that before them lay the land of fresh opportunities.

In Chicago, the cradle of the skyscrapers that shadowed every-day urban life everywhere, the 1893 World's Fair used architecture to declare the pre-eminence of the New World. On the exposition grounds, filled with the pride of places and nations, a great Ferris wheel circled. However, it was not that spinning wheel that made American prophet Henry Adams dizzy. Instead, he puzzled over the meaning of another turning invention at the fair: the dynamo, whose rapid revolutions generated electricity. In his notoriously pessimistic *The Education of Henry Adams* (published shortly after his death, in 1918), he asserted that no metaphor at hand could even grasp the wild and savage exponential change that machines and the human accumulation of power augured. He found no icon to minister to the rush of images and power. For him the transforming and metamor-phosing world was fragmenting, breaking apart, accelerating at atomic speeds. The world hereafter was without narrative for him.

Most telling, the world travelled ever less on foot. Ships, trains and trams began to shuttle multiplying numbers of things and humans back and forth. In 1903 travel went skywards. In that year on a North Carolina beach – so distant from the urban skylines of London, Paris, Chicago and Detroit – the Wright brothers, bicycle shop owners, launched their first successful flight at Kitty Hawk. Powered by a specially made light petrol engine of 12 horsepower, with a spinning propeller and a set of light and strong surfaces, the machine took flight – on the design of its wings humanity began dreaming of flying itself to the stars.

A decade later, a step in terrestrial transportation irrevocably transformed land travel for the whole of society. Everyday life would no longer be conducted almost exclusively on foot as it had since the first migrations off the African steppe to the rest of the world almost two million years ago. The specific event occurred 1 December 1913, when Henry Ford initiated the assembly line at his Highland Park Plant in the Detroit metro area. Ford revolutionized the ways cars were manu-factured, and subsequently many other industrial products, across the world. The mass-produced economical cars changed thereafter the way people lived, worked and enjoyed leisure time. The 'affordable Ford', promptly followed by other car manufacturers, put democracy in full motion, creating interlocking local and national networks. People's sense of place and time, work and leisure, was changed.

OF DESIGN AND INVENTION

Other than those great and irreversible events of revolution and war and the profound changes of population, mobility, the phenomenal spread and diversification of markets and centralization of the state, another characterization of the transformative power of modern Europe and its effects on everyday life lies in its advancing reliance on design and inventions in material matters and social organization.

The roots of design lay deep in the human spirit. It belongs to the disposition to make and embellish things. Things enhance power, magnify self and venerate the gods. Evidence compounds that humans were ever makers, improvers and beautifiers of all things. Civilizations, with the varied array of their achievements, testify to humans as creators of their own materials and shapers of their own environment. They harnessed animals to their needs and labours and built ships and wheeled vehicles to extend their reach. Engineers taught principles of moving earth and water, while architects undertook the great projects of designing walls and gates, raising temples and building elaborate villas, residences and gardens. In surrounding countryside agronomists and peasants shaped their fields, pruned their forest, built ponds, irrigated and fertilized their crops and improved their farm buildings. Similarly, craftsmen, especially boat builders and metal and weapons workers, whose capture was an object of classical warfare, held a privileged status just as arch-craftsman Daedalus did in Athens.

Modern history itself was built on the productivity of medieval fields and the labour of peasants, immense building projects (especially of churches, cathedrals, walls, towers, roads and towns themselves), medieval inventions (exemplified by mills and clocks) and a full horizon of craftsmen working with metals, wood, cloth and jewels. In conjunction with emergent science, modern thinkers fused invention and science. They opened the skies to speculation – calculation of celestial bodies, explanation of earthly and heavenly forces – and they explored and explained the human body. Later, the combination of pumps and steam engines profoundly enhanced human power to transport liquids, to manufacture heavy structures and to build and adopt specialized machines to satisfy needs and plans.

The eighteenth-century Enlightenment elite presumed to gather the knowledge and skills of the past, rethink and call for the reformation of institutions, and broadly call for the improvement of the world. Their positive appraisal of themselves and their potential rested on the ground floor of spreading manners, literacy and refined leisure; technically advancing crafts, confident rational science, enlarged European and global markets; and finally rational and directive states. Infecting the whole world, the European upper classes were virulent with the spirit of improvement, be it on farms, in shipyards, along canals, on roads, tracks or in the air. It predicated the utopian notion that humanity could be enlightened and come to achieve its own earthly happiness. The great European philosopher Immanuel Kant declared of his own times that humanity had 'come of age'.

The material, technological, social and political revolutions of the century concretized and popularized the reality and popularity of progress. They collectively denied that there existed an impenetrable, ever repeating and ordinary common life. Progress brought design, invention and applied science into every phase of life. It subjected everyday life to improvement by design.

Design was intertwined with invention. It was about more than a set of skills and techniques involved in making and promoting things. It could not be limited to such closed spheres as clothing and interiors of homes. It surely included architecture, and the planning and engineering of entire landscapes.

Design, at least according to my lights, was a disposition of mind. Its first premise was transformative. It would redraw, shape and make all things anew. It would subject all things, places, appearances, functions and means of manufacture to its scrutiny and arts.

Not to be circumscribed by a single end, design aimed to make things more attractive, saleable, efficient and functional. A major and assumed goal increasingly was to make everyday life less painful and onerous and more comfortable, appealing and beautiful. In some future perspective it matched dream and earthly application, wish and fulfilment. In spirit, it became as bold and limitless as future possibilities could be imagined. Of course, it burned bright with a pride to create and a drive for profits and place in expanding markets.

Democratization fed design's hegemony. The popular classes sensed it was their hour – their *aion* and *kairós*. Design should serve affordability, the abundance and leisure of having what the likes of their superiors had. Design on this count was truly a wing of progressive democratic society. Welcomed to do macrocosmic planning of landscape, cities, manufacture, transportation and communication, it also took up the microcosmic matter of mass comfort and of individual and personal choice. With ever more consumers with rising income, choice and display grew. Of course, fashion and glamour were one of design's favourite arenas, for their money and fantasy were companions.

DESIGN ALL AROUND

Design and invention's influence on daily life could be appreciated by naming the inventions that make everyday life at home and work and on the street. Lists of inventions and inventors astronomically increase across the course of the nineteenth and twentieth centuries. According to the u.s. Patent and Trademark Office, requests for patents for inventions, which began in 1840 at 735 and rose to 39,673 in 1900, exceeded 500,000 in 2011, increasing approximately 10 per cent a year; whereas design patent applications, first recorded in 1880, started with 634 and advanced in an irregular growth to 2,225 in 1900, while reaching 30,467 in 2011. In any one given year, half or more of the applications for inventions ('designated utility') and design patents were normally granted.[20]

Classification of inventions and designs requires that one distinguish tools, machines, objects, materials, paints, cleaners, glues and industrial and chemical processes involved in making the modern farm and city run. Classification takes place in the context of an ongoing, incremental and accelerating fusion of scientific theory and invention, with vast implications for all facets of the material and intellectual bases of everyday life and the forms of work, transportation, communication, information, control and understanding of daily life. Indeed, as the economic historian Robert Fogel declared was the case with contemporary economics as a science, so students of everyday life are without standard quantitative means, though they have much more agreed-upon qualitative means to measure and judge the impact of innovation, invention and design on everyday life.[21] A special issue of National Geographic divides what it calls '100 Scientific Discoveries that Changed the World' (March 2012) into four main subjects: 'The Power of Information: Computing Communications and the Nanoworld'; 'Engineering the Body: Health and Medicine'; 'Invisible Forces: Physics and Engineering'; and 'This World and Others: Earth Science and Astronomy'.

Without reference to the continuing emergence of drugs, plastics, new metals, computers, medical scanners, nanotechnology, biotechnologies and stem cells that characterized innovation in the second half of the twentieth century, the Industrial Revolution produced a steepening ascent in the production of such primary fields as the textile industry and the extractive and mining industries, and the birth of the nascent chemical industry, with soaps, cleaners and explosives. The improved eighteenth-century steam engine ultimately made possible steam boats and ships, steel-making, the railway system and fundamental powered tools of civil engineering. Of diverse but dramatic impact was road construction, photography, electricity, the petrol engine and the car and aeroplane. This list cannot exclude rubber and Bakelite, high-grade steel, aluminium, processes of manufacture and tool-and-die making and new systems of factory production.

The influence of these and many other inventions on everyday life is found, to choose a single volume, in Marjorie Quennell and C.H.B. Quennell, A History of Everyday Things in England: The Age of Production, 1851–1934.[22] After a frontispiece featuring a colourful merry-go-round, expressing the pleasure of a new mechanical ride, they offer chronological charts synchronizing changes and innovations in the spheres of politics, society (especially education and public health), the arts, and science and industry. There we find a choice chronology, from which I select in turn: from 1851, the Great

Exhibition; 1856, manufacturing of aniline dyes; 1857, Pasteur's paper on fermentation; 1858, first cable to America; 1864, London sewerage system; 1865, mechanical vehicle goes six-and-a-half kilometres/ four miles an hour; 1867, Lister's work on antiseptics and Monier's patent for reinforced concrete; 1869, opening of the Suez Canal; 1876, Alexander Graham Bell's telephone and Lester Allan Pelton's water turbine; 1880, first cargo of frozen beef from Australia to England; 1884, Daimler invents motor engine; 1885, Carl Benz builds his motor-car and, 1888, Dunlop perfects the tyre patent; 1890, first electrified urban railway, London's underground 'tube' which operated in deep tunnels, and nine-mile cantilever Forth Bridge over the Firth of Forth; 1892, diesel engine patented; 1893, Ford's first car; 1895, Röntgen discovers X-rays; 1897, Marconi patents a completely wireless telegraph; and, 1909, aviator and engineer Louis Blériot invents the first single-engine monoplane.

The everyday historian need only consider the many thousands of inventions and designs to imagine the profound alterations of daily life in every quarter of its activities and experiences. One can find such seemingly trivial matters as floating soap, celluloid substitutes for ivory pool balls and beer cans. And then there are far more significant inventions such as bicycles, pontoon bridges, safety razors and female sanitary products; and housewares, including bedding, cleaning appliances, cooking appliances, containers, dishes, decorations like wallpaper and Venetian blinds, flooring, furniture, lamps and heating and cooling machines, including refrigeration. Entire worlds of packaged, prepared and instant foods that have profoundly changed the way we prepare meals and eat. The very matrix of everyday life can be constructed though, of course, never completely inventoried, in terms of inventions and new industrial processes and their effects. They equalled changing households, altered workplaces (with new machines, assemblage and safety laws and devices) and transformed city streets, whose increasing flow of traffic was regulated by punctuated public transport, the installation of paved roads, uniform pavements, lifts, traffic lights and road signage.

The everyday historian can pick his way through a multitude of works on everyday life and things as well. In *Breakthroughs*, Charles

Panati offers a guide to very recent innovations. Dividing them into the three categories of medicine, science and technology, he distinguishes medical technologies through computers and microelectronics; communications making a smaller and more convenient world; the whole realm of alternative energies furnished by biofuels, wind and solar power, geothermal heating and cooling, and fusion and the continuing revolution in transportation.[23]

With direct relevance to everyday life, a second work by Panati, *Extraordinary Origins of Everyday Things*, offers a brief account of the origins of five hundred common objects. Belonging to the nineteenth and early twentieth centuries, they are such things as the can opener, safety pins, the bikini, crisps (potato chips), chlorine bleach, the brown paper bag, window glass, the lawn mower and the rubber hose. His objects are found, to mention only half of the sites, 'at the table', 'around the kitchen', 'in and around the house' and 'in the bathroom'. Later everyday life has the true luxuries of flush toilets, toilet paper, tissues, nylon bristle toothbrushes and safety and electric razors. Our vanity tops feature no end of vanities – cosmetics, rouges, lipsticks, creams and hair colouring.[24]

Entire industries are dedicated to people's bodies, health and appearance, their houses and gardens, their social relations, and trips and sports in the countryside. The patents, products, production and research of any one company can command large swathes of daily life. Quick to my mind is my own home state Minnesota's 3M. Starting at the turn of the century in northern Minnesota as a small company devoted to developing sandpaper, it went on to manufacture various types of adhesive tapes, signage and a large range of products developed for cleaning, painting, bandaging and waterproofing. Telling us a lot about how 3M has taught us to mark and stick things together and still be able to unwrap them and take them apart, was one of its more recent inventions, commercially introduced to North America in 1980: the omnipresent Post-it note.

In the same spirit of selecting representative transformers of everyday life, historian of design and technology Henry Petroski takes up the history of the pencil, the tines of a fork, pins, paper clips and zips, showing how big changes in manufacture, industry, use and design are caused by what are considered small and largely assumed and forgotten objects.[25] Essays in Michela Nacci's *Objects of Daily Use* feature the neon light, the electric calculator, the dashboard, the washing machine, the radio, the video telephone, the clock and the nutcracker.[26] In entirely different ways these objects, to which dozens – no, hundreds – more could be added, teach us how technology shapes our daily experience: bodily movements, senses, deployments of energy as well as how we avoid pain and tedium, spend time and accumulate leisure. They inevitably change the experience and meaning of light and darkness, day and night, water and the weather, and the whole outdoors.

Daily rituals, taken to be the repository of continuity in human life, are increasingly shaped by (I offer but the smallest list) redesigned chairs, beds and mattresses, processed, canned and refrigerated food, refashioned clothes and footwear (the tennis shoe reveals a history of materials, glues and design) and ever improved cars and trucks. In a word, I partially repeat, technologies shape our movements, work and action, and they form our experience, emotions and their expression. Inventions literally make verbs and describe situations (with a screw loose, we screw things up, before we pin them down). Brand names alone populate common language, offering a new lexicon of acts, images and metaphors, and wishes and dreams.

As if endlessly malleable to improvement, everyday life since the late nineteenth century has been virtually defined by the introduction of 'new and improved products'. Everything could be sold as new and curious, as shown by constant fads and fancies, and in the extreme by the popularization of glamour and stardom.[27] Mass commercial advertisement offered the fruits of design and invention in terms of its primary matrix of manipulation: the need to entice all to purchase in order to own, and thereby be a better-off somebody and a more important someone.

The spirit of design, continuous with the spirit of the crafts, has always moved forwards on the belief that in the smallest things – screw and screwdriver, tin and tinfoil – there is 'always room for improvement'. This spirit has been at play in the largest architectural structures and greatest machines as well. The idea of improvement was radicalized in the nineteenth century with industrial manufacture, machine design, competition for new markets, mass advertisement and the profoundly democratic idea that daily life could be improved for all, in all ways. The ideal of and the thrust towards improvement multiplied as invention and design played leapfrog from one invention and design to multiplying others. Inventors such as Alexander Graham Bell, the Wright brothers and Henry Ford were revolutionaries of everyday life and mind. In the smallest workshops and garages, and on out of the way beaches, they aimed at altering the human relation to sight, sound and space.

WE MAKE THE THINGS AND SPACES THAT MAKE US

There are countless ways to illustrate this dominant truth of modernity, so alive since humans fashioned wood at fires, made stone hand tools, made shell scoopers, packed mud into bricks, wove grass into cloth and twigs into thatch. We make the things and spaces that make us.

Anthropologists, as we first saw in Chapter One, have given truth to the proposition that we not only live in and amidst things and the space they define, but we think through them. Goods are thought. Tools open fields and make meaning. Pluralistic things like homes and boats offer the greatest and richest metaphors about having security and risking journey.

We accumulate things by day, year and lifetime, on our own and living with others. These things in fact and mind interact, creating new spaces and situations as well as juxtapositions and hierarchies in our senses and thoughts about order. Shopping and consuming and decorating, displaying and storing things make the environment around us and furnish the metaphors we use to understand the world at large. The messy house can be the first and lasting model of a person or the chaos of the world.

A further wrinkle: things and spaces have for us an inside and outside. On the one hand, we live within containers of a sort. We spend domestic life largely indoors, in beds, rooms, apartments, homes and dwellings – as private individuals and intimate selves. At work and school we are also encapsulated in types of interiors, cubicles, offices, buildings. We move through our days in bodies, cockpits and cabins of cars, trucks, buses, planes, boats and ships. What we have and value is – I borrow a page from Bachelard's *Poetics of Space* – within coats, pockets, drawers, books or vaults. Indeed, in the course of everyday life, we establish our more personal and private selves in interior realms of things and space, while our public identity belongs to more open and shared exterior spaces, and our place and self-representation in them.

At the same time that the masses started to live by purchased goods and chosen quarters, society itself transformed the environment. Engineering took space in eye and hand. Steam power, iron and concrete, steel and dynamite, mixed with ambitions, set Europe hurtling through time. Dreams followed from an unrivalled capacity to dig, push, mound and dredge the earth; shape rivers, build bridges and criss-cross landscapes with canals and tunnels; and set arid regions blooming thanks to aqueducts and irrigation systems. As European hinterlands and peasant societies were swept clean, subordinated, metamorphosed and brought under the designs of national markets and governments, so individual and imperial ambitions settled North and South America and Siberia in a matter of decades. The world had become a drawing board for prospects and designs of countless forces.

In North America, the rapid depletion of forests, the uninterrupted opening of prairie lands and the draining of waters in what was once thought to be inexhaustible nature, especially as focused in the iconic West, created a new environmental consciousness in urban elites, which was to spread across the twentieth century. Conceiving of nature itself as vulnerable – seeing the extinction of the passenger pigeon and the imminent loss of the iconic buffalo – conservationists declared government action imperative. Fragile nature must be preserved against Goliath industrial society.

MAKE STRAIGHT THE WAY OF THE NEW LORD

Europe, America and the world were increasingly joined in the nineteenth and twentieth centuries. The globe was explored at its poles and in its deepest jungles. Industrial, commercial and national society measured, standardized, partitioned and regimented all. The world was to be made ready for the great transactions and redistributions of peoples and things. Networks of volume, speed and efficiency netted more and more places. Everywhere, on tracks and roads, in cities, houses, factories and the inside of machines, surfaces were made straight, level and smooth for the touching hand and running wheel.

As I wrote in *On Foot: A History of Walking,* inner and outer surfaces were levelled for easier, quicker and safer movement. Sliding and gliding were learned in early modern Europe and became prerequisite for all civilized and polite feet by the end of the nineteenth century. The even, level and smoothed, the ideal of courtly garden, ballroom floor, palace floors and furniture, became a primary category of architecture and interior design. Smooth surfaces increasingly held a key to democratic urban life. Machines, thanks to tool making and oil, moved interiorly on a frictionless round – be they the gears of complex lathes or the ball bearings of wheels.[28]

Broken walkways, pitted roads, open cesspits, rickety and precarious stairs – all found at the beginning of the century – had to be repaired in the course of the century for society to advance efficiently and fashionably. Open and passable surfaces, roads and pavements, fulfilled the first rights and wants of worker, consumer and parading citizen. Accordingly, urban design increasingly took account of growing traffic, the mounting distance between work and home, city centre and suburbs. Orderly traffic belonged to the following century, with the completion of public transport systems, street routing, traffic signals, city cops and city-wise and mannered pedestrians and commuters, who kept democratic passage going against mounting traffic.[29]

Roads, which often followed and usually supplemented the routes of railway tracks, sped up the integrating grids of national life in countryside and city.[30] Roads multiplied at the end of the nineteenth century, serving carts and bicycles, and veritably multiplying touring petrol-driven cars and commercial trucks. Well in advance of the car, the bike (a developing marvel of nineteenth-century invention and design) put in a first claim for level roads. As an alternative to the expensive horse, whose wastes proved an abiding attraction and magnet for sparrows, the bicycle integrated the outskirts of village, town and even city. Known in the vernacular as the *iron horse*, the bike was a wheeled and self-propelling vehicle. It first went on running and balancing feet and ran under the alternative name *velocipede*. With each of its component parts worthy of a separate history – frame, handlebars, gears and brakes – the bike's light spoke wheels and pneumatic tyres played a special role in accelerating speed and levelling on bumps and providing traction on uneven surfaces from hard clay to light gravel to cobblestone.[31]

However, it was the car that ultimately put wheels under democracy and set humanity racing and chasing. In the course of the twentieth century it pushed the bike off or to the side of the road as it most recently has in China. The car, nuts and bolts, wheels and motors, pieced its way into existence; it was a design of a thousand inventions that spawned a million dreams about ways to travel and places to go. First came the matters of a chassis, number of wheels, steering wheel and brakes; and then there was the question of an engine for this new rolling land horse until inventors eventually settled on the small, light, economic and powerful cylinder-driven petrol engine.[32]

With experiment going on in barns, garages, bicycle shops and machine sheds across America, France, Germany and England, the car excited possibilities and focused inventions. It could be a truck, tractor and tank – or even a speedy roadster or perhaps a touring car or hearse. Unlike the train, individual schedule and choice of company ruled. It went wherever its owners wanted, if the engine didn't fail, weather permitted and smooth, passable surfaces allowed. Eventually, swing doors, back seats and running boards let a whole family of eight in (and four or six on the side boards); primitive headlights pierced the night, and later, windshields and cabs prepared its driver and passengers to face the elements and darkness.

Henry Ford, who further and profoundly changed the face of Detroit, was the first to standardize and mass manufacture and, thus, produce the car at an affordable price. He lured the many into the car, put them behind the wheel, gave them command over a dashboard, and, once in, they would not relinquish control. The car became a member of the family. A car, the horse of all, was a claim to being a lord of the road – with the right to travel the city, countryside and nation. Simultaneously the icon of manufacture, design, speed, freedom and so many other invented attributes of contemporary life, the car concretely (road by road, intersection after intersection) defined and required planning as it enhanced suburbs and organized the life of farmers and villagers.

In sum, the car was a great revolution in daily life. It defined daily rituals, weekend jaunts and even two-week summer holidays. It determined place of work, extension of commerce and range of travel.[33] Individual makes of car stated one's well-being and were advertised as modelling lifestyles. Cars hosted distant dating and romance. As the second most expensive item in a family budget, they taught their owners about borrowing and paying back, maintenance, trading in and depreciation. Citizens lived their biographies on wheels and in cars. They held the memory of first dates and long solemn drives to the cemetery.

Like early man's biface tools, the car increasingly organized the space and time of work, daily life and leisure in society. Like an elemental wrapper, it enclosed driver and passengers in a cocoon of comfort and speed. Its cockpit proved a multifaceted prism for seeing, conceiving and being in the world. As no other object-machine-commodity, it encapsulated life in contemporary society. Like first roads for great kings, the car opened a smooth and straight way ahead. It made all who could drive lords of choice. Contracting space and joining place, it put the world under the driver's wish and the tread of tyre. The world was seen extended through the windshield. It made everyday life reach to where we could drive and made true nature where our cars couldn't reach. Aeroplanes extended this democratic revolution in mobility and lordship in the second half of the twentieth century.

DESIGN TRUMPS ALL

By the start of the twentieth century, design was in the driver's seat. Inventions multiplied, and multiplied again, in a world in which, again to rely on Henry Petroski, 'there is no perfect design' and everyday life is classified as imperfect for reasons of invention and profit.[34] Places – whole societies, cities and great regions – were put on the planning boards. Reform took aim at public problems.

Science, with an enhanced place in universities and as a set of systematic disciplines, extended its range of research. Offering knowledge probing into everyday life – the common why and what of nature, things and processes – it was harvested, at increasing rate, for practical applications. The distance between discovery and invention diminished. Physics, chemistry and biology – which opened the atom, the molecule and the cell to theoretical consideration and practical application – carried us inwards to deeper sources of matter and life.[35] Knowledge of such invisible realities provided new tools to measure and envision all things in atomic images and gave us means to enter into the very making and manipulating of materials. The science of the first half of the twentieth century, so important to medicine and industrial and chemical production, anticipated the awesome awareness of the second half of the century, notably the atomic bomb, genetic and stem cell research, nanotechnology and bioengineering.[36]

With knowledge of the small and invisible, interior spaces and micro-sources of energy came a radically enhanced capacity to alter materials and shape surfaces. Atomic and molecular production, chemistry's domain, further extended the presumption that life in all its facets was malleable to improvement. The macro world responded in unison with the transfiguration of skylines, tunnelling, near endless paved roads and buildings and structures. Skyscrapers reached higher and subterranean networks of tunnels, water mains and sewer pipes went deeper. Visibly and above ground, businesses and transportation grew.

The built world was rebuilt before the eyes of each generation. Factories multiplied, commerce grew, standards of living increased – growth stamped promise on the face of things. Smoother and brighter surfaces stole eyes and won the velvety touch of hands. Window-shopping whetted appetites. Blinking lights and flashing signs lit marquees and regulated traffic. The printing industry sheeted over the world with the printed page. Headlines announced the day as if the world belonged to the readers of the daily paper. Societies, increasingly dependent on literacy, transmitted information, offered education and spewed and churned with national and imperial ideologies, swamping common, traditional and popular ways and language. Words, images and numbers, on a scale never before seen, said, read and counted, fabricated the modern and contemporary mind – became the fuel of daily life and work.

Nothing revealed the modern city's persuasion over the hearts and minds of its dwellers more than telling time. The clock, as we saw at the beginning of the chapter with canals and trains, synchronized and sped up the movement of the modern citizen in modern national society. 'The clock, not the steam engine, is', the American historian of technology Lewis Mumford contends, 'the key machine of the modern industrial age', for accurate timing is indispensable for standardization, automation and, alas, nationally integrated mobilization and war production.[37]

The clock became omnipresent in the second half of the nineteenth century.[38] In ports, railway stations, factories, schools, in kitchens and bedrooms and on wrists, the clock dictated people's actions. 'The best proxy measure of modernization', the clock wrote time on the inner impulses of both the urban and, belatedly though ultimately, rural citizen.[39] Time increasingly became a category of everyday perception and action. It doled out sleep and leisure, work and holiday. The clock found its way to the kitchen wall and the alarm clock stood guard at bedside.

AMERICA, THE WORLD'S NEW EVERYWHERE

The nineteenth-century quest for an improved life continued in full force in post-First World War America. For Europe, the First World War was a great tragedy. Its plans for a quick war to end all wars dashed hopes. It mobilized all its resources – its science, economies and peoples – to engage in unprecedented mechanized destruction and slaughter. Only in 1929, the year the Great Depression began, did the European economy return to its pre-war vigour. Conversely, America, which entered the war late but decisively, suffered comparatively slight losses of life and emerged from the war materially, technologically, financially and politically pre-eminent in the world – and England's creditor. In turn, the American body did not suffer radical social dislocation or radicalization of its ideologies.

Without dismissing undercurrents of uncertainty, suspicion, anxiety and fear, along with sharp prejudices and organized hate groups, Harvey Green captures a progressing America in *The Uncertainty of Everyday Life, 1915–1945*.[40] The nation's fourteen million immigrants and their children lived securely in their own enclaves in town and country, and did not, despite the fears of old Anglo-American stock, prove subversive by virtue of their Roman Catholicism, Judaism or old-country radical socialist or anarchist ideologies. The nation's farmers prospered in the immediate post-war period, while the nation itself, with regional variation, started its century-long urbanization. By 1933, half of all Americans lived within a half-hour drive of a city of 100,000 or more, and approximately 20 per cent of the population tilled the soil or raised livestock. Industrial work and management and clerical jobs replaced farming.

Green further details the urbanization and industrialization of life:

> Industrial productivity increased 40 percent in the 1920s, although the boom was unevenly distributed. The textile and coal industries and agriculture either stagnated or collapsed. The value of real estate showed the largest gain, followed closely by consumer goods and automobiles.[41]

Technology and science, great sources of hope, closely followed the spread of electricity, which went from the city to the countryside in the 1930s and '40s. It did away with the ordeal of pumping on the farm, while indoors the cheap electric motor lightened housework and the radio blared away the blues.

'Between 1915 and 1929', Green wrote, 'application of mechanization to production and mass advertisement accompanied a substantial increase in real wages for white- and blue-collar workers.

After virtually no gain between 1890 and 1915, wage earners' power increased 20 percent between 1915 and 1926.'[42] Homemade goods were virtually eliminated. Mass-produced products, testifying to the spread of design as a means of appeal and profits, were made more colourful and shapely. 'Beginning in the mid-1920s, typewriters, lipsticks, cameras, plumbing fixtures, towels, and bed linens, suspenders, underwear, and cheap silverware were offered in colors.'[43] Everyone was told he was now better off than the nobility and aristocracy of times past and things considered once-in-a-lifetime were pitched in multiples; not one but two were the way to go.

Cultures, of course, imagine and worry at the extremes, no matter how clear the general course towards better days. Self-help by books, university extension services, which offered education and training programmes, and the YMCA taught course upon course on how to manage one's manners and govern one's house. Government reform, which on the state and local levels regulated elections, introduced civil service hiring regimes and took power from party machines, and also made a long and ultimately failed reach into people's houses, pleasures and ethnicity with Prohibition, established as an amendment to the U.S. Constitution in 1919.

With changes in everyday life, it was a struggle to keep abreast of daily changes and happenings. The popular world registered new sounds, with jazz, gangsters and crimes, uncensored movies and 'the new woman'. Unlicensed worlds sprung up on American shores. The age unanimously projected itself in terms of heroes of every ilk: from Henry Ford and Charles Lindbergh to Babe Ruth, Johnny Weissmuller, Bill Tilden, Enrico Caruso, Rudolph Valentino and Al Capone, who was fast with guns and cars. This world looked back to the home it sentimentalized and ahead to the certain advance in space and movement and a future popularized in fresh and modernistic designs and cartoons. But the everyday life of one's age never equals times nostalgically venerated and times anxiously but ambivalently awaited. So the daily life of the 1920s, so varied for individuals, generations, immigrants and the employed and unemployed, entered unknowingly into the future through the Great Depression and the Second World War. Between emerging abundance and the developing Cold

War, different pleasures, hopes, fears and anxieties framed the 1950s
– and it became hard for American historians and Europeans alike
not to record the daily life of the twentieth century as a staccato
matter of events and decades and remain unobservant about the
trends linking the closing decades of the nineteenth century and the
beginning of the twenty-first. The issue abides for the everyday historian to write a narrative alive to the coordinates of place and time,
especially in this era of accelerating change and concentrated forces.

7

Compounding Minds

Culture is ordinary, in every society and every mind.

Raymond Williams, 'Culture is Ordinary'

As we have seen, moderns and contemporaries ever more live out their daily lives in the orbits of central states and great markets. They live in the expanding arcs of spreading manufacture and design.

This new world born of industry and its products shapes and develops our senses, perceptions, organizations and values. It literally transforms our experience and consciousness. On this landscape our senses fill, change and are replenished. Country and city eyes are filled with new sights, shapes, forms and colours. Farm tastes and smells give way to the odours of cities, industry and synthetic chemicals. Ears seek and are filled by new sounds; noise and music, not always distinguishable, come with and define new environments – and surely accompany industrial life at work and play. Bodies are spared roughness and unevenness, while, unless gloved for labour and thorns, hands anticipate a smooth and even touch of things.

Machines and goods, the agents of modern and contemporary transformation, proliferate. They make and remake our experience and consciousness. They redefine composing elements and parts of daily life. Magnifying our energies, capacity and imagination, machines, dare I say, do almost all things to the world. Machines, transforming body and the world we work on, make the world easier to lift and push, walk and ride, roll and climb, warm up and keep cool. They make packages and wrappers, facilitating storage and transport.

They expand, accelerate, encrypt and yet broadcast information of every sort.

Goods and structures, the fruit of industry and commerce, along with science and technology, multiply, as pointed out in the preceding chapter, to meet our expanding wants and pleasures. They make for indoor and outdoor worlds of growing comfort, increasing pleasure, greater efficiency and accelerating speeds.

At the head of the list of transformers of everyday life, and most worthy of the attention of the historian of daily life, is the prominence of the self-contained home. In conjunction with the car, the home away from home, the home (as real and idealized) becomes increasingly autonomous. It is detached from immediate dependency on the extended village, neighbourhood and community, which themselves are on the wane in countryside and city. Its autonomy grows along with the nuclear family and the self-sufficiency that comes with assured regulated heating and cooling, and water, electricity, and energy supplies, as well as access to home delivery, repair people, police and ambulance. In the contemporary home and apartment, not only the perennial household tasks of cooking, washing and cleaning can be carried out but household members have access to stored supplies, recreation and games, off-the-shelf and pharmaceutical medicines and communications by phone, radio, television and computer with the world close and far. Filled with things and furniture softer and smoother to the touch, the home – increasingly for the majority – offers more internal space and places and rooms for leisure, hobbies and small businesses; and increasing reasons to stay at home.

The outdoor world likewise is shaped for convenience and amenities. As roads and pavements multiply and are made more level and direct, so private and public motorized transportation increases. At the same time, there are more recreational public spaces, parks, gyms, swimming pools and ponds, museums, zoos and department stores and shopping centres, offering for those with means a full spectrum of the most recent and advanced goods of all sorts. With considerable unevenness, abundance and amenities are brought closer to the larger and richer markets. And for those who can afford it, the car and public transportation are given as their means to participate. A need for higher specialization and a desire for the most exclusive goods and pleasures may in the future require that daily life be increasingly budgeted and even lived for frequent trips and elaborate holidays to acquire these.

Engines and machines, in effect beyond all approximations here, define the modern world in its common work and ordinary play. They convey us through space at ever greater speeds and define our homes with ever more comfort and autonomy. Each object, however seemingly small and mundane, incrementally changes our senses, wishes and possibilities. Expecting science and invention to advance, the public looks to new materials and goods. For in truth, it is containers, paints, glues and medicines, instead of ideas, causes and political parties, that are the true revolutionaries of everyday life.

MATERIALS AND GOODS

Glass and plastic are two examples of materials, one ancient, one contemporary, that have not only changed the surface of everyday life and formed our containers, but have also profoundly altered how we see and value the world and ourselves. Glass, whose origins date to early civilizations as a glaze for pottery, for jewellery and as a transparent container for liquids, came in the West to furnish the great Renaissance and early modern optical tools, the microscope and telescope, that extended eye and imagination, knowledge, invention and design to what lies beyond. It played, in turn, a great role in the late nineteenth-century revolution of light, brightness and cleanliness in everyday life. As an architectural material it opened our dwellings to light, and its lenses extended our captive gaze into things within and around. Alan Macfarlane and Gerry Martin wrote in their *Glass: A World History*:

> Anthropologists have long seen technology as a mix of things and ideas, of ideas embedded or congealed in objects . . . Nowhere is this more obvious than the simultaneous development of ideas and techniques in the making of glass. It is both a tool of thought and tool with thought

embedded in it. What is peculiar about it, is that it is the only substance which directly influences the way in which humans see their world.[1]

Developed and refined in the early modern period, plate glass filled the scintillating courts of Europe with reflecting self-images of luxury and beauty. Mass-produced in the nineteenth and twentieth centuries in all sizes and shapes, it served a see-through world of windows and windshields. Its role in modern window-shopping and as the crowning glamour of the late nineteenth- and early twentieth-century department store allowed all – through proximity by sight and touch – to imagine and actually enter a dawning era of abundant and luxurious commodities.

Mirrors, which are vastly expanded by advertisement and images, helped create the sense of a self-contained consumer middle class. They were installed in furniture and decorated the walls of homes and gave many – if only a sneak peak at the mirror in their compact – a self-identifying and reassuring glimpse of themselves. With mirrors as the eye of the other, people saw in advance how they would appear when they stepped out in public, turned up at work or took to the dance-hall floor. The mirror also added self-indulgent consciousness to the new individual's private days and ways. At home and alone, in the intimate quarters of bedroom and the private space of the bathroom, mirrors served as Narcissus' pond. It gave anybody who dared throw a glance the chance to ponder if he or she were 'fairest of them all?' or if 'such a face as this' presaged a special destiny. With improved lenses all could take a more complete and accurate view of themselves.

Plastics are the distinguishing material of the second half of the twentieth century. As Chinese ceramics sparked porcelain kilns for the royal hearts and aristocratic taste of seventeenth- and eighteenth-century Europe, so everyday life in the last four decades of the twentieth century belonged to plastics and the polymers, as made clear by Susan Freinkel's *Plastic*.[2] Derived from the Greek word *plastikos*, meaning a potential to be moulded or shaped, plastics first appeared in everyday nineteenth-century life in natural form as chewing gum, shellac and rubber – that elastic hydrocarbon polymer first vulcanized and synthesized under the pressure of imperial Japanese expansion in East Asia – which rolled cars, trucks and all sorts of wheeled containers and tools into our future.

Plastics were fundamental to the materialization of the products, movement and environment of emergent mass democratic order. From coal tar and then petrochemicals, chemistry wove long string of polymers that came to command our lives. Beginning with Lucite, vinyl and Bakelite, plastics took control of more tools, goods and surfaces. Though DuPont first used nylon (a result of the quest for synthetic silk) for the bristles of toothbrushes in the late 1930s, they attracted more attention when they used it to veil women's legs and strengthen parachutes for flyers. DuPont's Velcro, patented in 1955, put people and things under tighter wraps with substitute fasteners for hooks, loops, snaps, buckles and zips. Out of polymers DuPont created 'stickless' Teflon and in the 1970s a second nylon: Kevlar. A material lighter and much stronger than steel, Kevlar proved ideal for the colourful shells and hulls of boats and canoes as well as the production of strong fabrics for sails and tyres for bikes and race cars. The chemical industry across the closing decades of the twentieth century made and patched daily life with polymers to form waterproof fabrics, time-release capsules for pills and replacement parts for human bodies.

Omnipresent! Everywhere alive to touch and eye! Far more than any material, plastic, as Freinkel vividly details, has become the epidermis, the inner lining and the substance of things and parts. More and more does contemporary research make plans for plastics to join glass in making the ever-present screens, touch screens, scanners and computer monitors of everyday life. Plastic, with a touch of poetry, can be considered the membrane of contemporary life: colourful, transparent, flexible, it holds, interfaces and substantiates almost all. Freinkel introduces her narrative with the drafting of plastic for the Second World War. In the company of such fresh recruits as polyethylene, nylon, acrylic and Styrofoam, plastic saw battle in all theatres, and none were decommissioned with war's end. She develops its story in terms of seven products: the comb, the chair, the Frisbee, the i.v. bag, the disposable lighter, the soda bottle and the credit card.

In the era of Plasticville, the average American consumes 300 pounds a year, and world consumption totals 600 billion pounds a year. Polyethylene found peacetime service in packaging. And along with that a by-product, propylene, can be made into polypropylene, which we meet in yoghurt cups, microwave dishes, disposable nappies and the bodies of cars. Acrylic fibre makes multiplying playing fields with greener-than-green Astroturf.

By 2010 the chemical industry had produced 70,000 different products, with polymers and plastics constituting about 80 per cent of the industry's worldwide output. Major markets for plastics include packaging and containers; home and commercial construction with great varieties of flooring, siding, covering and lining, as well as piping and hoses vital to the transport of electricity, air, water and other liquids along with agricultural drainage. Plastic forms the insides and outsides of cars, planes, ships and trains, while diverse polymers also have a significant role in paper, inks, tapes, signs and electronic and medical goods. In hospitals plastics are humbly cast as bags, tubing, syringes, 'nappies', surgical covers and bedpans and play vital roles in dialysis machines, incubators and the construction of artificial hips, knees and hearts. 'Plastic scaffolding', Freinkel notes, is used to grow new skin and tissues, making it in some measure the new face and body.

Nevertheless, as if to show that into every daily life poisons of one sort or another must fall, plastic also plays a villain in Freinkel's narrative. Under the subtitle of 'A Toxic Love Affair', she notes that certain bits of plastic act like sponges, absorbing carcinogens DDT (dichlorodiphenyltrichloroethane) and PBBS (polybrominated biphenyls) while other non-biodegradable plastics litter oceans, waters and lands, destroying ecologies and strangling wildlife. Everywhere plastics form the reality, confirm the practice and are the icon of a throwaway economy.

Freinkel anecdotally paves the way for the historian of everyday life to consider plastic as the informative material of our time. Furnishing the covers, linings and materials of so many of our products and tools (from credit cards to dustbin lids), plastics define what daily life takes to be the texture, colour, strength and malleability of things. Plastic transforms our sense of the genesis and cost of things and determines our expectations of the sounds, strength and types of transparency and solidity as well as contributing to our language, gestures and habits.

The French philosopher and theorist Roland Barthes gave protean plastic a mythological potency. In a 1957 essay, he wrote:

> So more than a substance plastic is the very idea of its infinite transcendence; as its everyday name indicates, it is ubiquity made visible . . . Plastic remains impregnated throughout with this wonder: it is less a thing than the trace of a movement.[3]

Barthes supplements its mythological endowment:

> And as the movement here is almost infinite, transforming the original crystals into a multitude: of more and more startling objects, plastic is, all told, a spectacle to be deciphered: the very spectacle of its end-products. At the sight of each terminal form (suitcase, brush, car-body, toy, fabric, tube, basin, or paper), the mind does not cease from considering the original matter as an enigma . . . And this amazement is a pleasurable one, since the scope of the transformation gives man the measure of his power, and since the very itinerary of plastic gives him the euphoria of a prestigious free-wheeling through nature.[4]

Plastic, Barthes has it, overlooking the place of aluminium and new metals, abolishes the old hierarchy of materials. It spreads everywhere, offering the proposition that all can be plasticized.

CROSSROADS OF INTERPRETATION

Everyday life is ordinary to those who live and think it. It becomes extraordinary by the experience, conceptions and habits and developments that carry people from one age to another. It is not made ordinary by the elevated pretence of high culture – the highbrow presumptions of art gallery and teashop – but instead becomes ordinary by the simple fact of living it and making it one's own.

I read the Welsh Marxist critic Raymond Williams to be saying in his essay 'Culture is Ordinary' (1958) that culture does not simply belong to the manipulation of outside forces and technology. Instead it is assimilated, though not without initial confusions and long suffering, by the human heart with patience, tenacity and persistence, and continued learning and adjustments. And in this way, culture, which is made habitual by repetition, endurance and disposition, serves as the mental glue of our ways and days. It keeps daily life a mixture of place and time and a balance of polarities. Born into the rural labouring classes, Williams writes on the basis of growing up in the country, studying at Cambridge and migrating:

> Where I lived is still a farming valley, though the road through it is being widened and straightened, to carry the heavy lorries north. Not far away, my grandfather, and so back through the generations, worked as a farm labourer until he was turned out of his cottage and, in his fifties, became a roadman. His sons went at thirteen and fourteen on to the farms, his daughters into service. My father, his third son, left the farm at fifteen to be a boy porter on the railway, and later became a signalman, working in a box in this valley until he died. I went up the road to the village school, where a curtain divided the two classes ... At eleven I went to the local grammar school, and later to Cambridge.[5]

Williams goes on from this autobiographical statement, fleshed out in his novel *Border Country* (1960), to shape his argument:

> Culture is ordinary: that is where we must start. To grow up in that country was to see the shape of a culture, and its modes of change. I could stand on the mountains and look north to the farms and cathedral, or south to the smoke and the flare of the blast furnace, making a second sunset. To grow up in that family was to see the shaping of minds:

the learning of new skills, the shifting of relationships, the emergence of different languages and ideas. My grandfather, a big hard labourer, wept while he spoke, finely and excitedly, at the parish meeting, of being turned out of his cottage. My father, not long before he died, spoke quietly and happily of when he had started a trade-union branch and a Labour Party group in the village, and, without bitterness, of the 'kept men' of the new politics. I speak a different idiom, but I think of these same things.[6]

On the autobiographical basis of having lived at the crossroads of rural and industrial, traditional and changing, and in a family of a place and on the verge of migration to new work and minds, Williams went on to complete his argument that 'culture is ordinary: that is the very first fact':

Every human society has its own shape, its own purposes, its own meanings. Every human society expresses these, in institutions, and in arts and learning. The making of a society is the finding of common meanings and directions, and its growth is an active debate and amendment under the pressures of experience, contact, and discovery, writing themselves into the land. The growing is there, yet it is also made and remade in every individual mind . . . A culture [thus] has two aspects: the known meanings and directions, which its members are trained to; the new observations and meanings, which are offered and tested.[7]

Alluding to the continuities of spirit and mind, even the disposition to learn, change and adapt, it is possible to contend, as Williams does, that there is a continuity to everyday life; there exists, in fact, a common culture making us ever one.

However, I believe that such an argument becomes increasingly tenuous. Not just in the villages and farms and neighbourhoods of industrial countries but in much of the world, the smallest towns lack people, institutions and coherent cultures to absorb 'the new'. They are utterly, profoundly and irreversibly transformed by industry, market and state, or simply have physically vanished altogether. The traditional way seems to weaken, lack stability and even those to remember, who could interpret the new and place it in the service of the old. Indeed, Heraclitus is not to be contradicted: change is not an illusion.

At least, I believe the historian of everyday life encounters significant changes in all phases of life in the last two centuries. As a historian I cannot but record those overwhelming changes that overrun place, community and mind despite culture's disposition through habit to adjust and bring coherence through repetitions to the ways of bodies and the attitudes of minds. Places, I would argue, simply lack sufficient density and autonomy, inherent institutions and abiding populations, to insulate and buffer themselves, on the one hand, or translate and integrate outside forces into their ways on the other.

Distinct languages, cultures and peoples have dramatically diminished everywhere since the last decades of the nineteenth century. Without the capacity either to buffer or absorb foreign influences, places have been subjected to the converging and concentrated powers of the outside world, which include the hegemony of centralized states, the dominance of distant markets, the pervasiveness of money in all transactions, the pull of new opportunities, the attractions of fads and fancies, and the emigration of local peoples and the coming of outside workers and leaders.

Indeed, countless memoirs chart lives in relation to the transformation of rural communities and local neighbourhoods. Old places are undone and new places only partially constructed.[8] In *Peasants into Frenchmen: The Modernization of Rural France, 1870–1914*, Eugen Weber charted how in the last three decades of the nineteenth century the outside world transformed the French countryside with the coming of government agents, railways and goods, visits from city cousins and the draft, public schools and party politics. His argument, which in measure I make my own, is that old rural France – its villages and countryside, which had held generally to their ways – was irreversibly and irrecoverably overwhelmed by the volume and combination of outside forces. Never again would it return to its local and traditional ways. Some identify different and earlier culprits and a different combination of forces starting in the late eighteenth century. Frédéric Chauvaud, for instance, stresses an earlier and greater interdependence between local affairs (and its issues, passions and honour) and central government and its courts. Weber, however, found his academic conclusions regarding the plight of rural France confirmed by others.[9] Three important sources for him were the folklorist André Varagnac, local historian and regionalist Guy Thuillier and Émile Guillaumin's memoir written in the form of a novel, *The Life of a Simple Man*.[10]

Indisputably, a major volume could be written on the literature of the changing countryside – its villages, regions, peoples and landscape – and its relation to the growing cities and metropolises in nineteenth- and early twentieth-century literature.[11] Debates and documentation, memoirs and literature could be used to outline similarities and contrasts from east to west – Russia to Germany to Spain – and south to north – from Sicily and the other regions of Italy to Scandinavia and England – with special places for Wales, Scotland and Ireland. Each would add to the profound and diverse ways that modernizing forces and emigrations altered daily lives and transformed minds. Peasants and their children became citizens, consumers and individuals; and villages were enrolled in regions, distant markets and national projects. In personal terms, I received half my education about Europe of the late nineteenth century and first half of the twentieth, not from the study of titanic events and battles of ideologies, but from changes in rural France and southern Italy. I have largely understood my own family as peasants under the Shadows of Chrysler as a long rural exodus to industrial Detroit on the eve of the First World War in one migration of Sicilians from the hills southeast of Palermo and another of Acadians, English, West Prussians and Irish who followed 'country paths' from Europe and New England along the Great Lakes to rural Wisconsin, and then Detroit just after the First World War.[12]

Although the United States was founded by immigrations and immigrants, the trans-Mississippi West was founded after the Civil

War (1861–5) by modern industrial engines, foreign (almost exclusively British) capital and metropolitan markets. It was born the cradle and harness of nation. However, daily life took form in small and distant villages and, regardless of the independence of separate states, rural America was born with the fact and myth of progress. Villages, farms and businesses, born together at hip, chest and head, were covenanted by the promise of a prosperous democratic future. They suckled at the breast of a nation run by and for cities; a nation that would embrace, with insignificant grumblings, car, tractor, movie shows, electricity, radio, television and synthetic chemical fertilizers. The countryside would receive (often immediately or within a decade or two) the best the city had to offer in goods, education and opportunities, and in exchange they would return their goods and sons and daughters to the advances and needs of the nation and its economy.

By the 1920s and '30s, even though farm prices were down, the everyday life of country villages and towns equalled that of larger towns and cities. Country folk had their movies, doctors, professional services – and even sewerage systems, paved roads and pavements. By reading, knowledge and benefits they surveyed the world from the top of the American mountains, even if clouded by the Depression. However, the Second World War marked the beginning of an irreversible demographic decline as labouring country folks filled out the draft, migrated for work opportunities in war industries, and veterans themselves in considerable numbers did not return home after the war but went on to a government-subsidized education or sought out distant chances to participate in the booming economy of the 1950s and after. The countryside shrank precipitously, with small and distant places (like those that filled the Dakotas and the Great Plains) getting smaller – and, if not vanishing altogether. Small towns everywhere grew progressively less capable of manning a Main Street offering what the majority of Americans now considered indispensable amenities and services. Surely, by numbers and wealth, the rural town could no longer keep pace with a prospering and specializing nation.

Diagnosis, therapy, education and entertainment were farther away. Those living in the country lived everyday life on the road, travelling for work, to see family and for holidays (when they could afford it), as well as seeking needed doctors, dentists and lawyers and the advice of specialists who resided in larger towns and cities. Even when at home, country people lived far away from home, thinking of and conjuring distant markets, opportunities and pleasures. As it became increasingly necessary for both husband and wife to work outside the home, the population sought places that offered multiple job opportunities. Localities at the same time had a harder time governing themselves and populations shrank, the elderly migrated to live near their children, and successful business people – traditionally a source of village and town leaders – retired or holidayed in preferred climates.

The rural landscape, not without parallel in town and city, has been increasingly depleted of small-town business families. A living was not to be earned and proud ownership to be affirmed on Main Street. With populations diminishing and more and more land belonging to fewer and fewer farmers (big 'operators'), commerce became dominated by large chain retailers and building and supply depots. Initiatives and employment steadily shifted to outside agencies or internal agents acting on behalf of outside government, institutions and markets. In step with declining populations the countryside aged, making many small towns and villages essentially care communities or housing for the broken, disadvantaged and the less ambitious. To speak, of course, in large generalizations, the countryside of the trans-Mississippi West, which was not incorporated by growing cities and new suburbs, has had an accordion life over the last 125–150 years. Counties and towns had rather prompt beginnings, marked by the coming of the railways, an immediate and even an extended expansion, depending on whether they were on a main line and how far west into dry lands it went; and then a certain and staged withdrawal occurred (from almost the founding decades until the 1950s) when most towns and counties from the Mississippi to the Rockies and beyond began an incremental, predictable and irrevocable compression. What were once vital and energetic localities defaulted to the old and memories of the past. Everyday life has shaped itself around mono-cultural and ever more genetically modified designed crops. There are fewer family farms and smaller families on them.

Shrinking rural populations increasingly resort to travel, visiting experts and computer screens for information, economy, education, health care and social connections. Rural communities divide, and even bifurcate, between the better off and the poor, fewer young and ever older, and declining villages and increasingly irrelevant Main Streets. Landscapes, across which no or only one or no-stop trains run, are now criss-crossed with different roads of all sorts and commercially defined by access or distance to main highways and by communities and food processing industries in search of ever more distant, deep and scarce water.

The countryside, to speak in far less than popular terms, has become a collection of colonies for which the national covenant of optimism and progress no longer holds. Of course, none of this is to deny that, with variation by place and region, a similar emptying has not occurred in city centres, ethnic urban neighbourhoods and even what are deigned old suburbs established just after the Second World War.

In 2013, in an essay titled 'The Extraordinary Ordinary and the Changing Faces of Place', I offered this introduction to the villages and towns of America and in measure Europe and the world. I quote and paraphrase:

> These first places have been or are being superseded nearly everywhere. At ever accelerating rates across the course of modern history, older places (villages, valleys, regions, towns, and even city centers and neighborhoods) have vanished altogether or significantly relinquished much of their economic, cultural, and political autonomy. They have surrendered and, in many cases, rushed to join fresh markets and newly formed nations; to participate in regional transportation; and to take advantage of education and literacy; and to join in the promise of a fuller and easier life. Places have become subservient, interdependent, mutable, and provisional . . . Standing in the shadow of new urban and interurban orders and central government – I think not just of Europe and North America, but of China, India, the

Near East, and Latin America – traditional places persist only in the memories of the aging and emigrated few or in the guise of Potemkin model villages for tourists to gawk and gaze.[13]

WHEN COUNTRY COMES TO THE CITY

When rural people from collapsing places in the countryside came to town – be that countrymen from the deep South or Appalachia, Sicilians from hill towns or peasants from Europe, the Near East or East Asia – their stories, proverbs, legends and myths fell to the wayside. The immigrant storytellers did not lose their memories, nor did their tongues fall out of their heads. But without listeners in their own youth and the world around, they fell silent. Exact places – towns, valleys and mountain passes – were forgotten and stories lost their footing in memory. Few knew the exact dialect; fewer, wishing to be modern and national citizens, cared to speak and lend hearts to old words and ways. Working parents and children lacked time and interest to indulge the storyteller whose repertoires seemed endlessly circuitous, filled with procrastinations and repetitions and references to unintelligible names and situations. In any case, storytellers couldn't compete with the doings of city people and rarely would be chosen when placed in competition with the movies, radio, television or what was out on the streets, at the dance hall or ballpark. A household of immigrants didn't generally have space, time, energy or interest to unpack old words and ways. Their treasures, when not buried alive, were converted to literary culture – gathered by folklorists and turned into memoir and literature by the eccentric and sentimental grandchild – or yet were carried to the larger ethnic community in dating and wedding dances or songs that voiced the plaintive hearts of the old when they were young and separated from place and love.

As words and stories did not provide new lives in old everyday shells, so goods from the old country were too few to frame new lives in small apartments, on the streets and at work. The goods, crafts and arts that survived passage from the Old World were ultimately meagre in comparison to the things needed and expected from the New. With considerable variation between the well-off and impoverished immigrants, newcomers brought with them the lightest, most valuable and what they judged to be indispensable possessions. With animals and farm implements left behind, they came with their best or only luggage – painted wood, canvas, leather or simply cloth – holding lace and linens, which often came with the woman's trousseau. Jewellery, candlesticks, a rug, a book or two and even decorated eggs might be carefully packed, along with needles and thread, a handful of tools and even a gun. Daily life in the New World was to be purchased by labour and enterprise, assisted by sponsoring relatives, and given form by freshly established immigrant neighbourhoods. Daily life, in turn, was shaped by needs to adapt and dreams of opportunities for a better life.

When ethnic communities and rural people from the same generation lived close by and formed neighbourhoods, older ways did take root and abide even in growing industrial cities like Detroit, Michigan. The father and oldest male remained the head of the household, called the breadwinner by virtue of his wages. The mother was heart and hearth of the home, even though many women were alone and worked outside the house. All were expected to contribute to the family. None of this suppressed the need to survive in the new cash economy or the competition to stand out and take advantage of the opportunities in this new land, which meant money, goods, a house and a measure of security, comfort and even privacy.

In this new land one could still keep and profess one's faith. Indeed, church and synagogue for many were their first definition of community in the New World. Churches and synagogues were primary social centres. In them members could meet and be with their kind; seek a favourable marriage within the faith; and share resources and make provision for newcomers, the old and lonely and those who had fallen on bad times. Also, churches were places to collect funds for local maintenance and new building projects. And, not to be forgotten, churches provided local places to pray, suffer, confess and hope for good fortune in light of their crossings and new beginnings. Churches also taught people about the tenets and practice of their faith, not mastered in the daily life of remote and unpopulated villages.

Sanctified and sanctifying churches, synagogues and mosques consecrated, celebrated and even offered special services and sacramental rites of passage – entrance into life, adult life, marriage, death and the priesthood itself. Congregations brought with them from the old country, procured or were assigned by bishops their own priests, ministers and rabbis, who functioned as community conscience, leader and promoter. Often with their own funds or the help of wealthy parishioners or the bishop or synod, congregations erected churches and synagogues in testimony of their commitment to the new way. Often these churches dwarfed anything immigrants had known in their former countryside and rivalled those in provincial capitals.

Beyond this, with faith came ties to fellow regional and national believers. Immigrants met in and through their religions believers with greater means, education and connections. In the case of more populous and established faiths, like the Catholic, faith meant access to schools, colleges, seminaries and the service of various religious orders with distinct missions and long records of establishing orphanages, hospitals, cemeteries and other charities. Indeed, bridging locality and ethnicity, village and new environments, religions offered an identity and means for living in secular, capitalist and national society at large. A vital institution in forming and negotiating everyday life, churches played a key role in organizing co-ops, insurance companies, businesses and even unions. They also interpreted and incorporated new ways to make them compatible with traditional faiths. Affording continuity and habits, on which all lives in measure insist, churches promised immigrants and their first-generation urban and rural offspring that their children could marry their own kind.

Everyday life then, even in larger metropolitan neighbourhoods, did not immediately abolish the old country and village way. On the contrary, older communities and beliefs were buffered and secured in accord with the ways of the old country – through marriage and relatives, neighbourhood help, the labour of children and wives. Even life in an industrial city such as Detroit up to around 1950 did not exclude gardening, keeping chickens in one's basement, making one's own wine, gathering greens in fields or fishing the city's river or canals. Weddings, cards, picnics, and birthday and holiday gifts and celebrations, bonded and kept relatives and friends close. Beyond this, adding to the old way, one took his worries and problems to the family counsel or even sought the help of a local saint or the auguring of a local teller, who, doing what institutions and doctors or even politics promise, predicted births and genders, the final outcome of undiagnosed and unmitigated disease, the coming of deaths and prospects for a serious undertaking.

On all these counts, despite the loss of language and words, strong remnants of culture, community, belief and even the basic arts of cooking, carpentry and other crafts abided. But much eroded, especially in cities, right from the first days of immigration. An unusual number of immigrants arrived single and stayed single and returned home, with cash, to wives and villages. Marriages no longer occurred for the sake of the family; they did begin to split apart because of alcoholism and other stumbling blocks of getting in step with the industrial order. Marriages outside one's ethnic group and religion became increasingly common. With school, entertainment and sports, youth became modernized, urbanized and nationalized and turned away from and even forgot the old ways. They forsook local and regional identities in the old country for national identities (fashioned by the upper classes and recent history). Sicilian villagers, for example, became Italian Americans, remaining equally ignorant of the histories of both nations, enthusiastically identifying with their new home city. In the case of east side Detroiters, it meant for young adults like my parents a growing place with work, cars, streetcars, a glistening and rushing river and a river park named Belle Isle. There were elm-shaded streets, hopping dance halls, good music and the colour of gangsters and blind pigs. In 1935 Detroit cheered for the World Series champions the Detroit Tigers, the football champs the Lyons and the Stanley Cup winners for the 1935–6 season, the Redwings.

The spirits of the children of immigrants migrated into the new, changing and urban world that tantalized and bewitched. They were drawn by the promise of having new goods, participating in new situations and being participants, if only as audience and witnesses, to famous events in arts, sports and music. Sensing themselves as part of a new generation and belonging to fashion-setting America, they could not resist the chance to be free, fresh and stylish in dress, manners and relations. They sensed they were on the threshold of being individuals – having distinct, private and intimate lives of their own.

Increasing numbers of post-First World War first- and second-generation American youth, as disposed by ethnicity, means, opportunity and ability, took direct aim at living a new and better life through higher education. Even in the course of the Depression years of the 1930s the young and new American working class chose unions (often formed by ethnic chapters) to insist on improved work and lives for themselves and their families. At the same time, as unionization advanced and poverty and unemployment reached unprecedented numbers, the federal government under Franklin D. Roosevelt and the Democrats promised to aid all in their search for material well-being.

With the Social Security Act of 1935 the social net was cast farther than ever before in the United States. The act aimed at establishing a worker–employer financed insurance fund for the unemployed, widows, fatherless children, and the old and retirees; of the latter, more than 50 per cent, as a consequence of the Depression and associated bank failures, had fallen into poverty as defined by the national government. With the Act's passage, everyday life had been transformed at its heart. Families and local communities relinquished care for the old and needy to a national system of care. Government, as was the case for old and wounded warriors, was no longer far off; its pensions and death benefits became a universal right of law and an integral part of daily life.

The structure of American law itself induced all, long-time citizens and immigrants, to base their everyday life on its rules, ordinances, laws, courts and legislatures. State and national law determined the purchase, holding and transmission of land, as well as goods and property. It afforded the means to negotiate and settle business contracts and transactions. More, it regulated behaviour and reinforced morals. It took the matter of justice and retribution out of community hands, affording immigrants new and no doubt what were at first alien means to protect children, determine their majority, punish abusive behaviour, reject forced marriages, and write wills, settle estates and assure distributions even when beneficiaries lived in other states and foreign countries. In a word, the law set the bounds of customs and manners. It moved the frame of justice and fairness in part out of the local and communal context, even at the extreme, placing unappeasable passions and calls for revenge by onerous vendettas and appeals to communal enforcers in the hands of the police and law.

HANDING BODY, PLACE AND LIFE OVER TO STATE, MARKET AND MIND

In North America, the West and much of the world, daily life today is distinguished by its comparative material prosperity, individual choices and expectations of social support. Life, in the broadest sense of the term, has been democratized. There is increased participation in the public world, and society aims at improved standards of life and increased choices and rights.

As a consequence of eighteenth- and nineteenth-century revolutions in politics, literacy and education, the majority, in turn, comes to believe in its own individuality. This sense is underpinned by the notion of an elemental right to participate in public life, enter contracts, profess loyalties and entertain valid opinions about all things public. When underwritten by standing constitutions, this individuality is more closely associated with the law and citizenship with full participation in society's open and free institutions.

Democratic individuality both fed and grew out of a broad optimism that one is living in an improving time which increasingly welcomes individual decisions. Everyday life is understood to benefit from state regulation and science, invention and design. Ideally, they allow one to see benefits from sacrifice and happiness as a consequence of individual work, initiative and risk.

Beyond this, I think an ever greater majority, as it moves from traditional rural place to modern democratic nation, considers its choices, pleasures and even opportunities a historical entitlement.

That is, to cite José Ortega y Gasset's classic *Revolt of the Masses* (1930), the majority, at some point, began in the early twentieth century to presume the past as destined to deliver the many to their pleasure, comfort and car, and indisputable sovereignty over change. Scientists and liberals, who strove and sacrificed for knowledge and freedom, were assigned the sole historical mission of procuring the happiness of the masses.

The great majority understood human control to mean less pain, more pleasure and greater fulfilment. Empowered by machines and tools, human control was equated with effective harvesting of nature, increased industrial production and unprecedented yields of energy and goods. The building of public structures and domestic housing reinforced belief in the beneficence of human work and design. Everywhere the majority found multiplying reasons to believe in the fruit of human industry and invention.

However, these conformities of belief in progress did not march twentieth-century peoples, groups and cultures lockstep into a homogeneous society of singular mind. Even the mounting fusion of high, popular, traditional and commercial cultures and their subordination to the mass culture did not mark the triumph of the collective whole over the individual. Despite being channelled by central powers and controlling ideologies, everyday lives remained diverse and were even increasingly variegated by belief and means. This was so for multiple reasons. Processes of modernization were not uniform in influence and combination. At the same time, daily life, at varying rates, gave way and resisted surrendering its old ways to new – and did it in different ways on different terms. Interactions occurred with the full differences of culture, class, place, region, status and nation.

As always, time differentiated life in all phases. Happenings, movements and global events initiated by the First World War intensified and dramatized distinctions and conflicts throughout the decade of the 1920s. The Depression and the 1930s fostered social and ideological conflicts, delivering the second global and total war in approximately twenty years.

Competing nation states showed unrivalled concentrations of power with global imperialism and intensifying arms races, which culminated for all in four years of murderous, mass and inventively destructive war. Daily life for millions of combatants became occupancy of stark, muddy and treacherous trenches in 'no-man's land', where they experienced, when not bogged down in boredom and cigarettes, continuous bombardment, charges through barbed wire and raking machine-gun fire, poisoning by low-clinging gases and impalement on bayonets. On the home front, where deaths were announced and families and hearts broken, cities, factories and fields were conscripted and bombarded. This tragic story, which killed and injured millions on the Western Front and even more on the Eastern, implicated the great authorities of state and national agencies of democratic promise and science and technology in death and destruction. It made suspect, and ultimately shaky, the middle class's governing promises of certain material and democratic progress. It cast a shadow, lengthened by events, over confidence. Everyday life trembled with each major subsequent event in the following decades.

Events, which brought profound insecurities and once unimaginable possibilities, entered people into parties, movements, ideologies and the national discourse. From contesting perspectives they looked to the nation for resolution. While no doubt many longed for and idealized the old days, contemporary lives and minds focused on the public order as key to achieving a secure and better life. In depression and war the populace as a whole recognized the primacy of government, its successes and failures, in determining their fate. Headlines ruled and newsreels unfurled the future and formed the global consciousness of the everyday mind.

Events of such global, surprising and monumental impact as came in the first half of the twentieth century turned minds farther away from villages and neighbourhoods. People looked for the foundations of their lives outwardly and in the future. Minds focused on national, and global, affairs. Everything and everyone was felt to belong to the same nation, world and economy. There was no way to ignore or flee them. One's daily bread and happiness, regardless of class and status, proved contingent on distant affairs, markets and their happenings. The autonomy of the daily order could not even be secured, at least for any length of time, by an attitude of aggressive indifference.

Events secured minds for outside orders. Daily life had been increasingly annexed to governments, laws and institutions, and markets and designs. Fates and fortunes increasingly were understood to turn on science and technology and on specialists and experts of all sorts. Life was conducted increasingly on a sense of contingency and expectation of 'what next?' A sense of collective destiny clouded individuals and places everywhere except on the most remote and out of touch places.

More encompassing, but more ethereal, was the dawning sense that we humans did what we wanted in existence. That is, humans were becoming independent from and even superior to nature in potency; humans were fusing new sources of energy and organization to a purposeful mind that willed its place in existence.

Reliance on science and the power of invention enhanced the overall sense that daily life was increasingly in the hands of the outer world. Physics with the atom, public health with 'the germ' and medicine and pharmacy with new powers of diagnosis, surgery and therapeutic drugs all recounted victories, along the path of human mastery over self. They gave credence and momentum to the notion that humans, ever potent and deadly, could know, invent and achieve what they wanted.

Today, local resources of knowledge and information have been superseded. Local understanding, therapy and counsel have been displaced by medicine, pharmacy, clinic and, to a degree, psychological counselling and specialized social work. And diagnosis and cure increasingly came to rely on X-rays, atomic scanners, microsurgeries and the pharmacy's inexhaustible chemical formulas. The reading of palms, faces or simple posture and comportment, along with sight, touch and senses, have been sacrificed to invisible realms composed of numbers and images intelligible only to experts and authorities at ever more distant and specialized clinics and hospital complexes such as the Mayo Clinic in Rochester, Minnesota, which draws patients from throughout America, the Near East and elsewhere. The dawning age of chemo, stem cell and gene therapies, along with the installation of pacemakers, microchips and other nano devices, carries daily imagination beyond past science and technology.

More than a century's social, material, technological and scientific progress has contoured imagination with new, even extravagant and utopian, notions of what is possible. The urban world, despite its horrors and injustices, and the nation state, despite wars and injustice, awake the majority to life's possibilities with fresh spaces, objects, entertainments and comforts. Beyond the attractions and the advantages of work and wage in the city, abundance and constant improvements in living conditions validated migration. Police, public health, utilities, libraries and social services increased security and prospects. In cities there were more dreams to be realized.

Selves that had more room, space, comfort and means were given over to their private and intimate lives: their emotions, wishes, imaginations and fantasies. In contrast to traditional society and fixed places, in cities selves experienced, if only vicariously but nearby, a wider range of taste, wants and feelings – and way of living. They projected themselves farther in space and time. Never knowing exactly who they were or what they wanted, many churned inwardly with conflicting feelings and aspirations. With new orders of possibility and individuality daily life burgeoned with wishes, plans and fantasies.

Contemporary society, or call it modern civilization, ploughs through the present with new energies, technologies and social agencies. The future bursts forth in change and promise, while the past with the old ways of parents is eroded, displaced and even violated. The past has become hidden. It furnishes the ghosts and revenants of community and times gone. So as progress exalts and nostalgia haunts, the everyday slips out of joint in place and time, jumping to an imagined future and intent on remembering a vanishing past.

To borrow a notion from Erving Goffman, the influential American sociologist, contemporary times metamorphosed the individual self. New places, things and societies presented new platforms and occasions for enacting the self.[14] In the contemporary world, the person – a complex of body, mind, actions, beliefs and social relations – lives not in one or two but in a multitude of changing, interactive and mutating everyday worlds. Daily life comes with inherent ambiguities, inner conflicts and even insoluble contradictions. The need to maintain work, family, friends, duties and beliefs brings choices and surprises with unsolved tensions. The everyday, in sum, is less and less experienced as static and predictable; it belongs more and more to change, design, individuality and subjectivity.

The everyday, which still orbits around habits and places, also turns more and more gyres in the mind. Mind leaps traditional borders and temporal boundaries. It follows imagination, affinity and empathy where they lead, making ordinary days of life extraordinary days of mind.

THE MARRIAGE OF THE MANY

Everyday life could be narrated in terms of housing, clothing, cleaning, cooking, animals, plants, machines, and as playing, working, fighting and healing. It equally could be narrated in terms of diverse geographies, distinct peoples, groups and classes, and the stages and ways of their lives. Portraits of the daily lives of the rich and eccentric, students and artists, and the poor, insane and criminal should be chapters in a book of daily life. Finally, everyday life could be described as a consequence of economics, demography and climatology; people's differentiations in space, migrations, wealth, income and consumption could equally form wholesome units in any volume on daily life.

Here, I have proposed that there are rich themes in contrasting rural and urban life and sets of associated contrasts beginning 10,000 years ago between dispersed and centralized societies, traditional and modern economies, oral communities and literate societies. I have particularly pointed to the attractiveness of exploring the ways in which village and peasant, local and regional societies, increasingly lost their autonomy and capacity to assimilate outside influences and in some way make them their own. I associate the retreat of traditional places and cultures not only with the increasing control of society by government markets and ideologies, but also the shrinking of the smaller units of family, village, crafts, and local institutions and government.

With special attention to the nineteenth century and the consequences of the two great revolutions, the French and the Industrial, centralizing agencies of government and ideologies integrated, while markets, technology and communication heightened emigrations. People became citizens of nations (at least in much of the world) and, if we borrow the critique of everyday life by Henri Lefebvre, all became consumers.[15]

Forces of change multiplied in nineteenth-century Europe. They were spearheaded by monumental building and civil engineering practices. Vast networks of transportation and new orders and speeds of communication wrapped continents together from the distant steppes of Russia to the high plains of the United States and Canada. Centralizing nations and expanding markets integrated places and peoples, regions and nations. Immense migrations within and out of Europe swelled in the course of the nineteenth century, as people left mountains for valleys, villages and small towns for large towns and great cities. Rural orders were drained of people and authority by new national and metropolitan orders. The redrawing of political jurisdictions, the formation of new groups and classes and the rewriting of cultural histories equalled a world of new and emergent identities by vocation, class, ethnicity, nationality, gender and race.

National, popular and mass cultures grew and fused together. Traditional everyday life could no longer subordinate its own people's wishes to long-standing ways and ends. Locals assembled around railway stations and ports. They heard distant factory whistles, where wages came in cash, and envisioned lands to break themselves. New possibilities punctuated old dreams.

Majorities professed a belief in movement and innovation and lent themselves to a collective belief in progress. Progress trumpeted a self-creating humanity. It postulated the powers of science and design and a social and therapeutic government. The promise of the present supplanted the ways of the past. Surely by the closing decades of the nineteenth century progressive ideologies had come of age and the old rural order, which had defined daily life for the last 10,000 years, was done for.[16]

The space and place of the old order had been overrun, in measure destroyed and annihilated. Education, news and information, which accelerated with each invention, diminished distances, undid old lands and increased contacts. The local rubbed elbows with the global. Travel dramatically increased. Among the upper classes, prevailing ideas and fashionable sentiment spread ever more rapidly across land and sea. Nations took up world missions and national emotions followed. Religions and philanthropies as well as envy and ambition also disposed peoples to look around and outward.

Starting in the nineteenth century and accelerating in the twentieth, national and international migrations increased profoundly, adding to the mutations of places, peoples and minds. Lives, things and ideas were increasingly mixed, composite and synthetic. Myths of authentic 'folk' were invented, often for the worst political reasons and narrowest psychological need of purity. Authorities stamped their people in languages of loyalty and the therapeutic and demographic languages of their ruling agencies and bureaucracies. Contenders, much indebted to past utopian democratic and social doctrine, moulded people into causes seeking new stages of humanity.[17]

The anthropologist Clifford Geertz argues that there has been a profound division in cultural understanding since the 1960s, when anthropology's standing theories were called into question by the acknowledgment of the West's colonial past.[18] Additionally, he contends that with the end of the Cold War in 1989, whole new agendas of study of contemporary life arose on all continents, including Europe. One must now account for places and peoples with reference to such global matters as

> ethnic discord, the formation of transnational identities, the spread of collective violence, and issues raised by migration of refugees, intrusive minorities, incipient nationalism, regional separatism, and yet civic and cultural citizenship and the operation of supra-national quasi-governmental agencies.[19]

Daily life, ever ministering to the human need for repetition and order with habit and local rituals and home and familiar spaces, increasingly met and was contradicted by alien realities. Life of the place and moment lost its continuity in the face of probable, potential and hypothesized change. At work and in play, in nation and world, disequilibrium was announced. Societies were caught in rivalries. There were growing imbalances between human uses and needs and nature's resources. In recent decades continents are said to be threatened by weather change, with its inescapable increasing droughts and rising seas. Worry sets minds and places awhirl.

The world at large is immersed in the changing flux of Heraclitus' river. No bank stands free of erosion and no man enters and exits the river the same. The closer their subject is to the present, the more historians must acknowledge the radical powers of time to transform and destroy. Everyday life implodes in the mind and explodes into space. Continuing from the commercial, industrial, national and democratic revolutions, humans have chosen and been compelled to leave home and make their inner temples spaces for dreams and designs.

With the phenomenon of multiplying and compounding minds, I believe we encounter a crucial distinguishing factor of contemporary everyday life. Everywhere and in most every way we note mind as consciousness, coming into play in daily life today. It emerges as we take up new collective identities, articulate our individuality or reach crossroads, where old thoughts and words, ways, friends and habits do not carry us forward.

Consciousness is called up by change. It is intensified by meeting differences and truly heightened when having to choose the new. It is occasioned by migration and encounters with new places, conditions, necessities, possibilities and choice. It comes with being an intimate individual and choosing work and friends, getting married and having a family, and all the choices of owning a house, acquiring goods and getting old. Consciousness comes when so much of life is lived by conjecture, judgements are so many and even memory is chosen and contested.

I think particularly mind, its emotions, thoughts and judgement, is called into play by contemporary changes of space. The places, buildings, homes and rooms in which we dwell are constantly built and arranged anew, making and remaking relations, emotions and habits. Screens and digital screens call our minds – our sensibility and understanding as well as desires and fantasies – to changing things, people and situations. The news notifies us of how place and globe are changing, calling out for attention. The streets and pavements on which we travel, themselves so frequently altered, feature a rapid and changing environment. Parades of new people with new faces pass. And soundscapes alert us with new sounds from new materials and engines, while music seeks to enwrap its public, lulling some to its wiles and in others stiffening consciousness against its intrusion and its sponsors' interests.

The everyday noticeable accelerates in all ways, calling attention to the world's change and mobility. For the sake of emotional peace and mental coherence, some seek to suppress and sublimate the world's mind-boggling change. Others, to defend the autonomy of mind and inner village, query and challenge the outer world. They ask, 'Is there a world without me and my consciousness?' They would have it be no more than the sum of one's interpretations.

In a more conscious mode, some philosophers would deem the world to be illusion, something that can pass through eye and ear but have no claim to heart. They would empty phantoms from their enlightened souls. Others, more of my stoic father's cut, would essentially reduce the world to their duty and what small pleasures and modest comforts they could find in its corners. Surely, most do not fasten their beliefs – be it in God's creation or Christ's spirit – to the everyday world of what commonly occurs and what they regularly do. That world is too inconsistent, calling doubly for salvation and condemnation, to support certitudes of beliefs and hopes. As much as they take everyday life as a thickening flux, they know they have no forecasting seismograph. They find, to borrow an idea from T. S. Eliot's 'The Hollow Men', 'a falling shadow between ideal and the reality', 'between the conception and the creation' and 'between the essence and the existence'.

The Poet's Field

Emigration does not only involve leaving behind, crossing
water, living amongst strangers, but also undoing the very
meaning of the world and – at its most extreme – abandoning
oneself to the unreal . . . [To] emigrate is always to dismantle
the centre of the world, to move into a lost disoriented one
of fragments.

John Berger, *And Our Faces, My Heart, Brief as Photos*

Everyday life in its first frame is, of course, a matter of analogy
and metaphor. If I say everyday life is a boat I can anchor at bay
or moor at dock, I stress how much it belongs to the repetition of
habits. Synchronized to millions of others across class, nation and
parts of the world (yet of course with near infinite variation), I
drink my morning coffee, read the paper, catch up on my emails,
press the children to get ready and chauffeur them to school before
starting on my long drive through heavy traffic towards work miles
away from my wife's workplace. So begins my son and his wife's
day and that of a considerable portion of young working couples.
At a nearby senior housing facility, a certain number ride down in
the lift to breakfast and the daily coffee klatch before walking their
dogs, preparing for company or their assistants, beginning their
day's chores, shopping, visits to doctors or games of cards or other
recreations. We can predict continuities and habits of large groups in
society as their everyday lives are shaped by age, condition and tasks;
determined by place and environment; yet more broadly moulded by
tradition, religion, social and health services, profit and non-profit

organizations, public institutions, the law and finally the influence of changing technologies, increasing mobility, multiplying forms of entertainment and the range of choices and alternatives. In a word, everyday life as a ship at anchor can be depicted, if not as stationary, then as a repeating cycle that is predictable in a matrix of varied but constant influences.

Conversely, everyday life can be depicted, as I here suggest, as a boat venturing into unknown seas. Body, matter and conditions are cut free by invention and design, the reach of markets and politics and the powers of wish and will. Mind, more ethereal, the sails of our ship, throws up more cloth. Consciousness goes free as traditional ways of village, neighbourhood, craft and class, and the knowledge that comes from living and knowing a place no longer, weigh heavy. Each person takes his individual and private self to be captain and compass of his course.

In the contemporary world we are all migrants – migrants in body, mind and even in class. Our experience is altered daily. Our senses are filled and refilled constantly with new sights, sounds, smells, tastes and touches. Consciousness and unconsciousness see-saw on the fulcrum of the quotidian with repeating occurrences, redundant words and phrases, unprecedented news, unimagined images and things and situations that in mind's quick snap are turned into metaphors.

Time itself is ever more changing. It is plastic. It is inflated by potency and possibility as contemporary science produces new syn-thetic materials, populations grow in numbers and wants, and the processes of market and politics – the tandem and tag-team of perpetual changes – keep the world awash in events, crises and devel-opments. The future dominates minds as it puts consciousness in a world of continuous projections and hypotheses. Possibility and probability, wishes, fears, dreams and prayers press around and both smother and excite minds on every level. Language, images, emotions and concepts expand themselves to ongoing, probable and future changes. In other words, past and present lose hold over conscious-ness. Future possibilities dominate. Variety and individuality of every sort grab the mind's attention. Time, thus, splits the atom of stability

– the mental and physical habits that give everyday life a nucleus of continuity and repetition.

Despite centralization, standardization and cultural fusion and homogenization, individuality multiplies. Its multiplication requires postulating infinity, a sort of innumerability. The individual is magnified by means and potency, wish and illusion. With whole choruses of law, legislation and public rhetoric, each is enjoined to be all he or she can be. Barely circumscribed by the biological rise and decline of bodies and minds, each generation is born afresh to changing conditions and altered selves. The young are differentiated by changing diets, regimes of child raising and social and economic conditions; adolescents by difference of family composition and means, influence of education, faith and career. Adults in turn are differentiated by their pasts, choices, home towns, marriages, friends, migrations and – not to be excluded – good luck. And old age, now a multiplicity of stages itself, reaching from fifty to a hundred, depends on a plenitude of factors that account for the past, health, opportunities, education and other intangibles differentiating each and every individual. In these ways the ordinary becomes extraordinary, the fixed and bounded, the unleashed and the boundless.

At all stages of life we are leaving behind, even casting over, things, groups, ways of body, speech and part of our being. Across life, as the old know well, we have all left behind so much – places, things, family, friends, communities, even lifetime homes and towns and cemeteries. Sentenced to travel because of need, want, whim, opportunity or ambition, we break away and become, to a degree, strangers to our own past because of irrevocable journeys in body and mind to other places and times.

Beyond our movements in space and consciousness, today everyday life, so committed to youth and progress, blossoms with changes. Once local worlds framed and reinforced the repetitions of everyday life and thought that served daily bodily needs and social habits. A sum of habits, fixed attitudes and lasting relations, which produced repeating emotions and thoughts, everyday life retained the capacity to absorb influences of the outside world as they arrived with strangers, officials, soldiers and goods. Everyday life in its largest frame and scope could take in alterations in the material world, the social order and even revolutions of ideas and rebound with a certain coherence and integrity.

But today, as much as common and repeating acts learned over several generations persist (like the card playing and bingo of the old and the morning coffee klatch of village adults), new habits and protocols of the body impose daily regimes (think of care of the teeth, the use of napkins, the taking of pills and doctors' appointments). People make daily, weekly and monthly payments for taxes, insurance and housing. The better off open their emails and read the stock market reports to calculate their place in the larger world. Anxious minds no longer read the physiognomy of faces and bodies or augur the skies to guess their fates and fortunes. Instead, they seek their diagnosis and therapy from trained specialists and experts. Daily life is continually reformed and validated by outside agencies, and one's own instincts and guesses are relegated to the bin of old wives' tales.

The habit-packed nuclei at the centre of daily life no longer holds. Habits of the body, starting with the aristocracy and upper bourgeoisie, have increasingly been brought under multiplying guides to manners. Now in the twentieth and twenty-first centuries, protocols and even laws and ordinances govern most behaviours around which people weave their ways and days. Police, public health and schools supervise our expression. Rules of one sort or another regulate our spitting, chewing, smoking, shouting and making noise. At every stage, starting with pre-school, people are enrolled, tested, graded, labelled and sorted out.

Since the threshold of the Victorian Age, language, gesture and even opinions and attitudes have been steadily brought under the canons of standard, correct, polite and moral. Mind itself in its reasoning, emotions, judgements and prognostications shifted in the twentieth century away from group and locality; villages, country and neighbourhood enclaves lost their authority and tradition. And families, ever diverse, almost uniformly lost their command.

At accelerating rates, everyday life gives way to intrusive worlds from without; and yet alien persons, institutions, thoughts and manners arise from within. Places no longer anchor or encapsulate lives. They do not hold a common order of experience. Everyday life, as the historian must probe and aesthetically represent, is truly metamorphosed. Heterogeneity and instantaneity of invention, design and governing institutions define what is and what is next. More simply, villages borrow from towns, towns from cities, cities from metropolises and yet nations from one another as they enter into commercial relations and contact with one another. For instance, after the Second World War America set the material dreams of modernity. America was about being fresh and on the move – and above all things the post-war French appreciated Americans for the comfort and convenience of their appliances.[1]

Hand and foot, which are constantly at work planting people in a place, no longer follow so consistently those short, repetitive and circling paths that once defined work, entertainment and life itself. Hand and foot, ever more often off the trail, no longer deliver people to recurrent experiences of senses and movements, things and society. People in work and play go farther afield in their encounters and travels. They physically move about in cars and planes, while mind feeds on phones and grazes for work and pleasure on screens. Alien images, streams of asymmetrical information, political slogans and the shrapnel of old ideologies invade the mind, and imagination seeks sense beyond the confines of our recurring lives.

None of this denies the tenacious power of attitudes, habits and even fixed words to secure us in mind and body in familiar ways. Habit, be it morning coffee, watching a favourite programme or simply being regular and punctual, can dull agitated awareness – can even silence the sirens of choice and the nagging call of conflicting responsibilities. Indifference, learned and calculated, becomes a way to stay constant to one's own days.

OF MIND AND METAPHOR

In its great variety and changes, contemporary daily life overflows the historian's experience and theory. Historians of everyday life entirely quit being companions with local, regional and ethnic historians;

they cannot ignore the insights of cultural and religious history, and they must learn from the case studies of sociology and anthropology. Doing all this, everyday historians do not escape the abiding paradox of seeking to research and represent the singular and unique, on the one hand, while relying on the framing powers of generalization and overarching narrative.[2]

Sources for the study of everyday life have been augmented dramatically. They came from the advent of the printing press – and the appearance of handbills and posters and the democratic thrust of daily chronicles, newspapers and books in the service of increased literacy. Public records amassed by governments and their agencies have resulted in gargantuan increases of information and data for the local historian. These documents include censuses of citizens, their locations and wealth, indices of settlements, business and manufacture, and records of projects born of government legislation and jurisdiction. All this is not to mention the swelling reams of online data about an expanding past and broadening present.

Available documents marked a true watershed in historical methodology in the early nineteenth century. The issue no longer turns on scarcity of evidence but, conversely, pivots on handling an overwhelming abundance of information about the world at large. As work on early periods hinged on conjecture and extrapolation from limited material artefacts and written manuscripts, so the study of the last two centuries overwhelms the historians with a plethora of materials. The selection and sampling relied on by quantitative historians prove with generalizations, trends and even probabilities alien to studies based on specific places and periods, biographies and anecdotes, and qualitative, exceptional and exotic sources.

Adding to the surplus of materials and potential evidence for modern and contemporary historians of daily life, there has been a rising tide of images, reaching tsunami proportions with public and private collections of photographs and films. Since the last half of the nineteenth century students of everyday life had to learn to read texts, letters and images from all theatres.[3] Photography born out of nineteenth-century science captures society spontaneously and casually, and not just portraits and ceremonial occasions. Images become the mirrors in which historians look to see the past and themselves.

Depiction and decoration forever framed perceptions and set interpretations. Renaissance and early modern painting, as exemplified by Brueghel and other Netherlandish and Dutch landscape painters, chose mundane subjects – studies of tables, bowls of fruit and everyday village and country life on the way to the field or at feast. In the form of realism and Impressionism, mid-nineteenth-century artists turned to the landscape, the colourful dress and flower-filled garden, the street scene, the beach, the café and dance hall. Taking their cue from this aesthetic, the camera and movies turned their lenses on the poised and self-parading middle class and the labouring poor caught in common activities and recreations.

Cameras recorded and celebrated democratic and industrial life. They shot all facets of the young nation America's Civil War, its valiant efforts and pathos. After the war, they depicted the face of defeat in the South and the grand openings of new ports, bridges, tunnels and train stations in the North and West. They offered iconic scenes, transformed landscapes and worn lives. They showed ordinary men and women caught in the extraordinary tangle of their times – wars, natural catastrophes and failed policies. By the 1920s and '30s photographs constituted a daily testimony to tragic and ebullient, common and mundane life. With an exceptional eye for detail, with words and images, the writer James Agee and photographer Walker Evans created a poignant portrait of the children, rooms and homes of impoverished Southern sharecroppers during the Dust Bowl in their famous *Let Us Now Praise Famous Men* (1936).

A picture was worth a thousand words – and a movie reel the equivalent of a book, story and national epic. Depicting movement and eventually colour, the motion picture showed how vibrant everyday life was. In the hands of the photographer, movie industry and the world of advertisement (which sells nearly all images), everyday life went graphic and celluloid – the world became infinitely divisible and representable. All the shots the kaleidoscopic camera could take became the essence of things. Society became an infinite set of snaps and scenes. The camera became the mirror in which the contemporary world saw and represented itself. Already by the beginning of the twentieth century lenses and screens carried souls not just to remote and distance places but into the small, hidden and invisible quarters of everyday life. Photography constituted a new aesthetic and epistemological activity. Everyday life became as poignant and tedious as a shot could be.

With X-rays and other beams science created new levels of imagery that stationed us, as unimaginable as this is, inside our own bodies, looking around. Atomic tomography the condition of our temporal and mortal selves. Truth itself – our mortality is now exposed by the click of the machine in distinct or shadowy images.

From this perspective everyday life itself flew up from surfaces as seen and vanished into the inner meaning of images on screens. Place and person lost their solidity and position in space. Of infinite poses, the exterior self became ever divisible by the snap of lenses – whose shudders and results are never to be seen. Without a secure hold in materiality and corporeality, the everyday person became interchangeable with the sum of images, social interactions and rituals – and at the same time a private, intimate self beyond and off all cameras.

THE VANISHING SELF

The conscious self increasingly distinguished itself from everyday life and sociality, as it valued itself for its individuality, privacy, intimacy and subjective transcendence. It came to believe that through friendship and love, surely composed by emotions of choice, it could join another person in the depths of the heart, superseding ties assigned by family and tradition or given by chance and necessity. In this way the self – perhaps we describe its beginning as the emotional Romantic self – bonded with select others, be they the beloved individual or an idealized collectivity of ethnicity, people, class or nation, and at the same time the self stood beyond on its own high, proud and windy hill. This self took itself to be of light in surrounding night.

The more self became the self-designated nucleus of being, the more everyday life melted into the background of consciousness – its emotions and ambiguities, and its sense of will and freedom. The spirit belonged to the self's fears, impulses and subtle conjectures. At the same time, the self identified with what aroused and captivated it. It was its project first to find order and meaning. An extension of the subjective self, the poet uses words and ideas to secure our place in discordant being, and so, wrote the poet James Orr, has his worth.[4] The poet furnishes the inner order that everyday life only outwardly supplies.

Self truly is emergent when it conjures itself, worlds, things possible, and dreams the beyond. The mobility and elusiveness of self, in combination with the vulnerability of life and community, explains why civilization's prophets and philosophers found in God their duty, obligation, explanation – the north star of a world in flux.

The self is transient. Moved by emotions, driven by passions, and thinking by ferrying analogies and bridging metaphors, the mind migrates across the domains of body, place, group, ideas and myths. Increasingly fuelled by a society of greater abundance, leisure, literacy and dramatic change, the contemporary self flies freer, higher and longer from the gravity of everyday place, life and habit. Analogous to Heisenberg's uncertainty principle, which affirms that we cannot simultaneously know the speed and location of a particle at the same time, the mutating mind cannot grasp movement and location at a fixing glimpse.

Psychology, at its boldest, suggests humans are in part or whole madly out of their minds. At least such a proposition drives Freud's depth psychology. Every person, for Freud, is on some level locked in an unresolved war with self. Self is part rational and irrational, enforcer and violator of the law. Endowed biologically with an id that searches for undifferentiated bodily gratification as sought by mouth, hands, anus and sexual organs, the same person, by Freud's construct, is profoundly censored from infancy onward by a superego enforcing society's discipline and order. Corrections first come exteriorly in admonishment, shame and punishment and then are internalized as the proper and repressive norms of social life. For Freud, out of this ongoing struggle between basic drives and internal regulation emerges the adult ego, whose success is measured by the capacity to work and be active sexually.

On these grounds, psychoanalysis locates a struggle at the foundation of self and everyday social life. From this perspective, family, tribe, culture, art and civilization, all that constitutes and frames everyday life, reside in repression and release from it. In accord with the thought of Jean-Martin Charcot, a French neurologist and professor of anatomical pathology, Freud found in his early patients that symptoms of neuroses were based on earlier suppressed traumas. As these were unveiled and resolved for patients by guided free association on his diagnosing couch, Freud found the unconscious expressed by a large number of seemingly trivial, bizarre or nonsensical errors and slips (*parapraxes*) as outlined in his 1901 *The Psychopathology of Everyday Life*. He saw these great inner repressed wars in the tragic conflicts of Old Testament and classical myths that told of violations of the taboo of incest and rivalries between sons and fathers to have mother and dominate kingdom.

However, proof of the existence of the irrational in everyday life does not require the depth analysis of psychoanalysis. Insanity peeks out of human existence at all times and points. Peoples unleash their envy, hostility and desires in their festivals and wars expose human brutality and cruelty. Some cultures incorporated types of madness into types of work, entertainment and military service. The insane also become the seers, tellers, 'the wise fool' in the tradition of Russian culture. Yet more often the extreme insane were judged to constitute a social problem. Along with beggars, blind people, physically disabled people and others, they were expelled and chased away. In Holland they were put on rudderless barges and cast on the sea. These 'ships of fools' were set on retreating tides to meet their fortunes on the sea. In late modern times, with increased public control, the most severe cases of insanity, especially cases of the helpless and dangerous, were institutionalized in prisons and finally treated in asylums.[5]

Of course, the insane, the bizarre and irrational, as well as the cruel and simply evil, filled crime blotters and made the daily paper's most compelling stories. Adding an unconsidered dimension to the possibilities of everyday life, the hideous and outrageous intrigued, fascinated and terrified readers. Foul deeds sold papers and set communities asking about the inner heart of mankind. Dostoevsky, whom Freud so admired for his penetration of the inner depths of the person, culled the paper for the irrational. Therein he found characters off the streets and out of everyday life engaged in extraordinary deeds, fascinating obsessions and the unadulterated logic of the mad. From his first works, like the novella *Notes from Underground* published in 1864, to his most complete novel, *The Brothers Karamazov* (1880), Dostoevsky penetrated hearts – as driven and spirited by pride and resentment, grudge and spite, kindness and love. Out of matters buried deep in the mind human actions come to form. In *Crime and Punishment*, published as twelve instalments in 1866, we meet a failed and ashamed father who drinks his family poor; his daughter, who prostitutes herself to save the family and ultimately by her faithful love redeems the protagonist Raskolnikov, a poor ex-student, underfed and delirious, who uses the most abstract philosophy of the rights of 'the person beyond the law' to axe a rich landlady to death and struggles profoundly to accept his guilt, which would return him to humble humanity.

To a marvellous degree, Dostoevsky illustrates the power of literature, especially starting with the novel in the middle of the eighteenth century and enhanced in flesh and spirit by Romanticism, to penetrate the inner side of private and anonymous lives. Whether Romantic or realist, aristocratic or democratic, nineteenth-century literature offered an anatomy of commonplace and truly bizarre. Literature often crossed paths with newspapers as it too (often syndicated by papers) sought to win the attention of new reading publics. In turn, literature in the late nineteenth and early twentieth centuries saw everyday life as having its foundation in enduring and perennial myths, while others conceived the everyday as anything but ordinary, treating it as an arena in which souls carried on great religious and existential struggles.

In his seven-volume *In Search of Lost Time*, which was started in 1909 and unfinished at the time of his death in 1922, Marcel Proust wove present sensations evoking memories of a life. The Irish Modernist James Joyce turned his experimental novel *Ulysses*, serialized over four years from 1918 to 1922, into an attempt to render everyday life by what it evokes in myth and the unconscious. *Ulysses* chronicled the encounters of a single character, Leopold Bloom, in Dublin in the course of one day in June 1904. Joyce transforms Bloom's quotidian way into an inner heroic journey akin to the mythic struggles of Ulysses on his ten-year journey home from the Trojan War.

In Franz Kafka's short story 'Metamorphosis' (1915), his principal character Gregor Samsa, a single working man supporting his mother, father and sister in a small apartment, awakes one morning unable to go to work. Overnight he has become a bug. Enduring all the opprobrium, pity and horror that the sight of him inspires, he lives out his quotidian life under the furniture, which he has known since childhood, between bare walls and by food slipped under his door until, lured into the front room by his sister's sweet violin music. He is mortally wounded by an apple thrown at him by his father. Everyday life, mutated in bed, could have undergone no greater metamorphosis. Gregor awoke to be his most extraordinary and hideous dream.

In a far more gentle way author James Thurber suggests that everyday life for the common man is a succession of dreams and fantasies. The protagonist of Thurber's short story 'The Secret Life of Walter Mitty' (1939) pushes his shopping trolley, imagining himself on bombing missions and being an emergency-room surgeon and a devil-may-care killer. In multiple genres, literature beginning in the nineteenth century probes the depths of ordinary consciousness in common circumstances and in raw and testing situations. Much of the literature has its axis and churn in the irrational and subjective mind – and teaches the everyday historian what lurks below the slippery surface of the ordinary.

THE POET'S AND THE HISTORIAN'S WORLD

Poets too explore and give voice to everyday life. With the spark of sudden unities and irreducible juxtapositions of things and appearances, they electrify the humble corners of the mundane. Walt Whitman, Carl Sandburg and Robert Frost, to choose but three American poets, spin great and universal tales out of common men and women.

The poet can start anywhere. He can draw the unusual connection and make a bold leap. Familiar laws and held truths do
not corral him. Following the advice of Ezra Pound – which more
than one writer did – the poet seeks the luminous detail. He dreads
abstract concatenations, or, to heed William Blake, 'Labour well the
Minute Particulars: attend to the little ones.'[6] The poet, to speak in
paradox, finds entireties in the pieces of the whole, waving insights
out of a stitch of words, sounds, connections and meanings. Yet the
poet is empty of all but self and what he fears and imagines himself
to be, and his mending words.

The poet takes apart to put together. With words he follows
the vines of sensation and emotion, the grip of habit and rituals, the
bonds of loyalty between the living and dead, the long reaching arms
of love, and the mixed mortars of gratitude, resentment and hate.
The Welsh poet Glyn Jones, who remembers the primordial ties of
mother, hearth and self in 'Goodbye, What Were You?', also tells of
her painful, brutal death in 'Easter':

> ... the star
>
> Of annunciation ...
> In death's stink now, with tears I watch her, old
> And hideous in dying – bitterly[7]

The poet weaves the details of inner and outer person, places
and things quotidian into a universal narrative of humanity. The poet
takes apart and puts together the subtle and glaring meanings of our
regular and ordinary – our peculiar, strange, bizarre and ineffable –
lives. The historian who seeks aesthetics in his accounting of modern
and contemporary lives can learn from the poet in listening to spirit
embodied in place and changing situations. A favourite poet of mine,
Giuseppe Ungaretti, teaches us to commemorate the forgotten individual. In 'In Memoria', Ungaretti remembers Mohammed Sceab, an
Arab living in Paris who committed suicide; 'And only I perhaps /
still know / he lived'.[8]

My poet friend Dana Yost wrote, in reply to my question of
how does the poet belong to the everyday, or even how does the

everyday belong to the poet: Poets are the workers of a place. They
make and repair things; they anchor and solidify a heart with words.
They provide a floor for our tenuous dance.[9]

In a poem called 'Sway' Yost talks about his daily routine and
common things that attach him to a place and tamp down the anxiety and insecurity that go with thinking about the world at large,
which he did as long-time editor of a local newspaper.[10] In 'Hands' he
reaches out to shake hands with the ordinary labourer:

> Hands and fingers: rough, scabbed,
> calloused, bent, thick,
> hands and fingers that do the rugged work
> of turning politicians' sweetly-spun
> words into the things . . .
> in a trench in the cold-water gush
> of a broken pipe, waist deep, rising.[11]

Yost writes too of humble daily ritual like that of his deceased diabetic
father in 'The Routine is What We Remember':

> Puncture marks
> the oddity
> of a diabetic's life.
> In my father's time,
> self-wounding
> for self-care
> in the minutes
> before bedtime
> seated at our kitchen table,
> white v-necked t-shirt lifted
> above his navel
> and a new syringe's
> orange plastic cap
> popped, needle
> dipped into squat
> clear bottle of insulin,

then the jab,
a speck of blood
and the ritual
completed.[12]

In 'Prairie Storm' Yost looks at the aftermath of a local tornado. In the second stanza, he recalled:

The bruised half-hour after a prairie storm . . .
The news comes for the dead, the shredded, the sobbing,
the images that can't be explained by science or God:
half a house in splinters, but the baby's bedroom left perfect
    and pink;
necktie rack blown forty miles, ten ties still attached, clean;
farmyard mud driven through the pores of the century-old
    farmhouse's walls, . . .
the wife on the front steps, wordless
and her palms as muddy as if she'd been swimming in earth,
    silently.[13]

However large their frame in space and time and their attempt to balance the common and ordinary with the singular and unique, historians must follow poets in their approach to the everyday world. They must knock their knuckles on its materiality and solidity while recognizing the pertinence of the quantitative, the irreducibility of the singular and the elusiveness of the ephemeral. They must remember minds are alert to the small things and swept up in the most grandiose ideas. As much as historians pride themselves on being aware of power and great forces, they should concur with poets that men and women, however high their station, live in the flats and folds of everyday life. In the end the historian must recognize that he is like everyone else: none of us knows where and how we fit into space, time, history and heaven. In these changing times, however, we do know that the courses of the most ordinary lives verge at every moment on becoming extraordinary.

References

Introduction: Writing Daily and Everyday Life

1 René Nelli, *La Vie quotidienne des Cathares du Languedoc au XIIIe siècle*, 3rd edn (Paris, 1969).
2 Paul Gruchow, *Grass Roots* (Minneapolis, MN, 1995), p. 6.
3 John Berger, *And Our Faces, My Heart, Brief as Photos* (New York, 1984), pp. 55–6.
4 Gruchow, *Grass Roots*, p. 7.
5 For an introduction to Guy Thuillier and his work, see Joseph A. Amato, review essay, 'Guy Thuillier: "Paris Will Save Nothing"', *Journal of Social History*, XXVII/2 (Winter 1993), pp. 375–80.

1 Bodies and Things

1 For an extended discussion of things, being, language and metaphor, see Joseph A. Amato, *The Book of Twos: The Power of Contrasts, Polarities, and Contradictions* (Granite Falls, MN, 2015), pp. 7–101.
2 One work of use for constructing material life and culture is Jean-Pierre Warnier, *Construire la culture matérielle: l'homme qui pensait avec ses doigts* (Paris, 1999).
3 Marcel Mauss, 'Les Techniques du Corps', *Journal de Psychologie*, XXXII/3–4 (March–April 1936), pp. 1–23.
4 For one view of exchange as essentially a matter of reciprocity required by gift, see Marcel Mauss, *The Gift*, trans. Ian Cunnison and E. E. Evans-Pritchard (London, 1990). For a broader notion of gift, including sacrifice and the gratitude and debt the gift incurs, see Joseph A. Amato, *Guilt and Gratitude: A Study of the Origins of Contemporary Conscience* (Westport, CT, 1982) and *Victims and Values: A History and Theory of Suffering* (New York, 1990).
5 Gabriel Marcel, *Being and Having* (New York, 1965), pp. 162–3.
6 In his seminal *Phenomenology of Perception* (1945), Maurice Merleau-Ponty devoted one of the three parts of his work to body, utilizing such rubrics as its spatiality and motility and expression

and speech. Among many others, Bill Brown utilizes theory from contemporary phenomenology in his helpful survey, 'Thing Theory', *Critical Inquiry*, xxviii/1, *Things* (Autumn 2001), pp. 1–22.

7 Francis Ponge, *The Voice of Things* [1942], trans. Beth Archer (New York, 1972).

8 For the relation between body and things from an anthropological view, especially as formed around the field of material culture (defined below in text and notes), see Judy Attfield, *Wild Things: The Material Culture of Everyday Life* (Oxford, 2000), and Daniel Miller, *Stuff* (Malden, MA, 2010).

9 For introductory works that suggest that self, composed of body and mind, is involved in a conversation with things, see Sherry Turkle, ed., *Evocative Things: Things We Think With* (Cambridge, MA, 2007), and Lorraine Daston, ed., *Things That Talk: Object Lessons from Art and Science* (New York, 2004); for a complex aesthetic of emotions and physical objects, see Peter Schwenger, *The Tears of Things* (Minneapolis, MN, 2006); for Philip Ball on the origins of science, see Philip Ball, *Curiosity: How Science Became Interested in Everything* (Chicago, IL, 2012).

10 Citation taken from Brown, 'Thing Theory', p. 3. Brown cites the original as Leo Stein, *The A-B-C of Aesthetics* (New York, 1927), p. 44.

11 Tim Ingold, *Being Alive: Essays on Movement, Knowledge and Description* (London, 2011), p. 239.

12 Tim Ingold, *The Perception of the Environment: Essays on Livelihood, Dwelling and Skill* (London, 2000).

13 For the pervasive use of lines in perceiving and conceiving life, see Tim Ingold, *Lines: A Brief History* (New York, 2007).

14 For the temporality of the landscape, see Ingold, *Perception of the Environment*.

15 For defining how bodies fit into things and make everyday life, see Daniel Miller's survey of the comfort of home in the case of thirty London homes, *The Comfort of Things* (Malden, MA, 2008).

16 A conversation between Brian Dillon and Steven Connor on 'A Philosophy of Everyday Things', 5 December 2011, can be found at www.podacademy.org. Two influential philosophers of body, things and consciousness are Martin Heidegger and Jean-Paul Sartre, especially the latter's *Being and Nothingness*, trans. Hazel E. Barnes (New York, 1956). How we speak to, articulate and dedicate ourselves

by subordinating our bodies is argued in David Bakan, *Disease, Pain, and Sacrifice: Toward a Psychology of Suffering* (Boston, MA, 1968), and Joseph A. Amato, *Victims and Values: A History and Philosophy of Suffering* (Westport, CT, 1990), esp. pp. 1–22. A philosophical study of how torturers seek to unravel the core of self and its secrets and principles through a discourse of pain with a person's body is found in Elaine Scary, *The Body in Question: The Making and Unmaking of the World* (New York, 1986).

17 Neil MacGregor, *A History of the World in 100 Objects* (New York, 1996).

18 Dillon and Connor podcast conversation on 'a philosophy of everyday things'.

19 A single work suggesting useful themes and approaches for historians regarding material culture is Andrew Shryock and Daniel Lord Small, *Deep History: The Architecture of Past and Present* (Berkeley, CA, 2011), which I reviewed in the *Journal of Social History*, XLVII/4 (Summer 2014), pp. 1101–3.

20 In 'Material Cultural Studies' Geismar Hardy offers a useful survey of converging theoretical interests that underpinned material culture and led to the creation of the *Journal of Material Culture* under the editorship of Daniel Miller and Christopher Tilley (*Comparative Studies in Society*, L/1, 2011, pp. 210–18). Early issues of *Journal of Material Culture*, starting July 1966, illustrate an impressive range of human interactions with things, objects and landscapes. A useful collection of essays on material culture comes from one of the two editors of the journal: Daniel Miller, ed., *Materiality* (Durham, NC, 2005), who also wrote *Material Cultures: Why Some Things Matter* (Chicago, IL, 1998). The second editor, the equally prolific Christopher Tilley, offers a guide to the philosophical sources of material culture, 'Interpreting Material Culture', in *Interpreting Objects and Collections*, ed. Susan Pierce (London, 1994), pp. 67–75. A longer history of material history in French and English thought is found in Victor Buchli's introduction to *The Material Culture Reader* (Oxford, 2002), pp. 1–22. Another useful guide to material culture is Dan Hicks, 'The Material-Cultural Turn: Event and Effect', *The Oxford Handbook of Material Culture Studies* (New York, 2010), pp. 25–98. For applied interest by American historians of everyday life, see Thomas J. Schlereth, ed., *Material Culture* (Lawrence, KA, 1985).

21 'Editorial', *Journal of Material Culture*, 1/1 (July 1966), p. 6.

22 For how things make minds and provide the metaphors and
    metonymy out of which humans make worlds, see Christopher
    Tilley, *Metaphor and Material Culture* (Oxford, 1999).

23 Of particular value for an archaeology of the relationship between
    humans and things, see Ian Hodder, *Entangled* (Oxford, 2011.) Of
    theoretical interest is Bjørnar Olsen, *In Defense of Things: Archaeology
    and the Ontology of Objects* (New York, 2010). Also of use is Joseph
    A. Amato, *Surfaces: A History* (Berkeley, CA, 2013).

24 For a recent collection of essays considering things as having
    meanings in themselves, see Amiria Henare, Martin Holbraad
    and Sari Wastell, eds, *Thinking through Things: Theorising Artefacts
    Ethnographically* (London, 2007).

25 For a single work on the organization of spaces, see Georges Perec,
    Species of Spaces and Other Pieces (New York, 1997), esp. pp. 1–96.

26 The book *Famous First Facts* (whose first edition dates from 1933),
    which records *First Happenings, Discoveries and Inventions in the
    United States*, offers the American historian a way to reconstruct
    material history over the past 150 or so years. The current version
    of the book (sixth edition, 2006), holding more than 7,500 entries,
    records an endless parade of patents, inventions and gadgets that
    have taken hold of our bodies, emotions, comforts, fancies – and
    thus literally made the things we embrace and the world which
    we have made and which makes us.

27 For a baptism into place and everyday life as a matter of things taken
    within the habits of body and assumptions of the mind, simply read
    – with an eye to things, tools, materials and mass production – a
    book on popular, social, cultural or everyday history. Off my shelves
    I pull Ivan Amato, *Stuff: The Materials the World is Made Of* (New
    York, 1997); Susan Freinkel, *Plastic: A Toxic Love Story* (Boston, MA,
    2011); Arjun Appadurai, ed., *The Social Life of Things: Commodities in
    Cultural Perspective* (Cambridge, 1986); Johnny Acton, Tania Adams
    and Matt Packer, *Origins of Everyday Things* (New York, 2006); and
    Michela Nocci, *Oggetti d'Uso Quotidiano: Rivoluzioni technologiche
    nella vita d'oggi* (Venice, 1998). Offering select parts of a history of
    things and their incorporation into everyday life in modern and
    contemporary times are Henry Petroski, *The Evolution of Useful
    Things* (New York, 1992) and *The Pencil: A History of Design and
    Circumstance* (New York, 1989), and also Witold Rybczynski, *One

Good Turn: A Natural History of the Screw and Screwdriver (New York, 2000); also see Tara Hamling and Catherine Richardson, eds, *Everyday Objects: Medieval and Early Modern Material Culture* (Farnham, 2010); Daniel Roche, *A History of Everyday Things* (Cambridge, 2000); and Marjorie Quennell and C.H.B. Quennell, *A History of Everyday Things in England: The Age of Production, 1851–1934* (New York, 1935). For design's ever-comprehensive hold on the making of everyday life, again see Henry Petroski – his *Small Things Considered: Why There Is No Perfect Design* (New York, 2003). Also see Catherine McDermott, *Twentieth-century Design: Design Museum* (Woodstock, NY, 1997); Jonathan M. Woodham, *Twentieth-century Design* (Oxford, 1997); Mel Byars, *100 Designs/100 Years* (Crans-près-Céligny, Switzerland, 1999); and George H. Marcus, *Masters of Modern Design* (New York, 2005). For literature's exploration and elaboration of everyday things see Liesl Olson, *Modernism and the Ordinary* (Oxford, 2011).

28 Sidney Mintz, *Sweetness and Power: The Place of Sugar in Modern History* (New York, 1985).

29 Only in the last decades of the nineteenth century and beginning of the twentieth century did city life start to come clean and mud, faeces, muck, dirt and what for me was the subject of a book, dust, lose their hold on everyday life, first in the city and only decades later in the rural countryside. Running water chased away the soot of coal-burning furnaces and steam engines and much else that went down the sewer and swirling bowl of the flush toilet. Roads, though still congested with pedestrians, carts and horses (which at the turn of the century numbered almost a million in London), were increasingly paved, widened and freed of potholes and mucky ponds. The flow of traffic was increasingly ordered and regulated; and the most luxurious avenues and boulevards were widened, made safe and lit for strollers, window shoppers and café sitters. The street, not just a thoroughfare to conduct people to market and work, became a safe and open stage of play and song – grounds for stepping out without stepping on.

30 Much of this 'By Our Skin' section is taken from Joseph A. Amato, *Surfaces: A History* (Berkeley, CA, 2013), pp. 1–16.

31 Here I am indebted to Clive Gamble's *Origins and Revolutions: Human Identity in Earliest Prehistory* (Cambridge, 2007). See esp. Chapter Four, 'Bodies, Instruments and Containers', pp. 87–110.

32 For an innovative analysis, which joined depth psychology and the study of language and metaphor and myth in cultural analysis and, in the spirit of the 1960s, sought sexual liberation from all oppression, see Norman Brown, *Love's Body* (New York, 1966).

33 This is a first premise of Amato, *Surfaces: A History*, esp. pp. 1–46.

34 A useful survey of skin is Nina G. Jablonski, *Skin: A Natural History* (Berkeley, CA, 2006).

35 'Skin', in *Oxford Companion to the Body* (Oxford, 2001), pp. 623–4.

36 The above quotations are found in Bergen Evans, ed., *Dictionary of Quotations* (New York, 1968), p. 68.

37 Stephen Jay Gould, 'Evolution by Walking', in *Dinosaur in a Hay Stack* (New York, 1995), p. 249.

38 To start with the most elemental families of life, bacteria are phototropic, using light to turn inanimate material into food. Some bacteria, additionally, are motile, moving with cilia and flagella. Bacteria that exhibit motility, that is, self-propelled motion, achieve it by one of three mechanisms: flagella, rotating axial filaments and the secret – yet to be understood – secretion of copious slime.

39 Life goes with light. Even bacteria react to it. The eye itself, which may have evolved out of chemoreceptors and photosensitive cells, appears only with the Cambrian, but it has evolved fifty to a hundred times since. The eye adapts and changes itself to meet the organism that bears it – hence the near perfect and complex human eye comes out of a simply coated optic nerve. The most primitive eyes, eyespots, which are photoreceptor proteins, can decipher light but not shape or direction. With the Cambrian explosion we encounter eyes that recognize the direction of light and begin image processing. From 'Evolution of the Eye', Wikipedia, accessed 16 June 2016.

40 Eyes are ever in action. They create images through details captured at the rate of thirty eye movements, or saccades, per minute, and stitch them together as if they were one. Visual perception focuses light on to the retina, whose outer cones permit night vision, while central clustered rods decipher high acuity and colour vision.

41 Colin Blakemore, 'Vision', in *Oxford Companion to the Body*, pp. 716–20. 'Sight', explains Stephen Apkon, 'is by far the most trusted of our senses. It is the one that has the greatest impact on reality.' Our eyes are the great gateway of our being. They bring enormous volumes of information (about surfaces, things and movements, including those of our own bodies). It is no accident,

Apkon continues, that up to 85 per cent of the brain is dedicated to processing and making sense of the visual stimulation that flows in. Stephen Apkon, *The Age of the Image: Redefining Literacy in a World of Screens* (New York, 2013), p. 75.

42 Paul Shepard, *Man in the Landscape: A Historic View of the Esthetics of Nature* (New York, 1967); also of use for a discussion of how we see and look, John Berger, *About Looking* (New York, 1980) and *Ways of Seeing* (New York, 1972).

43 Shepard, *Man in the Landscape*, p. 7. Shepard's notion that sight accounts for our 'widespread philosophical tendency to see the world dichotomously as infinite antinomies' is generalized and at play throughout Amato, *Book of Twos*.

44 Twos come with human bodies. Arms and hands, hands and fingers, feet and legs, eyes, ears and nostrils make us bisymmetrical creatures. Other parts of the body can be taken as juxtapositions, such as head and stomach, head and feet and mouth and anus. So bodies stamp our brains in twos, shaping perceptions, forming conceptions and structuring imagination. Bodies furnish the words and metaphors by which we join and distinguish what comes to mind. For two different approaches to the body as the metaphorical source of our creation, see Chapter Eleven of A. Richard Turner, 'The Body as Nature and Culture', in *Inventing Leonardo* (New York, 1993), pp. 191–209, and the entirety of Brown's *Love's Body*.

45 Hands can be understood to be the midwives of a pluralistic and multivalent reality. From their work comes comprehension born of action and yet derived thoughts and metaphors. More precisely, they deliver us to the world of twos: on this count, philosophy, religion and science might be understood as crafts rather than abstract theories. On this point, the whole of pragmatism and Heidegger find common ground, Martin Heidegger, 'Letter on Humanism' [1946], in *Martin Heidegger: Basic Writings*, revd edn, ed. David Farrell Krell (New York, 1993), pp. 217–65.

46 Hands do so much in telling us where we are in the world and taking 'in hand' our place in it. Fingers and nails establish heat, hardness, dimensions and texture. They also register vibration, pressure, temperature and granularity. With the grip of an opposable thumb and fingers, hands take hold of things, determining size, shape and weight, and find their point of balance. Hands match, test, break apart and join surfaces to surfaces, things to things. For a brief

discussion of 'handiness' (*Zuhandenheit*) and readiness to hand
in Heidegger, see Daniel O. Dahlstrom, *The Heidegger Dictionary*
(London, 2013), pp. 88–9.

47 Diane Ackerman, *A Natural History of the Senses* (New York, 1991),
esp. pp. 65–124.

48 Frank Wilson, *The Hand* (New York, 1998), esp. pp. 8, 15–16, 36–7.

49 Canadian psychologist and neurologist Merlin Donald postulated
a pluralistic human consciousness for *Homo sapiens*. In two earlier
stages spanning millions of years, human brains, he contends,
were first enlarged, not by tool making, but by social interaction:
mimetic skill allowing the duplication of voluntary action; and then,
in a second stage, with spoken language, which composed 'mythic
cultures' that still exist today. Finally, humans made a great leap to
becoming 'a symbol-using creature' that deals simultaneously with the
creation of 'mosaics of meanings'. Merlin Donald, *The Origins of the
Modern Mind: Three Stages in the Evolution of Culture and Cognition*
(Cambridge, MA, 1991). Following the lead of Donald, Professor
Henry Plotkin seeks to join knowledge to biology. He conceives
adaptation as a process of constant iteration, an act of repetition
that approximates the goal (teleology), assuring an ever more
successful fit with the world and into the structure of learning and
the organization of life. In this way the organization of an organism
– its limb structure, camouflage or means of movement – is made by
the environment. Henry Plotkin, *Darwin Machines and the Nature
of Knowledge* (Cambridge, MA, 1994), pp. 51, xv. Philosopher Barry
Allen notes that, for Plotkin, knowledge operates in the gene pool
and is expressed as adaptations that constitute what he calls 'Darwin
machines'. Barry Allen, 'Knowledge and Adaptation', *Biology and
Philosophy*, XII/2 (1997), pp. 233–41.

50 For an up-to-date summary of interpretations of bipedalism, see Ian
Tattersall, *Masters of the Planet: The Search for Our Human Origins*
(New York, 2012), pp. 6–44. Occurring an estimated six to seven
million years ago in the earliest hominids in Africa, bipedalism freed
hands from the ground for locomotion. Shaping the brain itself,
powerfully gripping hands and arms and the precise, manipulating
fingers picked up and examined things and made a variety of tools in
order to alter the environment. At the same time, the upright posture
of bipedal hominids, compared with quadruped animals, freed the
brain from the dominance of the olfactory sense, allowing the head

and the eyes to rotate freely and constantly focus between immediate things and distant horizons. For an introductory and conjectural discussion of bipedalism, see Joseph Amato, *On Foot: A History of Walking* (New York, 2004), pp. 21–3, notes 4 and 5.

51 The crucial evolutionary step involving the arrangement of muscles, bones and joints that allowed the movement is known as *opposition* – the ability to bring the thumb in contact with fingers. Sarah Goodfellow and Sheila Jennett, 'Hands', *The Oxford Companion to the Body*, p. 334.

52 A half century ago, in September 1960, in his article 'Tools and Evolution', physical anthropologist Sherwood L. Washburn contended that the use of tools antedated man, and that their use by pre-human primates gave rise to *Homo sapiens*. *Scientific American* (September 1960), p. 62. We still do not have a clear history of 'handy man'. In fact, 'he' has been a subject of controversy since Louis Leakey introduced a fossil in 1959 of the hominid *Australopithecus* in the company of coarse tools in the Olduvai Gorge in Tanzania, east Africa. He was christened *Homo habilis*, 'handy man', when linked three years later in 1962 to two distant cousins. As if to electrocute those he had already shocked, Leakey and his wife, Mary, introduced from excavations in the same gorge two specimens approximately 1.75 million years old whose larger skeleton and bigger brain size could more deservedly lay claim to the associated tool finds and title of 'handy man' than could exceptionally small-brained and big-toothed *Australopithecus*.

53 A rich two-volume collection of essays, authored by such thinkers as Carl O. Sauer, Lewis Mumford, Karl Wittfogel, Pierre Teilhard de Chardin and Charles Darwin, and edited by William Thomas Jr, was gathered and published in 1956 around what was then the prescient title *Man's Role in Changing the Face of the Earth* (Chicago, IL, 1956).

54 Hodder explicitly relies on C. Tilley's *Metaphor and Material Culture* (Oxford, 1999), *Entangled*, p. 121.

55 I borrowed the juxtaposition of tools and containers from Gamble's *Origins and Revolutions*, esp. pp. 87–110.

56 Nicholas Humphrey, *A History of Mind: Evolution and the Birth of Consciousness* (New York, 1992). For his examination of consciousness itself, see Humphrey, *Soul Dust: The Magic of Consciousness* (Princeton, NJ, 2011).

57 Humphrey, *A History of Mind*, pp. 46–51.

58 Cited in Colin Renfrew, *Prehistory: The Making of the Human Mind* (London, 2007), p. 122. For Bachelard's own discussion of the house and the house in the universe, see Gaston Bachelard, *The Poetics of Space*, trans. Maria Jolas (Boston, MA, 1969), pp. 3–73.

59 Ian Hodder, *The Domestication of Europe* (Oxford, 1990), esp. pp. 41–3. Hodder focuses with much imagination on various relations humans have with things – and their lives developed in, through and by things – in his *Entangled*. He offers specific study of a place and time of everyday life among and by things in his edited *Religion in the Emergence of Civilization: Catalhöyük as a Case Study* (Cambridge, 2010), esp. p. 336; and in his *The Leopard's Tales: Revealing the Mystery of Catalhöyük* (London, 2006), pp. 109–40.

60 The study of the place of the hearth in the classic home is found in the Second Book 'The Family', in Numa Denis Fustel de Coulanges, *The Ancient City: A Study of the Religion, Laws, and Institutions of Greece and Rome* (Baltimore, MD, 1980; orig. Fr., 1864), pp. 32–108.

61 Lewis Mumford, *The City in History* (New York, 1961), p. 17. For Hodder's repeated demonstrations of things that become metaphors and symbols of thought and actions, see his *Symbols in Action* (Cambridge, 1982).

62 'Appropriating the Cosmos' is the useful title of Chapter Nine of Renfrew's *Prehistory*, pp. 153–71.

63 Cited in Renfrew, *Prehistory*, p. 122.

64 Glyn Jones, 'Goodbye, What Were You?', in *Goodbye, What Were You?* (Llandsyul, Wales, 1994), p. 13.

65 Mumford, *The City in History*, p. 17.

66 For two overviews of human evolution and development, see Ian Tattersall, *Masters of the Planet*, and André Leroi-Gourhan, *The Hunters of Prehistory* (New York, 1989). For a useful view of humans as a migrant creature, see Clive Gamble, *Time Walkers: The Prehistory of Global Colonization* (Cambridge, 1994).

67 For a brief summary of Renfrew's 'sedentary revolution', see Gamble, *Origins and Revolutions*, pp. 207–8.

68 For this formulation of building in one's cosmic image, see Trevor Watkins, 'Building Houses, Framing Concepts, Constructing Worlds', *Paléorient*, XXX/1 (2004), pp. 5–23.

2 In a Place at a Time, with Changing Orders and Rising Spires

1 For definitions of 'Wilderness in the Medieval West, see part two of Jacques Le Goff, *The Medieval Imagination* (Chicago, IL, 1988), pp. 47–59.
2 For a discussion of the place and power, see Marcel Mauss, *The Gift*, trans. Ian Cunnison and E. E. Evans-Pritchard (London, 1990), and Joseph A. Amato, *Guilt and Gratitude: A Study of the Origins of Contemporary Conscience* (Westport, CT, 1982).
3 Marc Bloch, *Feudal Society*, 2 vols (Chicago, IL, 1961).
4 Marjorie Quennell and C.H.B. Quennell, *Everyday Things in Ancient Greece*, revd edn (New York, 1954); Jérôme Carcopino, *Daily Life in Ancient Rome* (New Haven, CT, 1940); Émile Mireaux, *Daily Life in the Time of Homer* (New York, 1959); Adolf Erman, *Life in Ancient Egypt* [1894] (New York, 1973); Jean Bottéro, *Everyday Life in Ancient Mesopotamia* (Baltimore, MD, 2001). The National Geographic Society offered two book-length collections of magazine reprints written by eminent scholars: *Everyday Life in Ancient Times: Mesopotamia, Egypt, Greece, and Rome* (1951) and *Everyday Life in Bible Times* (1977). Also of interest is Michael A. Malpass, *Daily Life in the Inca Empire* (Westport, CT, 1996), Davíd Carrasco, *Daily Life of the Aztecs* (Westport, CT, 1998), and John Manchip While, *Everyday Life of North American Indians* (New York, 1978).
5 A classic example of transformation from everyday primitive to modern life, and back again, is offered in Nick Hazlewood's *Savage: The Life and Time of Jemmy Button* (New York, 2001). When a mere boy, Jemmy Button was literally kidnapped from Tierra del Fuego by the English exploratory ship the *Beagle*, of Darwin renown. They took Jemmy, representative of millions of non-Western people, to England. Taken in body and trained in mind, over the years Jemmy became civilized until called on to serve on another expedition to Tierra del Fuego, where through a set of circumstances he reverted to his earlier life and became a leader of his people's resistance to the whites.
6 For definitions and a short history of feudalism, see F. L. Ganshof, *Feudalism*, 2nd edn (New York, 1961), and Bloch, *Feudal Society*.
7 This section, 'On the Ground Level', is based largely on Joseph A. Amato, *On Foot: A History of Walking* (New York, 2004), esp. pp. 42–70.

8 Amato, *On Foot*, pp. 45–6.

9 Chiara Frugoni, *A Day in a Medieval City* (Chicago, IL, 2005).

10 Paul B. Newman, *Daily Life in the Middle Ages* (Jefferson, NC, 2001).

11 Jacques Le Goff, ed., *Medieval World* (London, 1987).

12 Ibid., p. 1.

13 For an introduction to medieval technology, see Frances and Joseph Gies, *Cathedral, Forge, and Waterwheel: Technology and Invention in the Middle Ages* (New York, 1994).

14 The discussion in this section is taken from Joseph A. Amato, *The Book of Twos* (Granite Falls, MN, 2015), pp. 95–101.

15 For a recent discussion of the place of lines in the human organization of space and life, see Timothy Ingold, *Life of Lines* (London, 2015).

16 Eva Feder Kittay, 'Metaphor as Rearranging the Furniture of Mind', in *From a Metaphorical Point of View: A Multidisciplinary Approach to the Cognitive Content of Metaphor*, ed. Zdravko Radman (Berlin, 1995), pp. 73–116. Also, see her *Metaphor: Its Cognitive Force and Linguistic Structure* (Oxford, 1987).

17 Kittay, 'Metaphor', p. 114.

18 Robert O. Evans, 'Metonymy', in *Princeton Encyclopedia of Poetry and Poetics*, ed. Alex Preminger (Princeton, NJ, 1965), p. 500.

19 One way to appreciate the immensity of the Christian symbolic and metaphoric system is to examine J. E. Cirlot, *A Dictionary of Symbols* (New York, 1962), Alphonse Napoleon Didron, *The History of Christian Art in the Middle Ages*, vol. 1 [1851] (New York, 1965), James Hall, *Dictionary of Subjects and Symbols*, revd edn (New York, 1974), and Marie-Madeleine Davy, *Initiation à la symbolique romane* (Paris, 1977).

20 For the symbolic and metaphoric dimensions of food and feast, see Martin Jones, *Feast: Why Humans Share Food* (Oxford, 2007), Gillian Feely-Harnik, *The Lord's Table* (Washington, DC, 1994), and Caroline Bynum Walker, *Holy Feast and Holy Fast: The Religious Significance of Food to Medieval Women* (Berkeley, CA, 1988).

21 For a study of suffering as a cultural value, whose form and use varies across the ages, see *Victims and Values: A History and a Theory of Suffering* (New York, 1990). For a study of the medieval formulation of Purgatory as part of the geography of the afterlife and an object of the Church's mediation of prayer and forgiveness, see Jacques Le Goff, *The Birth of Purgatory* (Chicago, IL, 1984).

22 Christopher Dawson, *Medieval Essays* (Washington, DC, 1954),
    p. 49. In *The Historic Reality of Christian Culture* (New York, 1960),
    Dawson examines the outlook for Christian culture in contemporary
    times in light of how fragmented and secular Europe has become in
    the last five centuries.
23 For the cathedral as a technological accomplishment and a symbolic
    creation see Jean Gimpel, *The Cathedral Builders* (New York, 1983),
    Philip Ball, *Universe of Stone: Chartres Cathedral and the Invention
    of the Gothic* (New York, 2008), and Robert A. Scott, *The Gothic
    Enterprise: A Guide to Understanding the Medieval Cathedral*
    (Berkeley, CA, 2003). Classics on the cathedral are Henry Adams,
    Mont-Saint Michel and Chartres [1903] (Garden City, NY, 1959), Otto
    Von Simson's *The Gothic Cathedral: Origins of Gothic Architecture and
    the Medieval Concept of Order* [1956], 3rd edn (Princeton, NJ, 1988),
    and that of Émile Mâle, *The Gothic Image: Religious Art in France
    of the thirteenth Century* (New York, 1972).

3 Many Times Make Many Minds

 1 Joseph A. Amato, *The Book of Twos: The Power of Contrasts, Polarities,
    and Contradictions* (Granite Falls, MN, 2015), p. 47.
 2 Amato, *The Book of Twos*, pp. 35, 46–7.
 3 Ibid., p. 36.
 4 Robert Pogue Harrison, *Dominion of the Dead* (Chicago, IL, 2003).
 5 Amato, *The Book of Twos*, pp. 37–8.
 6 For an introduction to Vico, see the translation of Thomas
    Goddard Bergin and Max Harold Fisch, *The New Science of
    Giambattista Vico*, 3rd edn (Garden City, NY, 1961), and for a
    useful introduction to Johann Gottfried Herder, see Hans Alder
    and Ernest A. Menze, eds, *On World History: An Anthology*
    (Armonk, NY, 1997).
 7 Carlo Cipolla, *The Economic History of World Population*, 7th edn
    (New York, 1978).
 8 Eric R. Wolf, *Europe and the People without History* (Berkeley,
    CA, 1982).
 9 Wolf, *Europe and the People without History*, pp. 390–91.
10 Wayne te Brake, *Shaping History* (Berkeley, CA, 1998).
11 Robert Muchembled, *L'invention de l'homme moderne: culture et
    sensibilités en France du xve au xviiie siècle* (Paris, 1988).

12 For a discussion of Hobsbawm's critical comments on the change
of historiography in his lifetime – especially starting in the 1970s
with a decisive shift from the analytic to the descriptive, the
quantitative to the qualitative and from macro- to micro-history
– see his autobiography, *Interesting Times* (New York, 2002). See
micro-historian Carlo Ginzburg's agreement and disagreement, as
well as his self-defence, in his own historiographical collection
of essays *Threads and Traces* (Berkeley, CA, 2012), pp. 126–8.

13 For surveys of Europe's population and family, as well as such topics
as migration, food, women and relation to nature and the sea, see
'The Making of Europe' series under the editorship of Jacques Le
Goff. See in particular Werner Rösener, *The Peasantry of Europe*
(Oxford, 1994), Massimo Livi Bacci, *The Population of Europe*
(Oxford, 2000), and Jack Goody, *The European Family: A Historico-
Anthropological Essay* (Oxford, 2000). Also of interest are Martine
Segalen, *Historical Anthropology of the Family* (Cambridge, 1986),
and Michael Mitterrauder and Reinhard Sieder, *The European
Family: Patriarchy to Partnership, from the Middle Ages to the Present*
[1977] (Chicago, IL, 1982).

14 See the work of leading English historical demographers, Peter Laslett
and E. A. Wrigley, who in 1964 co-founded the Cambridge Group
for the History of Population and Social Structure and its journal
Local Population Studies, and especially Laslett's *The World We Have
Lost* (New York, 1965) and Wrigley's *Peoples, Cities and Wealth: The
Transformation of Traditional Society* (Oxford, 1985). For a guide and
bibliography to printing and literacy, see Elizabeth Einstein, *The
Printing Revolution in Early Modern Europe* (Cambridge, 1983), and
R. A. Houston, *Literacy in Early Modern Europe*, 2nd edn (London,
2002). Others, borrowing from the natural sciences, calculated seasons
and weather and the fate of crops, and measured the coming and
departing of famine and plagues. Carlo Cipolla offers a succession of
books on early Europe's battles against disease, *Faith, Reason, and the
Plague in Seventeenth-century Tuscany* (New York, 1979), *Fighting the
Plague in Seventeenth-century Italy* [1978] (Madison, WI, 1981), *Contro
un nemico invisibile: epidemie e strutture nell' Italia del Rinascimento*
(Bologna, 1985) and *Miasmas and Disease: Public Health and the
Environment in the Pre-industrial Age* [1989] (New Haven, CT, 1992).

15 For a single recent volume on deep history, see Andrew Shryock and
Daniel Lord Small, eds, *Deep History: The Architecture of Past and*

Present (Berkeley, CA, 2011), which I reviewed for the *Journal of Social History*, XLVII/4 (Summer 2014), pp. 1101–3.

16 The first generation of the Annales School was composed of Marc Bloch and Lucien Febvre; the second: Fernand Braudel, Ernest Labrousse, Pierre Goubert, Georges Duby, Pierre Chaunu and Robert Mandrou; the third: Jacques Le Goff, Emmanuel Le Roy Ladurie, Marc Ferro, Pierre Nora and Philippe Ariès; and the fourth generation: Roger Chartier, Jacques Revel, André Burguière and Bernard Lepetit. For Braudel's place in modern historiography, see Georg Iggers, *Historiography in the Twentieth Century: From Scientific Objectivity to the Postmodern Challenge* (Middletown, CT, 1997), Philippe Carrard, *Poetics of the New History: French Historical Discourse from Braudel to Chartier* (Baltimore, MD, 1992), Peter Burke, *The French Historical Revolution: The Annales School, 1929–1989* (Stanford, CA, 1990), and Marc Ferro, ed., *Social Historians in Contemporary France: Essays from Annales* (New York, 1972).

17 Fernand Braudel, *Afterthoughts on Material Civilization and Capitalism* (Baltimore, MD, 1977).

18 Ibid., pp. 4–5.

19 Ibid., p. 5.

20 For an introduction to Thuillier and his critique of Braudel's Marxism and disregard for everyday life and events of places, see Joseph Amato, 'Guy Thuillier: "Paris Will Save Nothing"', a review essay focused on Guy Thuillier and Jean Tulard, *Historie locale et régionale* (Paris, 1992), which appeared in *Journal of Social History* (Winter 1993). Additionally, Braudel's heavy reliance on social science theory deprives history of its decisive turning points – tests of freedom and moments of uplifting victory and irreversible catastrophe. For Braudel's adherence to models and laws, see his 'History and the Social Sciences', in *Economy and Society in Early Modern Europe: Essays from the Annales*, ed. Peter Burke (New York, 1973).

21 Fernand Braudel, *People and Production*, vol. II: *Identity of France*, trans. Siân Reynolds (New York, 1990), e.g. pp. 158–61.

22 In a lengthy passage from *Homo Ludens* (1938), worthy of reflection by the everyday historian interested in the history of the mind and mentalities, Huizinga wrote, contradicting Burckhardt, of the great cultural watershed between medieval spirituality and modern

aesthetics – and ultimately old-time faith and humanistic empathy. 'The great divide in the perception of the beauty of life comes much more between the Renaissance and the Modern Period than between the Middle Ages and the Renaissance. The turnabout occurs at the point where art and life begin to diverge. It is the point where art begins to be no longer in the midst of life, as a noble part of the joy of life itself, but outside of life as something to be highly venerated, as something to turn to in moments of edification or rest. The old dualism separating God and world has thus returned in another form, that of the separation of art and life . . .'. Quotation cited in translator Rodney J. Payton's preface to *The Autumn of the Middle Ages* (Chicago, IL, 1996), pp. xv–xvi.

23 Quoted in Maarten Van Ginderachter and Marnix Beyen, eds, *Nationhood from Below: Europe in the Long Nineteenth Century* (Basingstoke, 2012), p. 4.

24 Another pertinent work of recent cultural history is historian Lynn Hunt's *The New Cultural History* (Berkeley, CA, 1989). Aside from Natalie Davis, to whom she dedicates the work as 'an inspiration to us all', Hunt offers other cultural historians as models: Michel Foucault, Marxist historian E. P. Thomson, influential anthropologist Clifford Geertz, historical epistemologist Hayden White and others.

25 Peter Burke, *Varieties of Cultural History* (Ithaca, NY, 1997), p. 212.

26 On varieties of madness from legal, demonic and psychological to altogether unexplainable foolishness, see H. C. Erik Midelfort, *A History of Madness in Sixteenth-century Germany* (Stanford, CA, 1999). For a study on the prevalence of magic and the intermixture of religion during the Reformation and beyond, see Keith Thomas, *Religion and the Decline of Magic* (Oxford, 1971).

27 Carlo Ginzburg strove to show the other side of everyday history and the myths that made culture in his *Il formaggio e i vermi: il cosmo di un mugnaio del '500* (Turin, 1976), translated into English by John and Ann Tedeschi, *The Cheese and the Worms: The Cosmos of a Sixteenth-century Miller* (Baltimore, MD, 1980), his earlier *Night Battles: Witchcraft and Agrarian Cults in the Sixteenth and Seventeenth Centuries* (Baltimore, MD, 1983, first published in Italian as *I benandanti*, 1966). Also there is his *Storia notturna: una decifrazione del sabba* (Turin, 1989). Of additional critical use is his *Clues, Myths, and the Historical Method* (Baltimore, MD, 1989).

28 For the origin of curiosity and science, see Philip Ball, *Curiosity: How Science Became Interested in Everything* (Chicago, IL, 2012), which I reviewed in *Fides et Historia*, XLVI/2 (Summer/Fall 2014), p. 104.

29 For the place of opposites in human experience, see Ginzburg, *Clues, Myths, and Historical Methods*, pp. 62–3.

30 An eclectic survey of the social and cultural richness of the period is found in Gamini Salgado, *The Elizabethan Underworld* (London, 1977), David Warren Sabean, *Power in the Blood: Popular Culture and Village Discourse in Early Modern Germany* (Cambridge, 1984), and Daniel Roche, *The People of Paris: An Essay in Popular Culture of the Eighteenth Century* (Berkeley, CA, 1984).

31 Michel de Certeau, *The Mystic Fable*, vol. I: *The Sixteenth and Seventeenth Centuries* (Chicago, IL, 1992).

32 For Piero Camporesi, see *Il pane selvaggio* (Bologna, 1980), *La casa dell'eternità* (*Fear of Hell: Images of Damnation and Salvation in Early Modern Europe*; Milan, 1990), *Il sugo della vita: simbolismo e magia del sangue* (Milan, 1997) and, for Camporesi's central themes, *Il paese della fame* (Milan, 2000).

33 I argued this on multiple levels in *Surfaces: A History* (Berkeley, CA, 2013), especially in the early parts, pp. 1–61.

34 Alain Corbin, *The Foul and the Fragrant Odor and the French Social Imagination* (Cambridge, MA, 1986), and William Ian Miller, *The Anatomy of Disgust* (Cambridge, MA, 1990).

35 For histories of the senses and especially touch, Diane Ackerman, *Natural History of the Senses* (New York, 1990), Mark M. Smith, *Sensing the Past: Seeing, Hearing, Smelling, Tasting, and Touching History* (Berkeley, CA, 2007), and Constance Classen, *The Deepest Sense: A Cultural History of Touch* (Urbana, IL, 2012), which I reviewed in *Fides et Historia*, XLVI/1 (Winter/Spring 2014), p. 76.

36 For emotions, see for example Barbara H. Rosenwein, *Emotional Communities in the Early Middle Ages* (Ithaca, NY, 2006).

37 Tom Lutz, *Crying: The Natural and Cultural History of Tears* (New York, 1999).

38 David Morgan's *The Embodied Eye: Religious Visual Culture and the Social Life of Feelings* (Berkeley, CA, 2012), esp. pp. 7–28.

4 Of Things and Selves I Sing

1 This paragraph and following paragraphs in the first section elaborate ideas in Joseph A. Amato, 'A World without Intimacy: A Portrait of a Time before We Were Intimate Individuals and Lovers', *International Journal of Social Sciences Review* (Autumn 1986), pp. 155–68.

2 Aside from Chapter One and its endnotes, see Joseph A. Amato, 'Little Things Mean a Lot: The History of Things, or Histories of Everything', *Historically Speaking* (July/August 2004), pp. 31–3; Charles Panati, *The Extraordinary Origins of Everyday Things* (New York, 1987); Johnny Acton, Tania Adams and Matt Packer, *Origin of Everything* (New York, 2006), pp. 31–3; Neil MacGregor, *A History of the World in 100 Objects* (London, 2002); Michael O'Hanlon, *The Pitt Rivers Museum: A World Within* (London, 2014); and Tam Hamling and Catherine Richardson, eds, *Everyday Objects and Early Modern Material Culture* (Burlington, VT, 2010).

3 For a useful guide to the world of peasants and life during the old regime, see Jerome Blum, *The End of the Old Order in Rural Europe* (Princeton, NJ, 1978), Carlo Cipolla, *Before the Industrial Revolution* (New York, 1976), Pierre Goubert, *The Ancien Regime: French Society, 1600–1750*, trans. Steve Cox (New York, 1973), Emmanuel Le Roy Ladurie, *The Peasants of Languedoc*, trans. John Day (Urbana-Champaign, IL, 1976), and Robert Mandrou, *Introduction à La France moderne* (Paris, 1974).

4 Lucien Febvre, *Life in Renaissance France* (Cambridge, MA, 1977), p. 20.

5 Ibid., pp. 20–21.

6 Ibid., pp. 4–5.

7 For a short history of sitting and the development of the chair, see Galen Cranz, *The Chair: Rethinking Culture, Body, and Design* (New York, 1998), esp. pp. 40–41, and Jacqueline Viaux, *Le Meuble en France* (Paris, 1962), esp. Chapter Two, 'Le Moyen Age', pp. 30–42.

8 Fundamental works for the contemporary study of the history of family and childhood are Philippe Ariès, *Centuries of Childhood: A Social History of Family Life*, trans. Roger Baldick (New York, 1962), and Peter Laslett, *The World We Have Lost* (London, 1965).

9 Eugen Weber, 'Fairies and Hard Facts: The Reality of Folktales', *Journal of the History of Ideas* (January–March 1981), p. 96.

10 Robert Darnton, 'The Meaning of Mother Goose', *New York Review of Books* (New York, 1962), p. 95.

11 Weber, 'Fairies and Hard Facts', p. 107.

12 For a useful chapter on the strengths and weaknesses of the history of mentalities, see Peter Burke, *Varieties of Cultural History* (Ithaca, NY, 1987), pp. 162–82.

13 This is essentially the thesis of Joseph A. Amato, *The Book of Twos* (Granite Falls, MN, 2015), and I've recently found it echoed in an abbreviated statement by Carlo Ginzburg on how we think in opposites, *Clues, Myths and the Historical Method* (Baltimore, MD, 1992), esp. pp. 62–3.

14 Piero Camporesi, *Bread of Dreams: Food and Fantasy in Early Modern Europe* (Chicago, IL, 1989), pp. 151–2.

15 Camporesi, *Bread of Dreams*, p. 33.

16 Joseph Lopreato, 'How Would You Like to Be a Peasant?', *Human Organization* (Winter 1965), p. 306.

17 Emmanuel Le Roy Ladurie, *Montaillou: The Promised Land of Error* (New York, 1979), pp. 10, 222.

18 This discussion of the dusty and dirty world of yesteryear is found in 'Of Times when Dust Was the Companion of All', the first chapter of Joseph A. Amato, *Dust: A History of the Small and Invisible* (Berkeley, CA, 2013), pp. 15–35, or more rudely and true to the etymology of dirt they were mired in faecal material and biological waste.

19 In *Purity and Danger: An Analysis of Concepts of Pollution and Taboo* (London, 1966), a classic study of the senses of chaos and contamination, Mary Douglas contends that dust and dirt are the detritus of cultural constructions.

20 Eugen Weber, *A Modern History of Europe: Men, Cultures, and Societies from the Renaissance to the Present* (New York, 1971), pp. 204–5.

21 Diane Ackerman, *A Natural History of the Senses* (New York, 1990), p. 61.

22 Cited in Fernand Braudel, *Capitalism and Material Life, 1400–1800* (New York, 1967), p. 22.

23 A useful introduction to manners is Jan Bremmer and Herman Roodenburg, eds, *A Cultural History of Gesture* (Ithaca, NY, 1991).

24 For a short study of Rousseau and self, see Joseph Amato, *Ethics, Living or Dead: Themes of Contemporary Values* (Tuscaloosa, AL, 1982), pp. 11–24.

25   For walking as a refined activity of court, manners and new and smooth milieus, see Joseph A. Amato, *On Foot: A History of Walking* (New York, 2007), pp. 71–100.

26   This complex story of manners, etiquette and appearance has been richly told, but most effectively taken up by German sociologist Norbert Elias in his pioneering two-volume *Über den Prozess der Zivilisation* (1939), published in English, trans. Edmund Jephcott, as *The Civilizing Process*, vol. I: *The History of Manners* (Oxford, 1969), and *The Civilizing Process*, vol. II: *State Formation and Civilization* (Oxford, 1982).

27   If the French taught the eighteenth-century Western world proper ways of walking and talking, the British upper classes proved themselves to be the most adept students and disseminators of the French way. Popularized among the nineteenth-century Victorian middle classes, English etiquette was readily adopted by respectable folk throughout the British Empire.

28   For clothes and appearance, see Daniel Roche, *La Culture des apparences* (Paris, 1989) and *La Mode en France, 1715–1815* (Paris, 1990), and James Laver, *Costumes and Fashion*, revd edn (London, 1995). For a thoughtful study of the relation of the human body, especially the woman's, and clothing, see Anne Hollander, *Seeing through Clothes* (New York, 1978).

29   Dorene Yarwood, 'Dress and Adornment', in *The New Encyclopaedia Brittanica*, vol. XVII (Chicago, IL, 1997), pp. 489–93.

30   Fielding is quoted in C. Willett and Phillis Cunnington, *The History of Underclothes* (New York, 1990), p. 71.

31   Roger Chartier, *Cultural History: Between Practices and Representations* (Ithaca, NY, 1988), p. 88.

32   The mirror itself travelled a long and complex trail from late medieval Venetian glassmaking to early modern French plate glass production and the successful manufacture of the large, flat glass mirror, which played a central role in palace design. It made its grand and singular entrance in 1678 with the construction of the Versailles Hall of Mirrors (La Grande Galerie or La Galerie des Glaces), which was installed during the third phase of the construction of Versailles. For a short introduction to mirrors, see S. Roche, 'Mirrors', in *Oxford Companion to the Arts*, ed. Harold Osborne (Oxford, 1975), pp. 70–574, and Sabine Melchior-Bonnet, *The Mirror: A History* (New York, 2001), pp. 70–98. For an additional luxurious Hall of

Mirrors, see François de Cuvilliés, the Amalienburg, Nymphenburg Park, Munich, Germany, 1734–9.

33 Melchior-Bonnet, *The Mirror*, pp. 270–71; brackets are mine.

34 James H. Johnson, *Venice Incognito* (Berkeley, CA, 2011), esp. pp. 242–3.

35 For gardens as nature sought and invented and life itself as a subset of gardening, see Robert Pogue Harrison, *Gardens: An Essay on the Human Condition* (Chicago, IL, 2008), esp. pp. 25, 47 and 87. Also, see as auxiliary studies, Kenneth Clark, *Landscape into Art* (London, 1949), and Mark Girouard, *Life in the English Country House: A Social and Architectural History* (New York, 1980).

36 For a set of essays on four centuries of gardens in European and American art, see Betsy Fryberger, ed., *The Changing Garden* (Berkeley, CA, 2003).

37 The English garden, which invited walking, had the effect of defining wilderness as a place in which humans never set foot. In *The Wildest Place on Earth: Italian Gardens and the Invention of Wilderness* (Washington, DC, 2001), John Hanson Mitchell argues that nineteenth-century American thinkers formed their conception of wilderness in opposition to the Italian garden, pp. 20–22, 90–103.

38 Different facets of the development of walking are found in Amato, *On Foot*, pp. 71–124; Laurent Turcot, *Le Promeneur à Paris au XVIIIe siècle* (Paris, 2007), and Walter Benjamin, *The Arcades Project*, trans. Howard Eiland and Kevin McLaughlin (Cambridge, MA, 2002). I reviewed Turcot in the *Journal of Social History* (Winter 2009), pp. 488–91.

39 The revolution involved in idealized garden visions of happiness is explored in Erwin Panofsky's famous essay 'Et in Arcadia ego', in *Meaning in the Visual Arts* (Garden City, NY, 1955).

40 Daniel Roche, *A History of Everyday Things: The Birth of Consumption in France, 1600–1800* (Cambridge, 2000).

41 For the growing importance of things in European domestic life, see Tara Hamling and Catherine Richardson, eds, *Everyday Objects: Medieval and Early Modern Material Culture and Its Meaning* (Burlington, VT, 2010).

42 Catherine Richardson's 'A Very Fit Hat', *Everyday Objects*, pp. 289–98.

43 The importance of natural things to science is reflected in and captured in three different ways in Philip Ball, *Curiosity: How Science Became Interested in Everything* (Chicago, IL, 2012), Madeleine Pinault, *The Painter as Naturalist: From Dürer to Redouté* (Paris,

1991), and Raymond Wolff Purcell and Stephen Jay Gould, *Finders, Keepers* (New York, 1992).

44 For an introduction to books and printing, see Elizabeth Einstein, *The Printing Revolution in Early Modern Europe* (Cambridge, 1983), R. A. Houston, *Literacy in Early Modern Europe: Culture and Education, 1500 to 1800* (London, 2002), and William Hoffman, University of Minnesota, 'Die Anfänge der Zeitungen', 16 March 1981, http://mbbnet.umn.edu/hoff/hoff_news.html, pp. 1–5. Also, for a critical view, see Jonathan Rose, 'Arriving at a History of Reading', *Historically Speaking* (January 2004), pp. 36–9.

45 For an overview of travel, see Joseph A. Amato, *On Foot*, esp. pp. 71–124.

46 Turcot, *Le Promeneur à Paris*.

47 Walter Benjamin's notebooks were published as *The Arcades Project* (Cambridge, MA, 2002).

48 Inventorying 3,000 extant wills after death, Annik Pardailhé-Galabrun depicts seventeenth- and eighteenth-century households and the development of sociability, comfort and home in Paris in *The Birth of Intimacy* (Philadelphia, PA, 1991).

5 The Mechanizing of Work and Thought, and the Acceleration of Life and Individuality

1 Note that the first half of the title of this chapter is borrowed from the title of Chapter Three of Carlton J. Hayes, *A Generation of Materialism* (New York, 1941), p. 88.

2 For a short history of the power of public declarations, especially in the modern world, see Maurice Richards, *The Public Notice: An Illustrated History* (New York, 1973).

3 Two useful works on a socially changing Paris, France and Europe are Daniel Roche, *La Ville promise: mobilité et accueil à Paris* (Paris, 2000), and David Garrioch, *The Making of Revolutionary Paris* (Berkeley, CA, 2002), esp. pp. 292–313.

4 For the representations and role of dress in revolutionary France, see Richard Wrigley, *The Politics of Appearances* (Oxford, 2002).

5 The noosphere, derived from Greek and meaning 'mind-sphere', is a term coined and shared by the philosopher Édouard Le Roy, the Jesuit palaeontologist Pierre Teilhard de Chardin and the Russian geochemist Vladimir Vernadsky in the 1920s.

6 William Rosen, *The Most Powerful Idea in the World: A Story of Steam, Industry and Invention* (New York, 2010).

7 Richard Shelton Kirby, *Engineering in History* (New York, 1990), pp. 450–56.

8 For the connection between eighteenth- and nineteenth-century manufacture, see Maxine Berg, *The Age of Manufactures, 1700–1820* (Oxford, 1986).

9 With origins in the early seventeenth century, windmills in the Zaan River region, alone numbering more than a thousand, kept the land above water while processing barley, rice, paper, wood, cooking oil, mustard, tobacco and hemp and making chalk, abrasives and dyes. In any case, windmills abounded and were abandoned in the centre and south of the Netherlands.

10 Only at the start of the nineteenth century did the actual term 'civil engineering', in contrast to military engineering, become an official field of studies. In its 1828 Royal Charter, the British Institution of Civil Engineers declared its goals to be nothing less imperial than the control, use, command and conquest of nature. The masters of great surfaces were to practise 'the art of directing the great sources of power in nature for the use and convenience of man, as the means of production and of traffic in states, both for external and internal trade, as applied in the construction of roads, bridges, aqueducts, canals, river navigation and docks, for internal intercourse and exchange, and in the construction of ports, harbours, moles, breakwater and lights, and in the art of navigation by artificial power for the purposes of commerce, and the construction and application of machinery, and in the drainage of cities and towns.' Institution of Civil Engineers, 'Charter, Supplemental Charters, By-laws and Regulations', available at www.archive.org.

11 By the middle of the nineteenth century, wrought-iron beams displaced masonry, providing an efficient, prefabricated method of skeletal construction. Cast-iron buildings had a great capacity to carry stone floors and to provide mills with fire protection. Starting in the 1850s, cast iron matched the mid-century Gothic Revival urge to decorate as displayed in commercial buildings in New York, churches in Liverpool, the Houses of Parliament, Joseph Paxton's Crystal Palace (which combined cast and wrought iron) and Victor Baltard's Halles Centrales, which he rebuilt in glass and

iron according to Napoleon III's prescription of 'vast umbrellas'.
T. K. Derry and Trevor I. Williams, *A Short History of Technology*
(New York, 1993), pp. 407–11.

12 The Romans worked with masonry similar to modern concrete.
Their cement was made from crushed rock, utilizing burnt lime as
a binder. Cement mixtures were made with great success in modern
Britain. Derry and Williams, *A Short History of Technology*, p. 406.

13 For an introduction to roads and their surfaces, see M. G. Lay, *Ways
of the World: A History of the World's Roads and of the Vehicles That
Used Them* (New Brunswick, NJ, 1992), esp. pp. 121–332, and Joseph
A. Amato, *On Foot: A History of Walking* (New York, 2004), pp.
158–9, 242–3.

14 As affirmed by historian Wolfgang Schivelbusch's masterful *The
Railway Journey*, notably subtitled *The Industrialization of Time
and Space* (Berkeley, CA, 1986).

15 Schivelbusch, *The Railway Journey*, p. 33.

16 Ibid., 'Tracks in the City', esp. pp. 178–82. For the organization
of transportation in London and Paris, see Amato, *On Foot*,
pp. 153–228.

17 For a discussion of the telegraph, see Tom F. Peters, *Building the
Nineteenth Century* (Cambridge, MA, 1996), esp. pp. 11–15, 16–17, 20.
The originator of the code, the American professor of art and design
Samuel Morse (1791–1872), made the 'magnetized magnet' practical
and commercial, creating the language of dots and dashes bearing
his name, the Morse Code.

18 For a short description of the Crystal Palace and its celebration in
the arts, see Francis Klingender, *Art and the Industrial Revolution*
(Frogmore, St Albans, 1975), pp. 144–6.

19 Jean-Marc Léri, *History of Paris: Illustrated by the Collections of the
Carnavelet Museum* (Paris, 1994), pp. 68–9. The *bateau mouche* –
the river boat service – ferried more than 40 million people in 1900,
while the tramway service would reach 700 million tickets in 1930,
the year it was eliminated, ibid., p. 69.

20 For a useful volume of extracts of artists' attempts to capture the
array of people and sensual impressions of the streets of nineteenth-
century Paris, see Gilles Durieux, *Le Roman de Paris à travers les
siècles et la littérature* (Paris, 2000), esp. for sounds, pp. 203–6.

21 John P. McKay, *Trams and Trolleys: The Rise of Urban Mass Transport
in Europe* (Princeton, NJ, 1976), pp. 157–62, and Nicholas Papayanis,

'The Development of the Paris Cab Trade', *Journal of Transport History*, VIII/1 (March 1987), pp. 52–65.

22 McKay, *Trams and Trolleys*, p. 240. France, the most populous state in Europe next to Russia, with 36 million people in 1850, added only three million people in the next fifty years, leaving it considerably behind Germany and roughly equal to Great Britain without Ireland. Between 1870 and 1910, Great Britain grew from 26.1 million to 40.8 million; Germany went from 40.8 million to 64.9 million; and Russia, from 85.5 million to 139 million, Edward R. Tannenbaum, *1900: The Generation before the Great War* (Garden City, NY, 1976), p. 92.

23 Jean-Pierre Goubert, *La Conquête de l'eau* (Paris, 1986); Stephen Halliday, *The Great Stink of London, Sir Joseph Bazalgette and the Cleansing of the Victorian Metropolis* (Phoenix Mill, Gloucestershire, 1999); Lawrence Wright, *Clean and Decent: The Fascinating History of the Bathroom and the Water Closet* (New York, 2000); Reginald Reynolds, *Cleanliness and Godliness* (New York, 1946).

24 Halliday, *The Great Stink of London*.

25 Joseph A. Amato, *Dust: A History of the Small and the Invisible* (Berkeley, CA, 2000), pp. 83–4.

26 Wolfgang Schivelbusch, *Disenchanted Night: The Industrialization of Light in the Nineteenth Century* (Berkeley, CA, 1988).

27 Cited in Amato, *Dust*, p. 85.

28 For a historical exploration of glamour born of celebrity, style, design and commerce, see Stephen Gundle, *Glamour: A History* (Oxford, 2008).

29 Eugen Weber, 'Commonplaces: History, Literature, and the Invisible', *Stanford French Review*, IV (Winter 1980), pp. 315–34.

30 Stefan Zweig, *The World of Yesterday* (Lincoln, NE, 1964), p. 3.

31 Jonas Frykman and Orvar Löfgren, *Culture Builders: A Historical Anthropology of Middle-class Life* (New Brunswick, NJ, 1987), p. 220.

32 Ibid., pp. 220, 221–61.

33 Ibid., p. 187.

34 For a guide to the intimate side of Victorian life, from privy to bathtub, see Ruth Goodman, *How to Be a Victorian: A Dusk-to-dawn Guide to Victorian Life* (London, 2013).

35 Peter Gay, *Education of the Senses* (New York, 1984); *The Tender Passion* (New York, 1986); *The Cultivation of Hatred* (New York, 1993); *The Naked Heart* (New York, 1995); *Pleasure Wars* (New York, 1998).

36 Theodore Zeldin, *France, 1848–1945*, vol. II: *Intellect, Taste, and Anxiety* (Oxford, 1977), and *An Intimate History of Humanity* (New York, 1994).

37 This is the argument of Edward Shorter and Michael Tilly, *Strikes in France: 1830–1968* (Cambridge, 1974), esp. pp. 343–6.

38 Maps of France for the period 1880 to 1900 reveal the popular use of four names, indicating the advent of the new Republican era. There was *Thiers*, president of the new republic; *Gambetta*, who led the protracted war and resistance against the triumphant Germans; writer *Hugo*, who died in 1885; and the word *République* itself. Daniel Milo, 'Street Names', in *Realms of Memory*, vol. II: *Traditions*, under the direction of Pierre Nora, ed. Lawrence D. Kritzman, trans. Arthur Goldhammer (New York, 1997), pp. 363–90.

39 Maurice Agulhon, 'Paris: A Traversal from East to West', in *Realms of Memory*, vol. III: *Symbols*, p. 541.

40 Pierre Birnbaum, 'Grégoire, Dreyfus, Drancy and the Rue Copernic: Jews at the Heart of French History', in *Realms of Memory*, vol. I: *Conflicts and Divisions*, pp. 406–9.

41 Howard Payne, *The Police State of Louis Napoléon* (Seattle, WA, 1966).

42 Eugen Weber, *France, Fin de siècle* (Cambridge, MA, 1986), pp. 60–61.

43 Ibid., p. 58; and his 'Commonplaces: History, Literature, and the Invisible', pp. 327–9. For those with curiosity, there is also Julie Horan, *The Porcelain God: A Social History of the Toilet* (Toronto, 1996), and Lucinda Lambton, *Temples of Convenience and Chambers of Delight* (New York, 1995).

44 Weber, *France, Fin de siècle*, p. 58.

45 Notion and data from France taken from Weber, *France, Fin de siècle*, p. 51.

46 Frykman and Löfgren, *Culture Builders*, pp. 174–220.

47 Weber, *France, Fin de siècle*, p. 53.

48 Frykman and Löfgren, *Culture Builders*, p. 55.

49 For an essay suggesting that 'the interrelation of country and town is more relevant than their antagonism', see Eugen Weber, 'And Man Made the Town', *American Scholar*, LVIII/1 (Winter 1988–9), pp. 79–96. For emerging views of the countryside, see Frykman and Löfgren, *Culture Builders*, esp. pp. 42–87.

50 Joseph A. Amato, 'The Sum of the Somme', *Buoyancies: A Ballast Master's Log* (Granite Falls, MN, 2014), pp. 66–7.

6 Inventing Our Ways and Designing Our Days

1 For the diverse ways we classify by comparison through differentiation, contrast and opposition, see Joseph A. Amato, *The Book of Twos: The Power of Contrasts, Polarities, and Contradictions* (Granite Falls, MN, 2015).

2 Gertrude Himmelfarb, *The Idea of Poverty: England in the Early Industrial Era* (New York, 1983), pp. 9, 12–13.

3 Himmelfarb, *The Idea of Poverty*, pp. 307–400.

4 For an introduction to the writing of E. J. Hobsbawm, see *The Age of Revolution, 1789–1848* (New York, 1962), *The Age of Capital, 1848–1875* (New York, 1975), *Workers: Worlds of Labor* (New York, 1984) and *On History* (New York, 1997).

5 E. P. Thompson, *The Making of the English Working Class* (New York, 1966).

6 Jürgen Kocka, *Industrial Culture and Bourgeois Society: Business, Labor, and Bureaucracy in Modern Germany* (Oxford, 1999).

7 Jürgen Osterhammel, *The Transformation of the World: A Global History of the Nineteenth Century* (Princeton, NJ, 2014), which was prefaced by his and Dr Niels P. Petersson, *Globalization: A Short History* (Princeton, NJ, 2005).

8 Osterhammel, *The Transformation of the World*, p. 914.

9 Ibid., pp. 918–19.

10 *La République au village* (Paris, 1970) is the title of Maurice Agulhon's local study of the dramatic transformation of the Var region in southern France in the decades starting with the French Revolution and lasting until the Second Republic born during the revolutions of 1848. Of course, studies from across the world could focus on the juxtaposition between local and foreign institutions, local and national markets, governments and minds.

11 For a study of the great separation of country and city in modern literature, see Raymond Williams, *The Country and City* (London, 1973), and his own novel, *Border Country* [1960] (Cardigan, 2006).

12 Of interest for changing sexuality in the nineteenth century are Edward Shorter's 'Sexuality and Illegitimacy: The European Experience' and Robert P. Neuman's 'Industrialization and Sexual Behavior: Some Aspects of Working Class Life', which form section IV 'Personal Behavior and Social Change', in *Modern European Social History*, ed. Robert Bezucha (Lexington, MA, 1972), pp. 231–69 and 270–98.

13 Of special worth for a study of private life, home, society and individuality see vols IV and V, *From the Fires of Revolution to the Great War* and *Riddles of Identity in Modern Times*, of Phillipe Ariès and Georges Duby's edited five-volume *Private Life* (Cambridge, MA, 1990, 1991).

14 For a resident observer's retrospective depiction of a single place, Salford, a borough of Greater Manchester, and the argument that the poor were a single oppressed group as depicted by Dickens and given ideological definition by Engels, who had their own measure of life and respect and saw significant improvement, particularly after the Great War and its aftermath, see Robert Roberts, *The Classic Slum* (Manchester, 1971).

15 For beginning reflections on home, see Gaston Bachelard, *The Poetics of Space: The Classic Look at How We Experience Place* (Boston, MA, 1969), Witold Rybczynski, *Home: A Short History* (New York, 1986), and Bill Bryson, *At Home: A Short History of Private Life* (New York, 2010).

16 For my sources, see section One 'The Improvement of the Material Basis of Life', pp. 2–25, and section Two 'Life in the Industrial Society', pp. 27–37, of part One 'The Forming of an Industrial Society', of *The History of Popular Culture*, ed. Norman Cantor and Michael Werthman (New York, 1968).

17 For an introduction to the city as the definer of modernity, see, for example, Yi-Fu Tuan, *Topophilia: A Study of Environmental Perception, Attitudes, and Values* (New York, 1974), esp. pp. 186–224, and Witold Rybczynski, *City Life and Urban Expectations* (New York, 1995). Also of use, Mark Girouard, *Cities and People* (New Haven, CT, 1985), pp. 255–324, and Sir Peter Hall, *Cities in Civilization* (New York, 1998), pp. 291–502.

18 I explore the transformation of exterior and interior surfaces in *Surfaces: A History* (Berkeley, CA, 2013), esp. pp. 163–222.

19 For a short history of chairs, see Galen Cranz, *The Chair: Rethinking Culture, Body, and Design* (New York, 1998), esp. pp. 24–65.

20 United States Patent and Trademark Office, 'U.S. Patent Activity, Calendar Years, 1790 to the Present', www.uspto.gov/web/offices/ac/ido/oeip/taf/h_counts.htm.

21 Robert Fogel, 'Catching Up with the Economy', *American Economic Review* (March 1999), pp. 1–21; of special interest, Figure 1, 'The Growth of World Population and Some Major Events in the History of Technology', p. 2.

22 Marjorie Quennell and C.H.B. Quennell, *A History of Everyday Things in England: The Age of Production, 1851–1934* (New York, 1935).

23 Charles Panati, *Breakthroughs* (New York, 1978).

24 Charles Panati, *Extraordinary Origins of Everyday Things* (New York, 1987).

25 Henry Petroski, *The Pencil: A History of Design and Circumstance* (New York, 1993) and *The Evolution of Useful Things* (New York, 1992).

26 Michela Nacci, ed., *Oggetti d'uso quotidiano: rivoluzioni technologiche nella vita d'oggi* (Venice, 1998).

27 For a discussion of the history and composing elements of glamour, especially a Romantic escape from the mundane and ho-hum bourgeois present to an alluring past or exotic future, see Stephen Gundle, *Glamour: A History* (Oxford, 2008).

28 Joseph A. Amato, *On Foot: A History of Walking* (Berkeley, CA, 2012), pp. 229–38.

29 Ibid., pp. 153–78, 229–54.

30 For the development of nineteenth-century transportation, particularly in London, see ibid., pp. 167–8.

31 Scottish inventor Robert Thomson developed the pneumatic tyre with inner tube in 1845, but his design was ahead of its time. The pneumatic tyre was reinvented in the 1880s by another Scotsman, John Boyd Dunlop, and became immediately popular with cyclists. Natural rubber is the main raw material used in manufacturing tyres, although synthetic rubber is also used. In order to develop the proper characteristics of strength, resilience and wear-resistance, however, the rubber must be treated with a variety of chemicals and then heated. American inventor Charles Goodyear discovered the process of strengthening rubber, known as vulcanization or curing, by accident in 1839.

32 Amid a long history of building engines of oil, kerosene and petrol, German Gottlieb Daimler is singled out for his 1885 invention of the prototype of the modern gas engine – with a vertical cylinder and with petrol injected through a carburettor (patented in 1887). Daimler first built a two-wheeled vehicle, the 'Reitwagen' (Riding Carriage), with this engine and a year later built the world's first four-wheeled motor vehicle, 'The History of the Automobile', http://inventors.about.com/library/weekly/aacarsgasa.htm.

33 For transportation and tourism, see Amato, *On Foot*, esp. pp. 120–21, 125–33, 268–9; Orvar Löfgren, *On Holiday: A History of Vacationing*

(Berkeley, CA, 1999), and Alain Corbin, ed., *L'invenzione del tempo libero* (Rome, 1996).

34 Henry Petroski, *Small Things Considered: Why there is No Perfect Design* (New York, 2003).

35 For an earlier guide to science's answer to an array of questions such as 'Do butterflies migrate?' or 'How do submarines come to the surface', see William Vergara, *Science in Everyday Things* (New York, 1958).

36 I took up the subject of the revolution downward towards infinity in Joseph A. Amato, *Dust: A History of the Small and Invisible* (Berkeley, CA, 2000), pp. 126–42. Useful for innovations in the biosciences, see William Hoffman and Leo Furcht, *The Biologist's Imagination* (New York, 2014).

37 Mumford elaborated, 'the clock has been the foremost machine in modern technics; and at each period it has remained in the lead.' Also, 'It marks a perfection toward which other machines aspire.' Quotations from Lewis Mumford's magisterial *Technics and Civilization* (1934) were prefatorily cited in David Landes's *Revolution in Time: Clocks and the Making of the Modern World* (Cambridge, MA, 1983), p. xix. Also for clocks and ordering of time and lives, see Stephen Kern, *The Culture of Time and Space, 1880–1918* (London, 1983); Carlo Cipolla, *Clocks and Culture, 1300–1700* (New York, 1978); G. J. Whitrow, *Time in History: Views of Time from Prehistory to the Present Day* (Oxford, 1978); Robert Levine, *Geography of Time* (New York, 1997); Carlene Stephens, *On Time: How America Has Learned to Live by the Clock* (Washington, DC, 2002); and for a very insightful review combing Kern's and Landes's works, see David Cannadine, 'Time', in *The Pleasures of the Past* (New York, 1989), pp. 209–18.

38 Landes, *Revolution in Time*, p. 287. Britain was the original definer of official time on land and sea, due to its paramount roles with sailing and railways. The Swiss and the Americans later led the advance of crafting and the manufacture of watches in the nineteenth century, eclipsing Britain as the world's clock maker, pp. 274–337.

39 'The consumption of timepieces may well be the best proxy measure of modernization, better even than energy consumption per capita, which varies significantly with the relative cost of fuel, climatic, and product mix', ibid., p. 325.

40 The remainder of this conclusion was inspired by the Introduction to Harvey Green's *The Uncertainty of Everyday Life, 1915–1945* (New York, 1992), esp. pp. 1–15.

41 Green, *The Uncertainty of Everyday Life*, p. 6.
42 Ibid., p. 8.
43 Ibid., pp. 8–9.

7 **Compounding Minds**

1 Alan Macfarlane and Gerry Martin, *Glass: A World History* (Chicago, IL, 2002), p. 195.
2 Susan Freinkel, *Plastic: A Toxic Love Story* (Boston, MA, 2011).
3 Roland Barthes, 'Plastics', *Mythologies* (New York, 1972), p. 97.
4 Barthes, 'Plastics' [1957], in *The Everyday Life Reader*, ed. Benjamin Highmore (London, 2002), p. 307.
5 Raymond Williams, 'Culture is Ordinary' (1958), in *Resources of Hope: Culture, Democracy, Socialism* (London, 1958), cited here from Highmore, ed., *The Everyday Life Reader*, p. 92.
6 Williams, 'Culture is Ordinary', pp. 92–3.
7 Ibid.
8 A recent examination of the importance of place in life is Wilfred M. McClay and Ted V. McAllister, eds, *Why Place Matters: Geography, Identity, and Civic Life* (New York, 2014).
9 Frédéric Chauvaud, *Les Passions villageoises au XIXe siècle: les émotions rurales dans le pays de Beauce, du Hurepoix et du Mantois* (Paris, 1995). Also of interest for the deeply passionate and brutal side of a village in rural France, which knew its advantages before its loyalties and even enemies, is Alain Corbin, *Les Villages des 'cannibales'* (Paris, 1990). For an overall view of France's changing demography and relations between countryside and cities and their changing composition, see Armand Frémont, *France, géographie d'une societé* (Paris, 1986).
10 André Varagnac, *Civilisation traditionelle et genres de vie* (Paris, 1948); Émile Guillaumin, *The Life of a Simple Man*, ed. and intro. Eugen Weber, trans. Margaret Crosland (Lebanon, NH, 1983). Also of interest are memoirs from two different centuries from Bretons raised in the countryside, Jean-Marie Déguignet (1834–1905), *Memoirs of a Breton Peasant*, trans. Linda Asher (New York, 2004), and Pierre-Jakez Hélias (1914–1995), *The Horse of Pride: Life in a Breton Village*, trans. Laurence Wylie (New Haven, CT, 1978).
11 A useful introduction to English literature as born out of the interaction between the countryside and London is Raymond Williams, *The Country and the City* (London, 1973).

12 For studies of my family, see Joseph A. Amato, *Jacob's Well: A Case for Family History* (St Paul, MN, 2008) and *Coal Cousins: Rusyn and Sicilian Stories and Pennsylvania Anthracite Stories* (Marshall, MN, 2008).

13 Joseph A. Amato, 'The Extraordinary Ordinary and the Changing Faces of Place', *Historically Speaking*, XIV/1 (January 2013), pp. 2–7.

14 A useful introduction to Goffman and his sociology of self is Charles Lemert and Ann Branaman, eds, *The Goffman Reader* (Oxford, 1997).

15 In his influential *Critique of Everyday Life* [1947] (New York, 1991), the Marxist Henri Lefebvre criticized contemporary middle-class everyday life as soul-destroying banality. Its obsession with things, goods, consumption and a secure and comfortable place alienated people from awareness of the hour and the call to action, whose end would be to make everyday life a creation of their own will and vision.

16 On this point I am singularly indebted to Eugen Weber's *Peasants into Frenchmen* (Stanford, CA, 1976). For other contributions Weber made to the study of everyday life in France and Europe, read my review essay, 'Eugen Weber's France', *Journal of Social History*, XXV/4 (Summer 1992), pp. 879–82.

17 This insight was borrowed and modified from Michel de Certeau, *Culture in the Plural* (Minneapolis, MN, 1997), p. 134.

18 Clifford Geertz, 'An Inconstant Profession', in *Life among the Anthros*, ed. Fred Ingles (Princeton, NJ, 2010), p. 194.

19 Ibid., p. 198.

Conclusion: The Poet's Field

1 A survey of French attitudes about America in post-Second World War France is found in Theodore Zeldin, *France, 1848–1945*, vol. II: *Intellect, Taste, and Anxiety* (Oxford, 1977), p. 137.

2 By the evidence they utilize, local and regional historians and genealogists advocate for detailed histories. Aside from interviews and fieldwork, they rely on town and county records, specialized museums of trades and inventions, church archives, school records, local newspapers and state/regional historical societies in the pursuit of place, family and local work and activities. All of these repositories are tenacious collectors and preservers of all types of artefacts, censuses, membership lists, memoirs, papers, catalogues, town

directories, business histories and complete runs of local newspapers and lesser publications. Any one county courthouse can contain such vital records as tax rolls, assessments, permits, easements, military records, sanity hearings, birth certificates, name changes, divorces, civil and criminal cases, contracts, property deeds and other legal logs. In each type of record one can examine the foundations of everyday life and articulate a type portrait of a community, and yet also probe its contested and clandestine side. Two works I have done with genealogy and local and regional history are *Jacob's Well: A Case for Family History* (St Paul, MN, 2008) and *Rethinking Home: A Case for Writing Local History* (Berkeley, CA, 2002).

3 Useful for literacy in reading images in the contemporary world is Stephen Apkon, *The Age of the Image: Redefining Literacy in a World of Screens* (New York, 2013).

4 James Orr, *Poetry as Survival* (Athens, GA, 2002). Of special interest is Chapter One, 'Poised on a Mountain Peak, Floating on the Ocean', pp. 13–23.

5 For an argument that a society defines itself by its diagnosis and treatment of the insane, see Michel Foucault, *Madness and Civilization: A History of Insanity in the Age of Reason*, trans. Richard Howard (New York, 1973). For judging and institutionalizing the insane for seventy years in a Minnesota prairie town, see 'Madness', Amato, *Rethinking Home*, pp. 113–27.

6 Pound and Blake are cited in Orr, *Poetry as Survival*, p. 100.

7 Glyn Jones, 'Easter', in *Poetry, 1900–2000: One Hundred Poets from Wales*, ed. Meic Stephens (Cardigan, 2007), p. 73.

8 Giuseppe Ungaretti, 'In Memoria', in *Selected Poems of Giuseppe Ungaretti*, trans. Allen Mandelbaum (Ithaca, NY, 1975), p. 11.

9 Author's correspondence with Dana Yost, email, 15 March 2014.

10 Dana Yost, 'Sway', in *The Right Place* (Granite Falls, MN, 2011), p. 106.

11 Dana Yost, 'Hands', *New Plains Review* (Fall 2012), pp. 4–5.

12 Dana Yost, 'The Routine is What We Remember', *Tossing Heavy Cable*, unpublished manuscript, pp. 21–2.

13 Dana Yost, 'Prairie Storm', *Lingerpost* (July 2012), p. 10.

Acknowledgements

Everyday Life: How the Ordinary Became Extraordinary organizes my reflections on everyday life and it acknowledges my gratitude for what has been given and learned. I hope it stimulates the reader's thinking and writing about everyday life.

Everyday Life is not a manual on how to organize and produce a book on daily life but, in the spirit of my *Jacob's Well: A Case for Family History* and my *Rethinking Home: A Case for Writing Local History*, it offers reasons for studying and writing everyday life.

Thinking about and giving form to an account of daily life is a humane craft. Whether elaborated theoretically or written personally and anecdotally, it constitutes a form of self-knowledge, for after all we know ourselves through days spent with others. Lives and selves run on ordinary tracks; they are a matter of familiar places, faces and ruts. Humans, then, take form around their situations and conditions, work, family, friends, and repeating dreams and abiding concerns. Or more poetically, we are alive and afloat on the currents of the seasons of our life.

In addition to wishing to honour truth as embodied, ordinary and communal, I confess to making the variety of our everyday lives a counter-truth against the homogeneities of contemporary theory, ideology and programmes. Enhancing the premise of abundant variety and worth across time, this book assumes that everyday life is a field of many fields. However theoretically everyday life is constructed and conjured to be a unity, it is in truth a composite of matter and spirit, place and time, community and individuals, internal and external forces. It invariably remains unique, mixed, eccentric and mongrel.

Accordingly, this work draws on a range of works that define and construct everyday history. Trained as an intellectual historian and a historiographer and philosopher of history, I naturally identified with social, cultural and micro-history. But nourished by the powers of myth and folklore I was also drawn to newer fields such as peasant studies and environmental, rural and demographic histories, and innovations in the practice of local, regional and rural historians. Additionally, while social psychology and psychology afforded me an array of insights into how humans value and imagine their selves alone and in society, economics and the history of technology emphasized the material side of life. They offered a plethora of insights into markets, production and work. Anthropology, which was relied on for early chapters of my *On Foot: A History of Walking* and *Surfaces: A History*, offered fundamental insights into pre- or deep history, underlining the power of tools and everyday objects, the fundamental place of gifts and exchange, and the urban revolution associated with the growth of agriculture, formation of cities and specialization, and the rise of civilization.

However, to return to my mother discipline, I use historical narrative to conceptualize the factors that make up everyday life. Its largest tracks can be followed from the material to the mental, the collective to the individual, the rural to the urban, from seasonal and repeating time to unique and accelerating time. And finally, my narrative advances from a world of principally ordinary, common, repeating and circumscribing boundaries into an open and changing world, one centred not on place, things and group but surprising invention, encompassing design, imagined projects and whole realms of individual choices and personal dreams.

All this delivers us to an unresolvable paradox or a contradiction, if you wish. On the one hand, everyday life belongs more and more to society, nation and the world at large, while on the other it increasingly falls under the power of individual conscious selves and minds, themselves differentiated by experiences, different religions, ideas and self-chosen identities, and cultivated aspirations. As time, place, community, tradition and self, the composing atoms of daily life have been split, blasted to smithereens, so that everyday – so mundane and ordinary – becomes unusual, even extraordinary. As much as to historian and social scientist, everyday life belongs, as I argue in the Conclusion, to the reach of writer and poet.

Gratitude for my understanding of everyday life has deep autobiographical roots; and its explanation, here concisely described, has turned what was a Preface into these Acknowledgements. What I know of everyday life and the richness I attribute to it for everyone derives from family and community life. It comes from nearly fifty years with my beloved wife, Catherine, a public health nurse who came from a small town in Anthracite Pennsylvania. Her Rusyn immigrant grandparents were storeowners on the one side and coal-miners on the other. Her mother, Catherine, was a schoolteacher and her father, Adam, a small town attorney, long-term mayor and local politician who showed me 'the way of everyday local things'. At every turn, our own four children, Felice, Anthony, Adam and Ethel (Beth), amplified for me, an only child, sensitivity to the range of human personality, the shaping and intrusive powers of outside society as a set of possibilities and fads and fancies, the fragility of tradition and the tenacity of loyalty and love.

Needless to say, my sense of the everyday has its deepest roots in my own childhood and family. Nostalgia makes what was my secure and cared-for youth one and whole – and a standard of what a desirable youth should be. I had a bedroom of my own in an ample house with basement and attic. The house was commanded and energized by my stay-at-home mom: resourceful, quick-tongued and generous Ethel. The second pillar of my youth was my loyal, stoic father. The son of immigrants, Joe taught by ex-ample how duty comes with a discipline that lasts across a lifetime. Always doing what needed to be done, practising moderation in all things (except keeping his clothes clean), cheering for the Detroit Tigers and the Univer-sity of Michigan and harbouring a passion to complete the day's paper and its crossword puzzles, Joe began work at age seven, helped to raise four sisters before marriage, and faithfully and intelligently served Western Union from age sixteen to 59, missing only two days of work almost from the day he graduated high school in 1928 to his retirement in 1971.

My folks brought me up in a brick home on a block of six houses facing six houses, with a street in front and alley in the back. It was a neighbour-hood rich in trees, stores and engaging alleys and fields on the far east side of Detroit. My neighbourhood was composed of the children of immigrants – from Germany, southern and Eastern Europe and Canada – who weath-ered the Depression in Detroit by not joining the ranks of the unemployed.

At eleven I began to caddy at the Country Club of Detroit, Grosse Pointe Farms. At the Country Club, I eventually ran the driving range when I was sixteen and seventeen. In the caddy house, on the driving range, in the locker room and behind the half-way house, I, a child of the working class of a great industrial working class, learned about the life of its exclusive rich – and got a feel for the effect of wealth across generations while grasping the great distance that existed between that and the everyday life of labouring Detroiters. This Detroit and my east side seem idyllic when I now visit the town that has undergone such depopulation, crime, flight, abandonment, decline and hideous metamorphosis.

My folks afforded me a rich inheritance. I had a public education and a democratic point of view, sharpened by a militant unionism and an un-questioned allegiance to the Democratic Party of Roosevelt and Truman.

I inherited a Catholic faith, which was learned and practised around the sacraments. It was keenly argued and made articulate by the Baltimore Catechism, while it was emotionally grounded in attending weddings and celebrations and frequent trips to the cemetery.

Later in life I came to label my mother's family my American family and my father's my Italian. I recently wrote about them in *Jacob's Well*. My mother's family was headed by my fine cooking, fishing, card-playing and always dreaming grandmother – poet one day, lawyer another – Frances Sayers Boodry Linsdau. Born into a family of twelve on the banks of the Wolf River in northeastern Wisconsin in the town of Maine, north of Shioctin and Appleton, Grandma embodied the essence of mixed and migrating Americans. Her maiden name, Boodry, originally Boudrot, can be traced back to the early years of Port Royal, Canada (founded in 1605) and Acadian life in the Bay of Fundy. Her family was exiled to Massachusetts in the great 1755 Expulsion; and then, after intermarriage with English-American families, they migrated to Maine and then pre-Civil War to central Wisconsin, where they intermarried with the Sayers, Wisconsin immigrants from St Lawrence County, New York. Frances met her beau, William Linsdau, in Appleton.

William was a son of Menasha, Wisconsin, a local town at the mouth of the Fox River and on the northwest shore of Lake Winnebago. He was the son of Jacob Linsdau, a teenage immigrant from West Prussia to Menasha, who was a woodworker and then opinionated bar owner and politician, who married, to his economic benefit, the girl next door. Jacob's wife, William's mother, was Mary Jane Allen O'Brien. She came from a family of pre-famine Irish canal diggers, who literally dug themselves west along the Great Lakes from the Eerie Canal until in the 1850s they finally settled in Wisconsin, working on the canals and dams of the lower Fox River, where they commanded a team of horses and a small group of workers. Grandpa 'Will' (Frances's affectionate name for William), who was a storyteller and prankster, maker of stilts and slingshots, entertainer of his young grandson, followed opportunity and ever restless Frances to Detroit. Arriving after the First World War, they moved annually and biannually from homes on the east side and beyond. Eventually securing a foreman's job at Hudson Motor, Grandpa Will helped raise one son, Bill, and three daughters, Ethel, her younger sister Mabel and Ellen, who, breaking Grandpa's heart, died at two.

My father's family was 'my Italian family'. They were recent Sicilian immigrants from the Madonie Mountains in northeastern Sicily. I have visited the island many times in the last forty years and recently wrote a book about it, *My Three Sicilies: Stories, Poems, and Histories* (2016). Nonna Rosalia Notaro's fate, home and temperament belonged by food, emotions and drama to the old country from which she arrived in 1908. She left her native Montemaggiore Belsito pledged by letter and photograph to marry my recently arrived grandfather, Antonino, who came from Cerda, a village just down the slope from nonna's Montemaggiore. Soon married, with one son born in Kelayres, Pennsylvania, they set out to Detroit to improve their lives.

After painful job-hunting during a pre-war downturn, work was found and a downpayment was made on what was most important of all, a house of their own – a true nest for family and everyday life. However, death had not been left behind in Sicily; Rosalia and Antonino's endured the death of their first son, Joseph, and later Antonino, still a young man of thirty-three, died of a burst appendix. My father and I never knew him.

Another marriage and three more daughters – Aunt Josephine, Carmela (Milly) and Pauline – did not lift the curse from Rosalia. Her second husband betrayed the family's most important trust and she – a Sicilian woman – bravely called the police and testified, sending him to jail. My whole youth up to the time I went off to the university, I enjoyed Rosalia's special love, which incorporated her love for my father, fruit of her first marriage. She had made sure that he graduated from high school, and it was on him that she leaned for support from the time he was seven and first sold fruit out of a cart to factory workers until he was twenty-five and married my mother.

Indeed, I was the child of two families and two worlds of dramatic emotions and stories. They taught me that no one entirely absorbs and assimilates the meaning of family and everyday life. My annual trip to Detroit's Mount Olivet Cemetery, where all four of my grandparents, baby Ellen, my mother's favourite aunt, Great Aunt May, and others are buried, takes my heart far beyond explanation and narratives.

Thanks of this sort, but of lesser magnitude, are owed to revelatory effects and the powerful teaching influence of neighbourhood families and especially families of friends of my youth. They naturally, though inadvertently, shared their ways and days and sometimes their angers, joys and most intimate secrets with me, a young boy. They helped educate me to the fact that material and mental are inseparable in the making of everyday life. They remain in plain view and yet forever impenetrable even to those who enacted those family lives and neighbourhood worlds.

At the same time, I bound over my travels and stays in the United States and Europe, families I knew in Quebec City; Rochester and Binghamton, New York; Riverside, California; Ayr, Scotland; and Montemaggiore and

Cerda, Sicily. I also wish to acknowledge three mentors: the intellectual historian Stephen Tonsor, the cultural-political historian A. William Salomone, and the cultural-social historian Eugen Weber, in addition to the historian of machine and city Lewis Mumford, the local and regionalist historian Guy Thuillier and the folklorist Luc Lacourcière, who instructed me in the power of anecdote and story. History colleagues at Southwest Minnesota State University like Michael Kopp, David Nass, Thaddeus Radzilowski, Maynard Brass and Janet Louwagie put me in touch with places, cultures and events that added to my sense of the variety and density of everyday life. This work itself embodies running acknowledgements to the cultural historians, philosophers and anthropologists who taught me to think of the various dimensions of everyday life.

However, I end acknowledging my indebtedness for this work to four individuals: poet and newspaperman Dana Yost, who so carefully and constructively reads much of what I write; poet Suzanne Noguere, who copy-edits and keeps my most recent works of philosophy, history and poetry on track; and finally, Ben Hayes of Reaktion Books, who accepted *Everyday Life* and thoughtfully shepherded it from prospectus to completion, which was improved in multiple places by the careful final editing of Aimee Selby at Reaktion. These three, along with my wife and companion, Catherine, helped me democratically describe and celebrate the long and extraordinary making of everyone's everyday life.

Finally, I express my enduring gratitude to and love of my wife Catherine, my mate for fifty years. She has been an abiding companion in body, family, spirit and faith in a common life.

Index